RADIAL ARM SAW TECHNIQUES

Roger W. Cliffe

 Sterling Publishing Co., Inc.   New York

Dedication

To My Parents

Books by Roger Cliffe

Table Saw Techniques

Radial Arm Saw Techniques

Edited and designed by Michael Cea

Library of Congress Cataloging-in-Publication Data

Cliffe, Roger W.
   Radial arm saw techniques.

   Includes index.
   1. Radial saws.   2. Woodwork.   I. Title.
TT186.C55   1986   684'.083   86-898
ISBN 0-8069-6280-1 (pbk.)

                        9   10   8

Copyright © 1986 by Roger W. Cliffe
Published by Sterling Publishing Co., Inc.
387 Park Avenue South, New York, N.Y. 10016
Distributed in Canada by Sterling Publishing
% Canadian Manda Group, P.O. Box 920, Station U
Toronto, Ontario, Canada M8Z 5P9
Distributed in Great Britain and Europe by Cassell PLC
Artillery House, Artillery Row, London SW1P 1RT, England
Distributed in Australia by Capricorn Ltd.
P.O. Box 665, Lane Cove, NSW 2066
Manufactured in the United States of America

Table of Contents

Acknowledgments

Radial Arm Saw Techniques was produced through the work and cooperation of many people. No project of this type can be done by the author alone. The photos were shot by Jim Schmitz and Bill Peters. The custom darkroom work was done at Bill Peters's Photography. Special thanks to photo models Jon Axelson, Mark Duginske, Steve Holley and Chris Sullens.

The drawings for jigs and projects were done by Lane Coleman, Brian O'Connell, Ron "Pete" Peterson, Rhonda Ross, and Don Simon. Their quality work will make project construction easier for the reader.

Comments and suggestions from Wallace Kunkel (Mr. Sawdust) have helped make this book more complete in its treatment of radial arm saws. This help was greatly appreciated.

Typing and revision work were handled by Loveda Paulus on her new word processor. Many thanks for her help and commitment to deadlines.

The help and encouragement of Cathy and Austin were very important to the completion of this project. Thanks.

Also greatly appreciated are the commercial photographs, line drawings and products furnished by the following people and organizations: Sharon Baazard, T. David Price, and American Design and Engineering; John Butler, Seda MacIntosh, and Black & Decker (U.S.), Inc., Professional Products Division; Marilyn Brock and Boice-Crane Industries, Inc.; Gene Sliga and Delta International Machinery Corporation (formerly Rockwell); Johnny Monday, Fred Garms, and DML, Inc. (Radi All™); Vic Kluesner and Emerson Electric; Fred Slavic and Fisher Hill Products (Ripstrate™); John Baenisch and Foley-Belsaw Co.; Jim Forrest and Forrest Manufacturing; Tim Hewitt and HTC Products; Aivars U. Freidenfetds and Tops™ Power Saw-Marvco Tool and Manufacturing; Paul Mertes and Mertes Manufacturing; Wallace Kunkel and Mr. Sawdust™ Inc.; Jeff Machacek and Northfield Foundry and Machine Co.; Catherine Hopkinson and Ryobi American Corporation; Mike Mangan and Sears, Roebuck and Company; Dick Riggins and Wisconsin Knife Works.

ROGER CLIFFE
CLIFFE CABINETS

Preface

There are 7 million radial arm saws in the United States. This extremely versatile and popular machine can be used for many jobs, and can be found in both the small hobby shop and the large industrial shop.

Radial Arm Saw Techniques addresses the need for basic information and explains the cutting techniques that all radial-arm-saw users have to know.

Included in the basic information core are topics such as:

1. Selection of blades for the radial arm saw.
2. Maintenance of blades and accessories.
3. Maintenance of the radial arm saw.
4. How to buy a new or used radial arm saw.
5. Design and construction of radial-arm-saw jigs.
6. Design and construction of projects that can be built with the radial arm saw.
7. Tips for operating the radial arm saw efficiently and correctly.
8. Safety tips and procedures for operating the radial arm saw.

Included in the operations core are topics such as:

1. Ripping and crosscutting procedures.
2. Simple and compound mitring.
3. Cutting feathers and splines.
4. Cutting and shaping edge joints.
5. Using the radial arm saw as a shaper.
6. Cutting drawer joints such as the rabbet, rabbet-dado, dovetail, and lock corner with the radial arm saw.
7. Using the radial arm saw to make door joints such as the lap, mortise-and-tenon, haunched mortise-and-tenon, and mitre joints.
8. Cutting coves and partial coves.
9. Setting up the radial arm saw for stroke-, spindle- or disc-sanding.
10. Setting up the radial arm saw for drilling and boring.
11. Using the radial arm saw for routing and pin routing.
12. Using the radial arm saw for scrolling or cutting irregular curves.
13. Constructing jigs for cutting tapers, irregular parts, splines, mitres and other joints.
14. Constructing household projects and furniture using the skills outlined in the book.

Radial Arm Saw Techniques was written for both the novice and experienced woodworker. The collection of special setups and techniques represents the knowledge of many experienced woodworkers and cabinetmakers with whom I have had the pleasure of working. While many experienced radial-arm-saw operators will be familiar with some of these operations, it is certain they will not be familiar with all of them. Also, many operations that are only performed occasionally are easy to forget; this book will serve as a thorough guide to those operations. It is certain that woodworkers will find in this book ways to use the radial arm saw to its fullest potential.

1

Introduction to the Radial Arm Saw

History of the Radial Arm Saw

The radial arm saw is an American invention. It was invented by Raymond E. DeWalt in 1922. (Today there is still one radial arm saw that bears the name DeWalt.) The original one (Illus. 1) was the model for production, which began 2 years later. Though this model was not as sleek and modern as today's radial arm saw (Illus. 2), it did the same job.

Illus. 2. Today's radial arm saw appears sleeker and more modern than the original, yet it is designed to do the same job. This machine bears the name of its inventor.

Illus. 1. The original radial arm saw invented by Raymond E. DeWalt in 1922. The radial arm saw is an American invention.

Since the original model went into production, many modifications have been made that have changed and improved the machine. And though the radial arm saw was invented in the United States, it is now manufactured around the world.

The invention of the radial arm saw was first hailed by carpenters who found it difficult to handle large lumber on a table saw (Illus. 3). The fact that the wood remained stationary while the blade made a controlled cut made rafter cutting much safer, more accurate, and less fatiguing. Carpenters soon built jigs and fixtures that increased the saw's versatility.

Many cabinetmakers and home woodworkers also favor the radial arm saw. It can do the work of the saw, boring machine (Illus. 4), shaper (Illus. 5), disc (Illus. 6), and spindle sander (Illus. 7) while using very little floor space. Few machines possess this kind of versatility.

Illus. 3. Large timbers are much easier to handle and control on a radial arm saw. This is because the stock remains stationary while the blade makes the cut.

Illus. 5. The radial arm saw will also do the work of a shaper. It will shape stock into moulding or trim for new work or restoration.

Illus. 7 (right). The blade on this radial arm saw has been replaced with an abrasive spindle for a spindle sanding operation. Irregular shapes can be sanded easily with this attachment.

Illus. 4. The radial arm saw can also do the work of a horizontal boring machine.

Illus. 6. The radial arm saw shown here is being used as a disc sander. It is sanding the face of the stock as it is fed under the guard.

Types of Radial Arm Saws

There are many ways of categorizing radial arm saws. The most common way is by overarm type; however, yoke type, drive type, and cutting type are also important categories. Each categorization describes certain qualities that the saw has. These qualities determine the capabilities and relative value of the saw.

Overarm Type The radial arm saw can have a single overarm, double overarm, or a retracting (gliding) over arm. The majority of machines in use today are single overarm saws (Illus. 8). These radial arm saws pivot off the column at the back of the saw. The single overarm has one limitation. A long left mitre cannot be done completely on the table (Illus. 9). As the cut is made, the blade follows a path that leads off the table.

Illus. 8. This is a single overarm saw. It pivots back at the column. The majority of machines in use today are of the single overarm type.

Illus. 9. In many cases, the blade leaves the table when a long left mitre is cut on a single overarm saw. A blade that extends past the table can be dangerous.

The double overarm or turret arm (Illus. 10) saw pivots from the end of the upper overarm. The lower overarm is attached to the end of the upper overarm. It is about twice as long as the upper overarm. The carriage (motor and blade unit) travels on the lower overarm. This pivoting method allows both right and left mitres to be cut over the table (Illus. 11). The carriage can rotate 360°, and the blade always cuts over the table.

Illus. 10. This is a turret or double overarm saw. The lower arm pivots off the end of the upper overarm. The carriage travels on the lower overarm.

Illus. 11. When a double overarm saw cuts a left mitre, the blade remains on the table for the entire cut.

The retractable or gliding arm saw (Illus. 12) has an arm that glides through the column. The entire arm moves when a cut is made. The advantage with this type of radial arm saw is that the worktable is completely clear when the saw is not cutting. This leaves the table clear for layout work. It also means that when you work, the arm is clear of your path and makes it possible for you to get closer to your work (Illus. 13). The disadvantage is that the machine cannot be placed as close to the wall as other saws. There has to be clearance behind the machine for the retracting arm.

The single overarm radial arm saw is the most widely used, probably because it has been on the market longest. Both other types work equally well and have been marketed for many years.

Yoke Type   Single- and double-overarm radial arm saws can be either single (open) or double (closed) yoke. A single- or open-yoke saw has only one motor mount (Illus. 14 and 15). The other end of the yoke is open. A double-yoke type has 2 motor mounts, one at each end (Illus. 16). It has a U or closed shape. The double-yoke machine provides greater vibration dampening and strength than the single-yoke machine. The double-yoke machine is much better for shaping and heavy dado work because the motor has more rigidity.

Illus. 12. This retractable or gliding arm saw has an arm that glides through the unit mounted on top of the column. This machine must be located away from the wall to allow clearance for the arm.

Illus. 14. This double overarm saw has a single or open yoke. The motor is attached at only one end.

Illus. 13. The chief advantage of the retractable arm saw is that the arm is clear of the table when not in use. This allows you to get closer to your work or use the saw table for layout.

Illus. 15. This single overarm saw has a single or open yoke.

Illus. 16. This single overarm saw has a double or closed yoke. The closed yoke makes the saw more rigid during heavy cuts or machining.

Drive Type Some radial arm saws have direct motor drive, while others have a clutch-and-drive belt (Illus 17). The clutch type will slip when overloaded. This reduces the strain on the motor. The clutch will require adjustment after severe overloading of the saw. Careful operation of the saw will help you avoid adjustment problems.

A direct motor-drive saw will stall when overloaded. Most direct motor-drive radial arm saws have a thermal overload protector (Illus. 18). It is a heat-actuated switch that opens when the motor becomes hot. This protects the motor from damage. The thermal overload protector will not close until the motor is cool enough to run safely.

Illus. 17. This radial arm saw has a clutch-and-drive belt. It causes the blade to slip when overloaded. The clutch will require periodic adjustment.

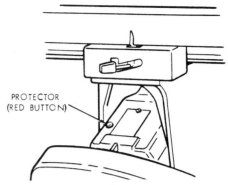

Illus. 18. Most saws will have a thermal overload protector on the motor. If the motor overheats, the switch opens and shuts off the motor. Consult your owner's manual for correct operation.

If the switch opens, shut the motor off and allow the motor to cool. Never attempt to hold the switch closed while turning on the saw. This is sure to damage the motor.

Cutting Type Some radial arm saws are unipoint saws. A unipoint saw begins all cuts from the same point in the fence (Illus. 19). A multipoint saw cuts a new kerf in the face for every change in the setup (Illus. 20).

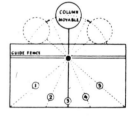

Illus. 19. The unipoint radial arm saw begins all cuts from the same point in the fence even when the blade and arm are tilted. The fence on a unipoint machine seldom needs replacement.

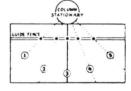

Illus. 20. A multipoint radial arm saw cuts a new kerf in the fence for every change in setup. After several setups, the fence must be replaced.

A unipoint saw makes it easier to begin the cut since you know where all cuts begin. Most unipoint saws are retracting-arm saws (Illus. 21). Retracting arms keep the work in view. With a multipoint saw, the fence has to be changed more often because every setup change puts a new kerf in the fence. As new setups are cut, more of the fence is cut away. The kerfs in the fence can trap sawdust

Illus. 21. This unipoint saw is a retracting-arm type. This keeps the work in view because the arm only moves over the table while the cut is being made.

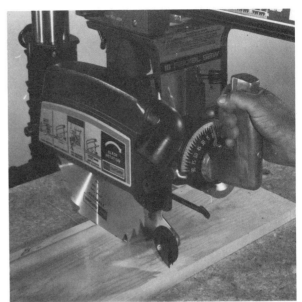

Illus. 22. Crosscutting is an operation where solid wood is cut across or perpendicular to the grain. Sheet stock may also be cut this way, but it is not always across the grain.

and affect the accuracy of the cut. Before long, there will not be enough fence to control your work.

Radial-Arm-Saw Cuts

The radial arm saw can make 8 cuts. The cuts with the blade in the vertical position are as follows: crosscut (Illus. 22), the ripcut (motor turned 90° [Illus. 23]), and the mitre cut (arm turned [Illus. 24]).

The cuts made with the blade tilted are the bevel or angular crosscut (also called end mitre [Illus. 25]), the bevel rip cut (motor turned 90° [Illus. 26]), and the compound mitre (arm turned [Illus. 27]).

Finally, there are the cuts made with the blade in the horizontal position: the edge slot (also called edge-grooving) or edge rabbet (Illus. 28 and 29), and the angular edge slot (blade tilted from horizontal slightly). This cut is used chiefly for making raised panels (Illus. 29).

Chapters 5 and 6 discuss all the procedures for making all these cuts in all positions. Study your owner's manual before beginning to work. Know which way to turn clamps and other mechanisms on your saw. This will prevent mistakes or damage as you make setup changes.

Illus. 23. A rip cut is made by turning the yoke 90°, so that the blade is parallel to the fence. The splitter behind the blade keeps the wood from pinching on the blade.

Illus. 24. A mitre is an angular crosscut made with the blade perpendicular to the table. Only the arm is turned for this cut.

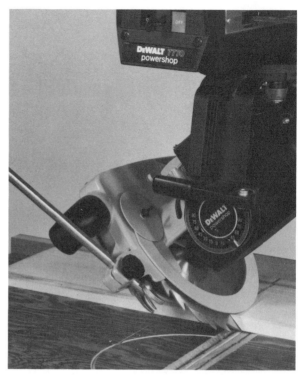

Illus. 25. A bevel crosscut is a crosscut made when the blade is tilted. This cut is sometimes called an end mitre. Note the lower blade guard. It protects your hands from slipping into the sides of the blade.

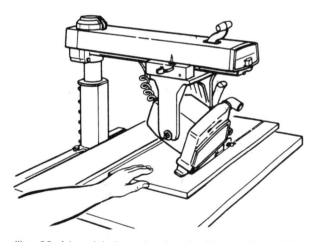

Illus. 26. A bevel rip is made when the blade is tilted while ripping. This cut is often made in stave construction.

Illus. 27. A compound mitre is made when the arm is turned and the blade is tilted. This cut is also known as a hopper cut.

Illus. 28 (left). An edge slot is cut when the blade is dropped into the horizontal position. A special guard may be used for this operation.

Illus. 29. When the blade is tilted slightly off the horizontal plane, a raised panel may be cut.

Radial Arm Saw Blade Diameter		Maximum Stock Thickness Cut	
Inches	MM	Inches	MM
8	203	2	51
10	254	3	76
12	305	4	102
14	356	5	127
16	406	6	152
18	457	7	178

It is possible to use a blade smaller than that specified on a radial arm saw. For example, an 8″ blade can be used on a 10″ radial arm saw. The smaller blade will have more power per tooth than a larger blade, but cutting capacity will decrease. This topic is further discussed in Chapters 4 and 5.

Determining the Size of the Radial Arm Saw

Blade Diameter   The most common indicator of radial arm saw size is blade diameter. Most radial arm saws are advertised according to the largest blade that can be mounted on it. Small radial arm saws will take an 8″ blade. The most commonly manufactured radial arm saw uses a 10″ blade or smaller.

Blade diameter is an important measure of radial arm saw size. A 10″ radial arm saw will cut a piece of stock 3″ thick in half. Saws with smaller blades will not be able to cut stock as thick as 3″. The chart that follows gives typical cutting thickness; these thicknesses will vary from one brand to another. Consult the manufacturer's specifications for maximum thickness of cut.

Table Size   The size of the worktable is an important aspect of radial-arm-saw size. The larger the work table, the easier it is to handle large or heavy pieces. Some owners add table extensions to the ends of the worktable to increase the worktable size. These extensions may be the folding or stationary type (Illus. 30). The typical table size on a 10″ radial arm saw is about 20″ deep by 35″ long.

Arm Travel   The length of the pull stroke is the arm travel. The longer the stroke, the greater the crosscutting capacity. Arm travel is usually specified as the crosscut capacity on stock 1″ thick. This capacity limits the maximum width of stock you can cut. When comparing radial arm saws, arm travel is an important consideration. Arm travel is usually greater on machines with larger diameter blades.

Illus. 30. Table extensions are sometimes added to radial-arm-saw tables. This makes it easier to handle and control larger pieces.

Maximum Rip The maximum ripping capacity of the radial arm saw is an important size consideration. The maximum rip can affect some operations. For example, when ripping 48″ panels in half, a maximum rip of 24″ is required (Illus. 31). Any radial arm saw with a capacity less than 24″ maximum rip would be useless. Maximum rip and arm travel are usually closely related.

Illus. 31. For cutting a sheet of plywood down the middle, the radial arm saw must have a maximum rip of 24″. Maximum rip and arm travel are closely related.

Horsepower Horsepower is a very important measure of radial-arm-saw size. Almost all motors appear to be about the same size physically, yet some are more powerful than others. This makes motor selection confusing and difficult. The following discussion will help you select the correct motor and clarify the terms used when horsepower is discussed.

Rated Horsepower vs. Peak Horsepower. Horsepower is a function of torque and rpms (revolutions per minute). The peak or developed horsepower is the horsepower of the motor when its only load is the saw blade. Rated horsepower is the horsepower under load. The rated horsepower is lower than the peak horsepower.

Generally, the best comparison between motors is the amperage rating. A 10-ampere, 110-volt motor has an actual horsepower of about 1. Under actual working conditions, the electrical supply can affect horsepower and radial-arm-saw effectiveness. There must be adequate voltage and amperage at the motor to gain total horsepower. A 15-ampere circuit is the absolute minimum. If an extension cord is used to connect the saw to the circuit, make sure the wire can handle the load without a large drop in amperage or voltage. Use an extension cord with a number 12 or 10 wire gauge. Consult your operator's manual for specifics.

How Much Horsepower Is Needed? Most radial arm saws come equipped with a motor from 1 horsepower (rated) to 7 horsepower (rated). This is a considerable difference in horsepower. The 1-horsepower motor would be found on an 8 or 10″ saw. This is because the saw turns a smaller blade and is not designed to cut thick stock.

A 12 or 16″ radial arm saw would have a 5 to 7 horsepower (rated). A 10″ radial arm saw could have a 1-, 1½-, 2-, or 3-horsepower motor (rated). The large variety is due to the different jobs these saws might perform. If a 10″ radial arm saw is used to cut framing lumber, a 2- or 3-horsepower (rated) motor would be selected. This is because framing lumber has a higher moisture content and is not as true as furniture lumber. Increased moisture in wood requires more horsepower to throw or eject the heavier sawdust.

Twisted or warped stock has a tendency to bind or pinch against the blade. This added stress requires more horsepower to keep the saw blade turning.

Radial arm saws that are purchased for heavy ripping or dadoing operations should be equipped with the largest available horsepower motor. Ripping requires about 5 times as much energy as crosscutting. Turning a large dado head and making dado cuts require much more power than general ripping or crosscutting.

In most cases, a 10″ radial arm saw is underpowered if it has a 1 horsepower (rated) or smaller motor. A 12-amp or about 2-horsepower (rated) motor should be the smallest one used on a 10″ radial arm saw intended for general service. A 10″ radial arm saw with an 8″ blade mounted on the arbor will have more power at the blade. More cutting power is available since less power is needed to turn the smaller blade. When using a smaller blade, make sure that the arbor hole and rpm rating are correct for your saw.

Larger horsepower motors can do a bigger job, but because they have more power they have more of a capacity for kickback (eject or kick stock towards you). Stock that binds on a smaller or lower horsepower radial arm saw is likely to freeze the blade rather than kick back.

Select the radial arm saw according to the work you do. Evaluate all available radial arm saws carefully before selecting one.

What Voltage is Desirable? Most 10″ radial arm saws draw 15 amperes or less. This is considered appropriate for 110-volt household circuits. Some saws can be modified to run on 220-volt household circuits. There will be more power and less strain on the electrical system when the saw runs at 220 volts. Most 12″ radial arm saws require

220 volts because they draw 18 to 20 amperes. This may be too much of a strain for the typical 110-volt household system.

The outlets for 110 volts (Illus. 32) and 220 volts (Illus. 33) differ in configuration. This eliminates the chance of using too much or too little voltage.

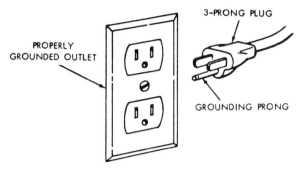

Illus. 32. The outlet shown here is typical of the 110-volt type used with a radial arm. This plug should not be modified in any way.

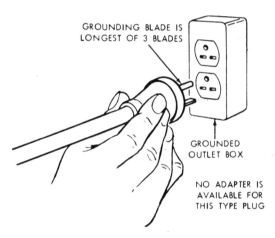

Illus. 33. The outlet shown here is typical of the 220-volt type used with a radial arm saw. Most 12" radial arm saws and some 10" radial arm saws run on 220 volts. This is because they draw too many amps for a 110-volt circuit.

Power Takeoff Shafts Many radial arm saws have a power takeoff shaft on the end of the motor opposite the blade arbor (Illus. 34). This shaft is designed to accommodate work accessories such as a drill chuck or router collet. There are many work accessories available for the radial arm saw. These accessories are discussed in Chapter 2.

The power takeoff shaft is usually threaded. Accessories are mounted on the threaded shaft. When the shaft is not in use, a plastic cap may be attached to it. This cap protects the threads from damage. On some radial arm saws, the power takeoff doubles as a brake (Illus. 35). The brake is removed and the braking wheel is unscrewed from the threaded shaft. The speed at which this shaft turns may be different from the saw arbor. Consult the owner's manual for specifics.

Illus. 34. Many radial arm saws have a power takeoff shaft opposite the saw arbor. This shaft is threaded to take accessories. This shaft may not turn at the same speed as the saw arbor. Consult your owner's manual.

Illus. 35. This braking mechanism must be removed for access to the power takeoff shaft.

2

Radial-Arm-Saw Controls and Accessories

Controls

There are 5 common controls on the radial arm saw: the power switch, blade elevation, motor or power unit angle, yoke adjustment, and arm swing or pivot. (Study Illus. 36–40.) In some cases, radial arm saws have a brake. This may be an electronic control related to the switch, or it may be mechanical.

Note: Whenever adjusting blade elevation, blade an-gle, arm angle, or yoke position, always make a cut in the table. Also, make a cut in the fence at the same time. Before cutting into the table or fence, make sure that the blade will only contact wood. Check for metal table clamps (Illus. 41) or table fasteners that may be in the blade's path. Contact with metal parts dulls or damages the blade and may cause injury due to flying metal parts.

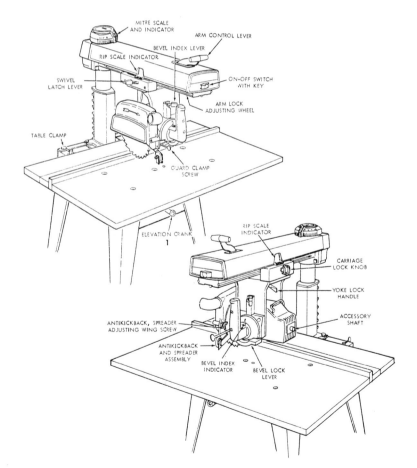

Illus. 36. Study the controls on this radial arm saw. Can you see how they are different from the controls in Illus. 37 and 38?

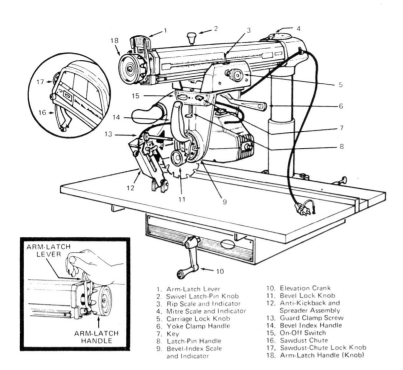

ARM-LATCH LEVER

ARM-LATCH HANDLE

1. Arm-Latch Lever
2. Swivel Latch-Pin Knob
3. Rip Scale and Indicator
4. Mitre Scale and Indicator
5. Carriage Lock Knob
6. Yoke Clamp Handle
7. Key
8. Latch-Pin Handle
9. Bevel-Index Scale and Indicator
10. Elevation Crank
11. Bevel Lock Knob
12. Anti-Kickback and Spreader Assembly
13. Guard Clamp Screw
14. Bevel Index Handle
15. On-Off Switch
16. Sawdust Chute
17. Sawdust-Chute Lock Knob
18. Arm-Latch Handle (Knob)

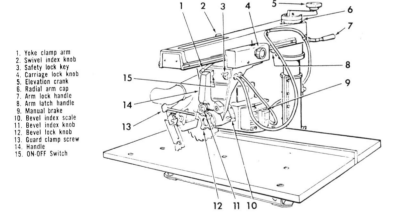

1. Yoke clamp arm
2. Swivel index knob
3. Safety lock key
4. Carriage lock knob
5. Elevation crank
6. Radial arm cap
7. Arm lock handle
8. Arm latch handle
9. Manual brake
10. Bevel index scale
11. Bevel index knob
12. Bevel lock knob
13. Guard clamp screw
14. Handle
15. ON-OFF Switch

Illus. 38. The blade elevation crank on this saw is on the column. Where is the elevation crank on the saws in Illus. 36 and 37?

Illus. 39. Some radial arm saws color-code the controls to simplify the setup. Study the operator's manual that comes with your saw to be sure you know how to set it up and adjust it correctly.

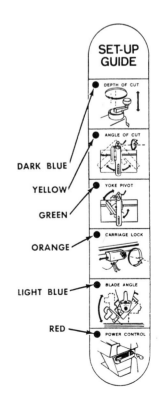

SET-UP GUIDE

DEPTH OF CUT

ANGLE OF CUT
DARK BLUE

YELLOW
YOKE PIVOT
GREEN

CARRIAGE LOCK
ORANGE

BLADE ANGLE
LIGHT BLUE

RED
POWER CONTROL

17

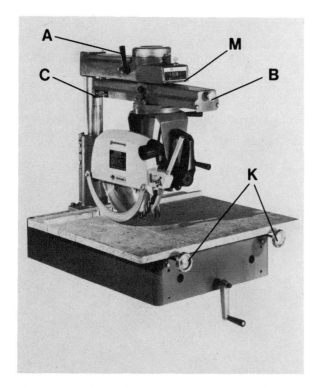

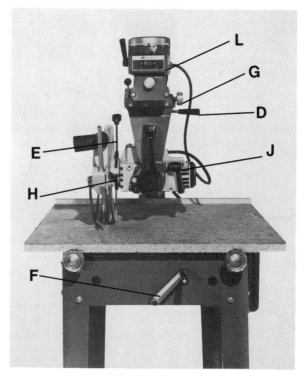

A—TRACK-ARM CLAMP HANDLE Controls swing of track-arm for all mitre-cutting operations. Locks track-arm at any angle for the full 360° rotation. To rotate track-arm loosen clamp handle and rotate arm. The arm will stop at the 0° and 45° positions right and left. To move the arm past these points the track-arm index knob (B) must be pulled out.

B—TRACK-ARM INDEX KNOB Locates 0° and 45° positions, right and left, of the track-arm.

C—YOKE INDEX KNOB Locates each 90° position of the yoke for ripping or crosscutting operations. When rotating the yoke, the yoke clamp handle must first be loose.

D—YOKE CLAMP HANDLE The yoke clamp handle must be loose when rotating the yoke to the rip or cross-cut position.

E—ANTI-KICKBACK DEVICE When ripping, the yoke is positioned and clamped so that the blade is parallel to the fence. The rear of the blade guard is lowered until it almost touches the workpiece. The anti-kickback rod is then lowered so that the fingers catch and hold the workpiece. Never rip from the anti-kickback end of the blade guard.

F—ELEVATING CRANK HANDLE Controls the depth of cut in all operations. Turning the crank handle raises or lowers the overarm.

G—CUTTERHEAD CLAMP KNOB Locks cut-terhead at any position on the track-arm. When ripping, the cutting clamp knob must be tight.

H—BEVEL INDEX KNOB Locates 0° and 45° and 90° positions of the motor when bevel-cutting. When tilting the motor for bevel cutting, the bevel clamp handle must first be loose.

J—BEVEL CLAMP HANDLE Controls tilt of motor for bevel-cutting operations. Locks motor at any desired angle on the bevel scale.

K—TABLE CLAMP KNOBS Allow the operator to quickly set the desired fence position.

L—ON–OFF SWITCH Conveniently placed at eye level, switch can be turned on or off in an instant for added operator protection.

M—SWITCH LOCKOUT Permits switch to be locked so that saw cannot be turned on—an extra safety feature that restricts unauthorized use of the machine.

Illus. 40. Notice that the double overarm saw has similar controls. Adjustment and setup is about the same on all radial arm saws.

Illus. 41. This table clamp was cut by the saw blade. Always check the blade's path before making a cut. Putting an auxiliary table over the front table would have raised the blade above the table clamps and rear table.

Power Switch There are many different types of power switches used on radial arm saws (Illus. 42–46). Some are push-button switches, and others are flip-type switches. For safety purposes, some of these switches are designed so that they are easier to turn off than on (Illus. 44). When color coding is used, red is off and green is on (Illus. 43).

The power switch is positioned so that the saw can be turned on and off easily without reaching. Some saws have the switch on the end of the arm. The switch can also be located close to the pull handle on the yoke (Illus. 45).

Illus. 42. This power switch is located on the upper over-arm. This position can be reached easily regardless of the operation.

This type of switch is handier for crosscutting, but when the yoke is turned for ripping, the switch is on the other side of the machine. The switch on some saws is located under the table. Newer machines have a better switch that is positioned for safety. Old radial arm saws have the switch at the back of the machine on the column. These switches are difficult to reach in a crisis.

On some power switches, a key has to be inserted before the radial arm saw can be used (Illus. 45). This type of switch keeps inexperienced operators and curious children from operating the saw. Key-actuated switches should always be used on tools found in a home where children live or visit (Illus. 46).

On high-voltage radial arm saws, a low-voltage switching system is used. The system uses a 24-volt circuit to the motor. This system activates a solenoid on the motor to the on or off position. The 24-volt circuit minimizes the chance of high-voltage electric shock to the operator.

Illus. 43. The off-switch is color-coded red while the on-switch is color-coded black or green. These switches are positioned on the arm.

Illus. 44. The on-button is housed on this radial arm saw. This minimizes the chance of accidental starting.

19

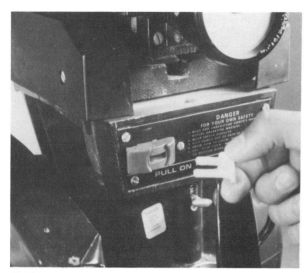

Illus. 45. This radial arm saw has a flip-type switch located on the yoke. This position is handy for crosscutting, but it is awkward when ripping. This switch has a removable key to prevent unauthorized use.

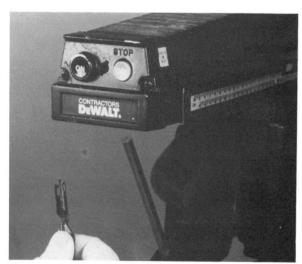

Illus. 46. This key-actuated switch also prevents un-authorized use. Switches of this type should be used in home shops where children live or visit.

Blade Elevation Blade elevation is controlled by a handwheel. This handwheel may be on top of the column or arm (Illus. 47), or it may be under the table at the front of the saw. Most handwheels have an arrow to indicate turning directions for raising the blade (Illus. 48).

Learn how much one turn of the elevating handwheel raises or lowers the blade. This knowledge will be valu-able to you when making minor blade-height adjust-ments. For instance, if one revolution of the handwheel raises (or lowers) the blade ⅛″, then ½ of a revolution of the elevating handwheel would raise (or lower) the blade

⅟16″. If you understand the relationship between the blade height and the elevating handwheel, saw setup will be easier and faster.

Some older machines have some lash (slop or looseness) in the elevating mechanism. This may allow the blade elevation to change as the operation is in progress. If lash exists on your radial arm saw, make the final blade-height adjustment by raising the blade. This will ensure positive gear engagement and prevent blade creeping (elevation change) during the operation.

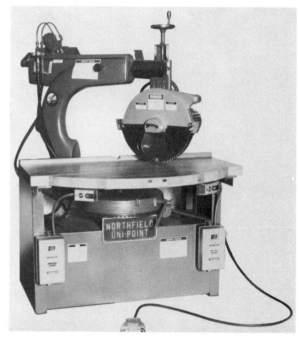

Illus. 47. The crank above the blade controls blade height. Note the power-feed unit attached to this machine.

Illus. 48. This elevation crank is located on top of the arm. Note the arrow on the handwheel. It eliminates confusion when raising or lowering the blade.

Arm Turning Arm turning is also known as radial arm swing or pivot. The arm is turned so that the radial arm saw can make angular cuts such as mitres (Illus. 49). The arm is usually locked and clamped in the O position. This is the position used for crosscutting (Illus. 50). The arm may also be locked and clamped at angles such as 45° left or right. When other angles are cut, the lock does not engage, but it holds the arm securely at the desired angle.

To pivot the radial arm, loosen the locking device and release the clamp. The lock and clamp are located at the front of the arm on some radial arm saws. Others have the lock and clamp at the top of the column. On turret-arm saws, the lock and clamp are found at the junction of the upper and lower arm. Make sure the blade is elevated above the fence and table before pivoting the arm. If the blade is not raised, damage could occur to the blade, fence, or table. Set the desired angle using the indicator on top of the column. Engage the lock (if possible) and secure the clamp.

A kerf must now be cut into the fence and table. Push the motor unit all the way back against the column and turn on the saw. With one hand on the handle, slowly lower the blade until it touches the table. Slowly pull the motor through the length of its stroke to cut a kerf. Return the motor to the column and repeat the process until the kerf in the table is ⅟16 to ⅛" deep. Before actually making mitre cuts, read Chapters 4 and 5. These chapters discuss safety procedures and mitre-cutting techniques that will help you do a safer and better job.

Illus. 49. The arm is turned when cutting mitres. For crosscuts, the arm is set at zero.

Blade Tilting   To tilt the blade, pivot the motor in the yoke. The blade is tilted to cut bevels, chamfers, and mitres (Illus. 51). When the blade is tilted and the arm is turned, the radial arm saw can make compound mitres or hopper cuts (Illus. 52). The blade tilt is also used when devices such as sanding discs are used to sand bevels or chamfers. (See Chapters 5 and 6.)

The motor is held in the O position (perpendicular to the table) with a lock and clamp. The lock and clamp also hold the blade in position at angles of 45° and 90° (horizontal or parallel to the table). When other blade angles are set, the clamp holds the blade (and motor) at the desired angle.

To tilt or turn the blade, raise the blade above the table while it is back at the column. Loosen the clamp and place your hand on the handle. Release the lock with your other hand, and twist the handle to tilt the blade. The indicator on the yoke will tell you when the desired angle has been reached. With some angles, the lock will fall into place. Other angles can only be held with a clamp. Tighten the clamp securely.

A kerf must now be cut into the fence and table. Turn on the saw with the motor all the way back at the column. With one hand on the handle, slowly lower the blade until it touches the table. Pull the motor through the length of its stroke. This will cut a kerf through the fence and into the table. Return the motor to the column and repeat if necessary. The kerf in the table should be about ⅟16 to ⅛" deep. Consult Chapters 4 and 5 before actually making any cuts. These chapters will provide information on how to do the job safer and more efficiently.

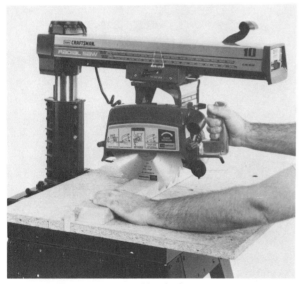

Illus. 50. The crosscut position is the most common setup for a radial arm saw. Note the kerf in the table and fence. Be sure to raise the blade above the table before turning the arm.

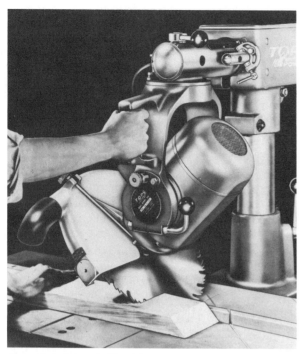

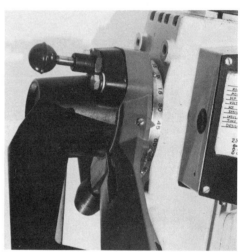

Illus. 51A (above). The blade is tilted and clamped in position. End mitres can be cut after the table is kerfed. Note the clamping knob and index scale at the pivot point in the yoke.

Illus. 51B (top right and right). Locking mechanisms are different on this double overarm saw. The scale is positioned differently (inset) on this saw.

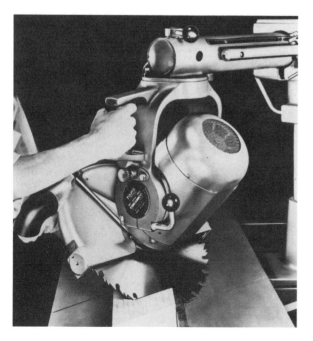

Illus. 52 (left). The blade is tilted and the arm is turned for the compound mitre or hopper cut. Lock all clamps securely after the saw is set up.

Motor and Yoke Pivot The motor and yoke are pivoted mostly for ripping operations (Illus. 53). The yoke is pivoted so that the blade is parallel to the fence. The motor and blade are attached to the yoke and pivot together. When the blade is between the fence and motor, it is known as in-ripping. When the motor is between the fence and blade, it is known as out-ripping. The motor or yoke is also pivoted for other operations such as shaping and sanding. These operations are discussed in Chapters 5 and 6.

To pivot the yoke, pull the yoke and carriage (unit that holds the yoke to the arm) to the middle of its stroke and lock the carriage. Release the yoke clamp, which is located between the motor and carriage. Lift the yoke-locking pin and turn the yoke to the desired position. A rip trough may now be cut (Illus. 54–57).

Illus. 55. Turn on the saw and lower the blade until it cuts the table lightly. Release and pull the carriage through its stroke. A slight trough will be cut.

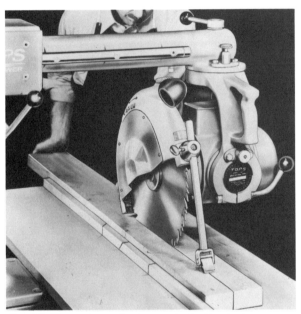

Illus. 53. The motor and yoke are pivoted for ripping operations usually, but there are other operations that require the yoke to be pivoted. Secure all locks and clamps before beginning any operation.

Illus. 56. Lower the blade again so the trough is about ⅛" deep. The blade may now be adjusted for ripping. Read Chapters 4 and 5 before attempting a rip cut.

Illus. 54. Position the saw blade slightly above the table and clear of the fence. Lock the blade in this position.

Illus. 57. The blade has been tilted here for a bevel-ripping operation.

Turn on the motor and lower the blade until it touches the table (Illus. 55). Grasp the handle securely and release the carriage lock. Move the carriage slowly throughout its stroke, being careful not to hit the fence. Lower the blade and repeat the process until the trough is ⅟₁₆ to ⅛" deep (Illus. 56). The blade may now be moved in the trough to adjust for any width of rip.

If you wish to bevel-rip your stock, tilt the blade to the desired angle after the rip trough has been cut (Illus. 57). This may require readjusting the blade height. Make this adjustment carefully so you do not hit the table and damage the blade.

Brake Some radial arm saws made today are equipped with an electronic brake. This brake stops the blade by sending a current through the motor. The current counteracts the motion of the motor, causing it to stop. An electronic brake can be retrofitted to most radial arm saws. For additional information, consult an industrial woodworking machinery catalogue or agent.

The brake makes the radial arm saw safer to operate. The operator does not have to wait for the motor to coast to a stop before changing the setup. The electronic brake causes no appreciable wear on the electric motor.

Note: When the radial arm saw is equipped with a brake, make sure the arbor nut that holds the blade in position is tightened securely. The sudden stop caused by the brake can cause the blade to loosen. Check the arbor nut for tightness periodically. Rapidly cycling a saw on and off when it is equipped with a brake can loosen the blade.

Other radial arm saws have a mechanical brake (Illus. 58). This brake goes over the auxiliary arbor. The auxiliary arbor is located on the motor opposite the saw arbor. The mechanical brake is depressed after the saw has been shut off (Illus. 35, page 15). Mechanical brakes are likely to be found on older radial arm saws. Newer saws will have an electronic brake.

Illus. 58. Some radial arm saws have a mechanical brake, which is usually located over the auxiliary arbor.

Accessories

There are numerous accessories available for the radial arm saw. These accessories make the radial arm saw more versatile, safer, and easier to use. Some accessories may come with the saw or may be sold as extras or options. Others are designed and made in the shop for a specific purpose.

Table Boards Most radial arm saws have 3 table boards, the largest of which is fastened to the saw frame. The 2 smaller boards are held in position with the table clamps (Illus. 59). These clamps may be actuated at the front or back of the saw. The fence is located between the table boards. The clamps hold it in position also.

Illus. 59. The table clamps hold the loose tables and fence against the stationary front table. Sometimes jigs and fixtures replace the fence. They are then clamped in position.

The widest table board is called the front table. The rear table is narrower than the front table and the narrowest piece is called the spacer board. There are 3 possible fence positions (Illus. 60): 1, the typical or usual position; 2, position for crosscutting wide pieces of 1" stock or for increased mitre and bevel capability; and 3, position for widest possible rip (saw in out-rip position [Illus. 61]).

Most table boards are made of ¾ or 1" particle board or plywood. Particle board holds up best. When the tables have been cut up many times for different operations, they are replaced. Holes are sometimes cut in the rear table to accommodate a spindle sander (Illus. 62).

Some woodworkers screw, nail, or clamp an auxiliary front table on top of the front table. This table is from ¼ to ¾" thick. The auxiliary table is easier to replace and keeps the front table in good shape. The auxiliary table also elevates the work, which is necessary when working with the blade in the horizontal position.

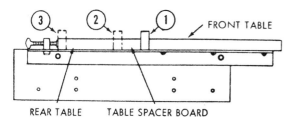

Illus. 60. Note the 3 possible fence positions. Consult the text for the use of each position.

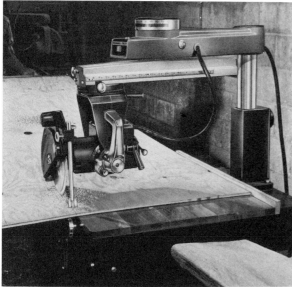

Illus. 61. This radial arm saw has the fence in position 3. The saw is set for out-ripping. This allows the operator to make the widest possible rip.

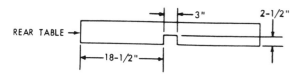

Illus. 62. Some rear tables are cut out for a spindle sander or other attachment. The dimensions listed here may not be correct for your saw.

Fence The fence supplied with the radial arm saw is usually made of ¾ or 1″ particle board. It is approximately 2″ wide and about the length of the front and rear table. The fence is replaced frequently, because the kerfs made for different operations weaken it or cause projections that affect accuracy.

Most woodworkers make replacement fences in different sizes and shapes for special setups and jobs. Some fences are made for a specific job and are only installed for that job. They are removed immediately after the job is completed. Thick fences may require that a different-sized spacer board be used. This is because the table clamps may not have enough adjustment to accommodate the thicker fence.

The fences shown throughout this book are of different thicknesses, widths, lengths, and shapes. They were made for the job at hand. Make up some extra fences as one of your first radial-arm-saw projects. That way, they will be ready when you wish to try some advanced setups. Make the fences out of particle board, plywood, or solid stock. The fence must be true, smooth, and rigid enough for the operation being performed.

Shaper Fence The shaper fence is a manufactured accessory for the radial arm saw (Illus. 63). It has 2 parts: an adjustable metal infeed fence and a stationary wooden outfeed fence. The adjustable infeed fence is designed to accommodate jobs where the entire edge of the work is shaped away. When the entire edge is removed, the fences must be offset. This fence system simplifies this adjustment.

Illus. 63. The shaper fence is a manufactured accessory. It is used for shaping and jointing operations where the entire edge is removed.

Guards There are 3 common guards used on the radial arm saw: the upper guard, the lower guard, and the shaping guard. The upper and lower guards are used for most common radial-arm-saw operations (Illus. 64). The shaping guard is used with the shaper head, planer head, or other accessories, but not with a common saw blade.

Illus. 64. These upper and lower guards are typical of those used on radial arm saws today. Sometimes the lower blade guard is made of clear plastic.

The purpose of these guards is to protect the operator from contact with the blade. Most radial-arm-saw guards attach to the motor housing. They are easy to remove, so setup changes and blade changes can be done easily.

Upper guards are usually made of metal, and lower guards are made of soft metal or clear plastic. Lower guards made of metal limit vision. The clear plastic guard offers more visibility, but tends to become scratched or blurred over time. Less damage to the blade results when a plastic lower guard comes in contact with it.

Lower guard contact with the blade is not uncommon. Movement of the stock under the lower guard can sometimes push the lower guard against the teeth. The lower guard is lifted over the work as the cut is made (Illus. 65). The upper guard does not contact the blade if it is installed properly and the correct blade has been mounted on the arbor. When in doubt, turn the blade over by hand to make certain it does not touch the guard. Do this with the power disconnected.

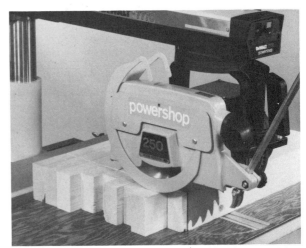

Illus. 65. When the cut is made, the lower blade guard hits the work. The guard is then lifted above the work.

The shaper guard is used when the blade arbor is positioned vertically, and has an accessory or blade mounted on it (Illus. 66). This guard is adjustable. It will move up and down to allow specialty setups (Illus. 67). Make sure this guard is securely fastened and adjusted before performing any operation. Check it periodically while in use.

The shaper guard can be made of metal or plastic. The metal guard is more durable and safer (Illus. 68). It resists the abrasion of wood chips striking it and affords greater protection against a flying cutter or carbide tip. Use the guards whenever possible. Do not work without either an upper guard or shaper guard. The lower guard must be removed for some operations.

Illus. 66. When the arbor is positioned vertically, a shaping guard is used. The knurled screw locks vertical adjustment of the clear plastic shield.

Illus. 67. This plastic guard is opaque. It has been adjusted to clear the work. The stock travels under the guard. Push sticks are being used to make the operation safer.

Illus. 68. This metal shaper guard resists abrasion better than the plastic guards. The clear guards provide better visibility until they become scratched.

Splitter The splitter and anti-kickback pawls (Illus. 69) are suspended from the upper blade guard. They adjust up and down and are locked in place by a thumbscrew or wing nut. The splitter and anti-kickback pawls are used only for ripping. They are raised out of the way for cross-cutting.

Illus. 69. The adjustable rod mounted on the upper guard supports the splitter and anti-kickback pawls. The splitter and anti-kickback pawls are used only for ripping.

The splitter rides in the saw kerf (Illus. 70) and holds the kerf open as the stock is cut. This minimizes the chance of the stock pinching the blade and causing a kickback. A kickback occurs when the stock is thrown towards the operator with great speed, possibly causing injury.

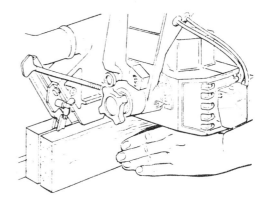

Illus. 70. The splitter rides in the saw kerf. The wing nut at the rear of the upper guard controls the splitter's position.

The anti-kickback pawls (Illus. 71) ride on the stock while it is being cut. These pawls are very sharp. If the stock begins to kick back, the pawls dig into the wood and stop the kickback. The pawls must be kept sharp and positioned correctly to be effective (Illus. 72).

There are other things you can do to minimize the chance of a kickback. Chapter 4 discusses kickbacks thoroughly and provides valuable information about identify-

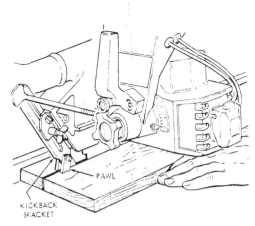

Illus. 71. The anti-kickback pawls ride on the work. If the work begins to kick back, the pawls dig into it.

Illus. 72. To be effective, the anti-kickback pawls must be positioned correctly. They must also be sharp so that the wood does not slide under them during a kickback. There is no splitter used with these pawls. The splitter is sold as an option with this saw.

ing accident-producing situations. Read it thoroughly before attempting any radial-arm-saw operations.

Crosscut Crank The crosscut crank is an accessory offered on large, industrial radial arm saws (Illus. 73). The crosscut crank drives the carriage through heavy lumber. The crosscut crank provides positive control of the carriage and eliminates the chance of the blade climbing the wood and jamming. It also prevents operation fatigue since human strength is not needed to resist blade climbing.

The speed at which the crank is turned determines the carriage or feed speed. Thicker stock will require slower

feed than thin stock. If the blade slows down during the cut, it is an indication that you are feeding too fast. Some saws have hydraulic feed for cutoff work (Illus. 47). These are operated by a foot pedal.

Illus. 73. The carriage crank controls the feed speed of the blade. The operator does not have to resist the blade as it tries to climb the work.

Return Spring The return spring (Illus. 74) is an accessory that pulls the carriage back to the column. When the carriage is released during a pull stroke, this spring-loaded accessory returns it to its rest position. The Occupational Safety and Health Administration (OSHA) has written legislation concerning this aspect of the radial arm saw. One of its guidelines is as follows: "Installation shall be in such a manner that the front end of the unit will be slightly higher than the rear, so as to cause the cutting head to return gently to the starting position when released by the operator." The return spring complies with the OSHA regulations concerning industrial use and makes the saw safer in a home or small shop operation. Some springs simply hook over the carriage lock knob (Illus. 75).

Arm Clamp The arm clamp (sometimes called arm stop, carriage stop, or carriage clamp) locks to the arm of the radial arm saw (Illus. 76). The arm clamp limits the movement of the carriage. This makes repetitive cuts safer. You cannot pull the blade beyond the work. Arm clamps can also be used for blind dadoes. When the carriage hits the clamp, blade travel stops.

Arm clamps are required by OSHA on saws doing repetitive work. Another OSHA guideline states:"An adjustable stop shall be provided to prevent the forward travel of the blade beyond the position necessary to complete the cut in repetitive operation." When arm clamps are not available for a particular saw, they can be made from wood (Illus.77) or a scrap can be clamped to the arm.

Illus. 75. Some return springs simply look over the lock knob or clamp on the carriage. These are easily removed for specialty setups.

Illus. 74 (left). The return spring located on the column pulls on the cable attached to the carriage. This ensures that the carriage will return to the column after every cut.

Illus. 76. This arm clamp locks to the radial arm. It limits the stroke of the carriage during repetitive cuts.

Illus. 77. This wooden shop-made stop can also be used as an arm clamp. Lock the stop securely before using the saw.

Featherboard A featherboard (Illus. 78) is a shop-made device used to help control stock. It is a piece of solid stock with several kerfs spaced along or with the grain. The end of the piece is cut at a 30 to 45° angle.

The featherboard is clamped to the table or fence. It holds stock against the fence or table. The featherboard acts like a spring. The feathers force stock against the fence or table. They help minimize kickback hazards and reduce vibration. Vibration is the chief cause of blade dulling.

The featherboard is referred to as a comb in OSHA regulations. Many safety-conscious people have tried to improve on the featherboard. The devices that have been developed are discussed under the heading Commercial Hold-Downs on page 31.

Illus. 79. The first stick is used to adjust the distance from the fence to the blade. This setting is equal to the desired feather size.

Illus. 78. These featherboards are being used with commercial hold-downs to keep stock positioned correctly.

Illus. 80. The first cut is made on both ends. The saw is shut off when the blade reaches the layout line. Allow the blade to come to a complete stop before moving the work.

Making a Featherboard The featherboard is an excellent radial-arm-saw project. Use 2 spacer sticks and the fence to space the kerfs evenly. One stick should be as thick as the desired "feathers," and the other should be as thick as one feather and a saw kerf. Select a piece of stock ¾" thick, 4" wide, and about 36" long.

Cut the ends of the workpiece at 30 to 45° before making any kerf cuts. Mark the feather length (about 4½") with a pencil. Position the blade for in-ripping, cut a rip trough, and install an uncut fence. Set the distance between the blade and fence with the thinner stick (Illus. 79). Lock the carriage in position. Turn on the saw and make the first cut (Illus. 80). When the blade reaches the layout line, shut off the saw and let the blade coast to a stop. Do not move the workpiece. Make the same cut on the other end.

With the blade still in the work, unlock the carriage

Illus. 81. Move the blade over using the larger stick. The work remains in contact with the blade. Lock the carriage at this setting.

and insert the thicker stick between the fence and work (Illus. 81). Lock the carriage in this position. Pull the work off the blade and move it over to the fence. Turn on the saw and make the second cut (Illus. 82). Let the blade coast to a stop when it reaches the layout line. Make the same cut on the other end of the work (Illus. 83). Continue this process until you reach the other edge. The last feather may be wider or narrower than the others (Illus. 84). It can be eliminated by simply cutting along the entire edge, thus sawing it off. Sand the featherboard lightly, and it will be ready for use.

Illus. 84. If the last finger is too wide or narrow, saw along the entire edge to eliminate it.

Illus. 82. Make the second cut. Cut both ends in the same manner.

Illus. 83. Continue making the cuts. Always stop at the layout line and allow the blade to come to a complete stop.

Commercial Hold-Downs Commercial hold-downs are devices designed to do the job of a featherboard. They hold stock down on the table and against the fence. The commercial devices are an improvement over the featherboard. There are 3 commercial hold-downs on the market today: the spring-steel type, the Ripstrate™, and the Shophelper™.

The spring-steel hold-down uses 4 spring-steel pieces to hold the work in position (Illus. 85). The position of the springs is adjusted relative to the work. Note that the outfeed side must be adjusted correctly (Illus. 85, inset) or the work will not lift the springs. Springs are held in position with a set screw. Shaper fence design (Illus. 86) accompanies the hold-down set. The spring hold-downs can be used for feed from either end of the saw.

The Ripstrate™ (Illus. 87) is designed to hold the stock in and down. The wheels pull the work towards the fence and hold them down on the table. The Ripstrate™ also acts as an anti-kickback device. If the work begins to kick back, the wheels lock and resist the work. The Ripstrate™ is completely reversible for feed from either end of the saw. A special fence is made, and the Ripstrate™ clamps to the fence.

The Shophelper™ hold-down holds the work in and down with large rubber plastic wheels. These wheels turn in only one direction, so they act as an anti-kickback device. Spring tension and positioning are infinitely adjustable. The wheels slide in and out of metal brackets that are screwed to an auxiliary fence (Illus. 88). The spring tension is adjusted by wheel movement and a wing nut on the end of the spring. Since the wheels turn in one direction, one pair (colored yellow) is needed for in-ripping, and one pair (colored orange) is needed for out-ripping.

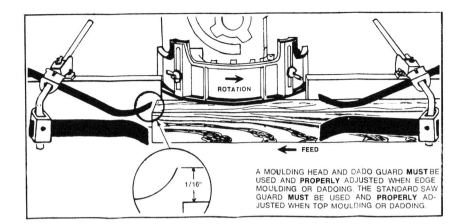

Illus. 85. This commercial hold-down uses spring steel for holding stock in position. The springs go under tension when work is fed against them.

ROTATION

← FEED

A MOULDING HEAD AND DADO GUARD **MUST** BE USED AND **PROPERLY** ADJUSTED WHEN EDGE MOULDING OR DADOING. THE STANDARD SAW GUARD **MUST** BE USED AND **PROPERLY** ADJUSTED WHEN TOP MOULDING OR DADOING.

1/16"

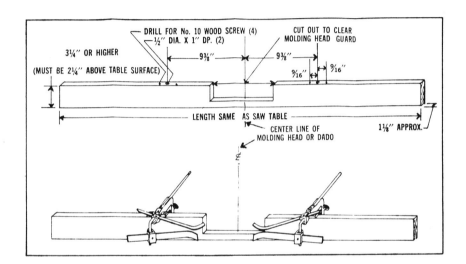

Illus. 86. This rip- and shaper-fence drawing accompanies the hold-downs. You will see this fence in use in Chapter 5.

DRILL FOR No. 10 WOOD SCREW (4)
½" DIA. X 1" DP. (2)
CUT OUT TO CLEAR MOLDING HEAD GUARD

3¼" OR HIGHER
(MUST BE 2¼" ABOVE TABLE SURFACE)

9⅜" 9⅜"

⁹⁄₁₆" ⁹⁄₁₆"

LENGTH SAME AS SAW TABLE

1⅛" APPROX.

CENTER LINE OF MOLDING HEAD OR DADO

Illus. 87. The Ripstrate™ holds stock down and against the fence during ripping operations. It may be used for both in-ripping and out-ripping.

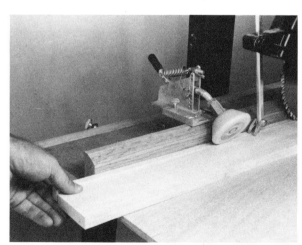

Illus. 88. The wheels on the Shophelper™ slide in and out of a metal bracket for easy adjustment. Tension is controlled by spring loading and positioning of the wheel. Note the thumbscrew for locking the adjustment.

Table Clamp The table clamp is a hold-down used for crosscut-type operations on the radial arm saw. The clamp hooks itself to countersunk eye bolts (Illus. 89), which are positioned in 4 locations on the front table. The table clamp holds small pieces securely and allows you to keep your hands well away from the blade.

The table clamp can also hold pieces with irregular edges or shapes. Stock that cannot butt to the fence may be clamped to the table. Irregular shapes can also be clamped to the fence (Illus. 90). The V-shaped groove helps ensure positive clamping. Note how the V groove is offset slightly on round stock. This forces the work against the fence. There are other devices that may be used to hold irregular pieces. They are discussed in Chapter 5 under Crosscutting.

The table clamp is designed for tables at least 1″ thick. It may be used on thinner tables if an auxiliary table is also used. Drill holes in the auxiliary table where the eye bolts are located and secure it to the front table. The auxiliary table keeps the top of the eye bolts from being higher than the top of the table. Always check your work after

clamping. The work should not move. Readjust the clamp if necessary.

Push Stick The push stick is a shop-made device. It is used to feed stock through the blade or cutter. It can also be used to hold stock against the fence or table. The push stick keeps your fingers clear of the blade and allows you to cut thin or narrow pieces safely.

Push sticks take on many different sizes and shapes. They are cut for the job at hand. Push sticks are usually cut with a sabre jig or band saw. This is because of their curved or irregular shape.

Note: Before doing any sawing, cut several push sticks and keep them near the saw. Plywood scraps make good push sticks. Many serious accidents can be avoided by using push sticks. Illus. 91A–91F provide several push stick patterns that you can use. Use these shapes or modify them to suit your needs. Be sure to round all edges and avoid sharp corners on the push sticks you make. Sharp edges and corners can easily split your skin if they are forced into your hand by a kickback.

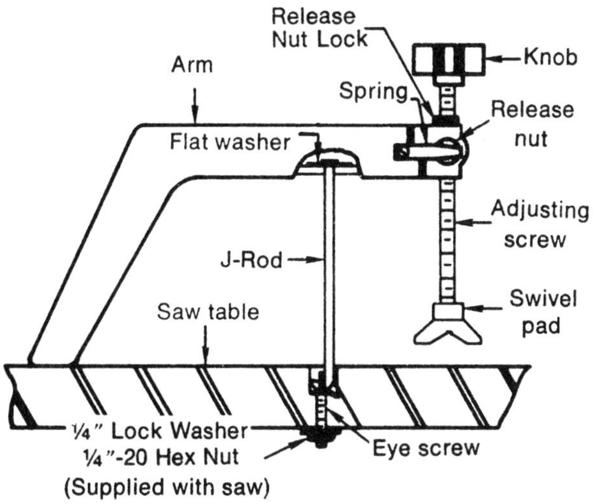

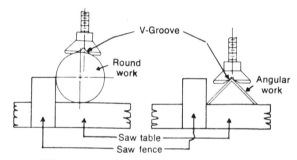

ALWAYS TEST THE WORK PIECE BY HAND TO BE SURE IT IS CLAMPED FIRMLY BEFORE MAKING ANY SAW CUTS.

Illus. 90. The table clamp will also hold irregular shapes in position for crosscutting. The table clamp also allows you to keep your hands well away from the blade while the cut is made.

Illus. 89. This table clamp locks to an eyebolt and holds stock against the fence and/or table during a crosscut. Make sure stock is clamped securely before making a cut.

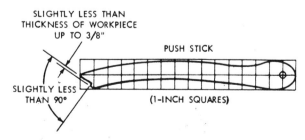

Illus. 91A. This push stick works well for ripping on the radial arm saw.

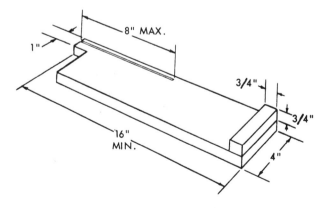

Illus. 91B. This push stick works well for narrow rips and some shaping operations.

33

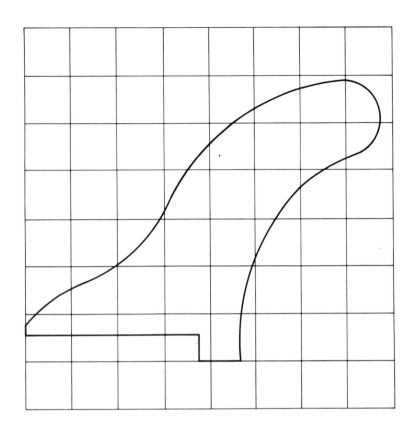

Illus. 91C. Use this pattern to make push sticks for your shop. Modify it to suit your needs, but avoid sharp corners and edges. This pattern and the patterns for 91D and 91F are on 1-inch grid that has been reduced.

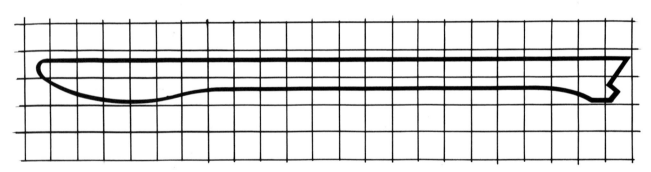

Illus. 91D. This push stick works well for some ripping operations.

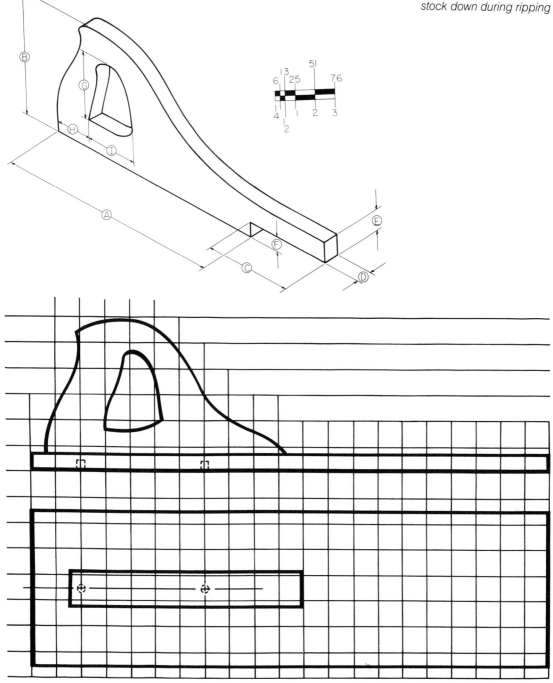

Illus. 91F. Use this push block for shaping and for raising panels. These squares can be used for making a template.

Dead Man The dead man or roller support (Illus. 92 and 93) is a device used to support long or wide stock being machined on the radial arm saw. There are many different types of supports. Some are commercial and others are shop-made.

Commercial supports are usually metal. Their height is adjustable, and they have a rolling device to support the stock (Illus. 94). Shop-made supports may also have a rolling device made of pipe, closet rod, furniture glides, or a rolling pin. The shop-made dead man may be adjustable or fixed.

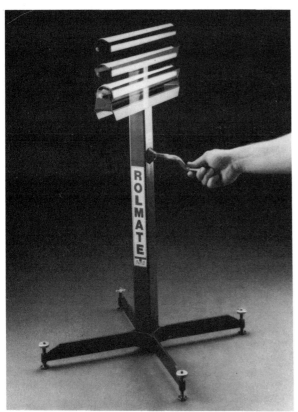

Illus. 92. This is an adjustable dead man. It will support long and/or wide pieces being machined on the radial arm saw. Turning the elevating handle controls height adjustment. This dead man locks at any desired height.

Illus. 93. This adjustable dead man folds compactly for storage. The lock knob clamps the unit at the desired height.

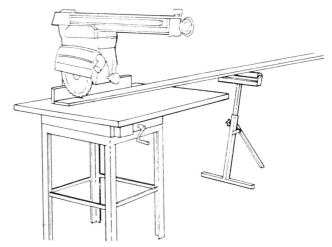

Illus. 94. The dead man holds the work at the correct height. The roller allows easy adjustment.

Some shop-made dead man devices are much simpler. They use a portable workbench sawhorse with a piece of stock or a roller. A sawhorse with a piece of stock clamped to it can also be used. The support or dead man is adjusted at the correct height to support the stock. For occasional use, the simple dead man is enough, but for frequent use, a better one should be made.

Built-On Tables   Built-on tables are tables added to the front or side(s) of the front table on the radial arm saw. These tables are designed to extend the working surface in one or more directions. Most often, they are adjusted so that they are in the same plane as the front table. This increases your control over long or wide pieces of stock.

Built-on tables can be categorized as stationary or portable. The stationary tables are permanently attached to the table (Illus. 95). Permanent tables are usually mounted on a saw that is used chiefly for crosscutting. These tables may be smooth or they may be made up of a series of rollers. The roller tables allow easy movement of stock for crosscutting and other operations. They also reduce friction between the stock and table. Since there is space between the rollers, sawdust does not accumulate on these tables. Sawdust accumulation between the table and the work can lift the work out of a true plane.

Smooth tables are usually made out of sheet stock. They are much less expensive than the roller tables, but they have some disadvantages, such as sawdust accumulation and increased friction. They have to have adequate support or they will warp or twist out of a true plane.

Portable built-on tables are easily removed for ripping or other setups (Illus. 96). The portable table may be removed completely or it may fold down next to the saw.

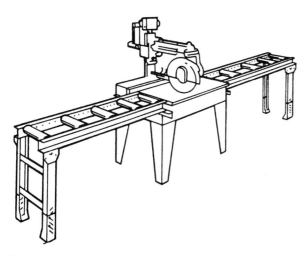

Illus. 95. These stationary conveyor tables are permanently attached to the radial arm saw.

Those which are completely removable usually have some quick-disconnect fastening such as a wing nut. Some radial-arm-saw owners have only one portable table with three quick-disconnect mounts. The mounts are located at the front and both ends of the front table. This allows the table to be quickly and easily moved to any position.

Illus. 96. This portable table is easily removed. It folds down and out of the way when not in use.

When the radial arm saw is used for ripping, usually no table is located on the feed end. This allows the operator to stand closer to the saw and have greater control over the operation. If the pieces are long, a table is usually

mounted on the opposite end. This gives the stock additional support when the cut is completed.

If you do a great deal of ripping, it is best to have portable tables. This allows you to rip from either end and still support the stock as you finish the cut (Illus. 97). A dead man can also be used for this purpose, but it provides much less stock control.

Illus. 97. This portable fold-up table allows you to rip from either end without interference. The table can also be stored when not in use.

Length Gauges Length gauges are manufactured devices used to control stock length when crosscutting. Two common ones are the Mertes LG 500™ and the Jig-fence™. Length gauges and stops are discussed more completely under Crosscutting in Chapter 5.

Mitring Jig The mitring jig (Illus. 98) is an accessory used to cut mitres without turning the arm on the saw. It even has a stop to control part length (Illus. 99). The jig is attached to an auxiliary fence. The auxiliary fence is clamped in position and aligned for cutting mitres. Shop-made and commercial mitring jigs are covered in Chapter 5 under Cutting Mitres.

Scrolling Attachment The scrolling attachment (Illus. 100) is a manufactured device that attaches to the saw's arbor. It has reciprocating action (moves up and down) that propels a blade similar to the one found on a sabre saw. The scrolling attachment allows you to cut irregular curves. This attachment increases the versatility of the radial arm saw. A complete discussion of scrolling setup and safety procedures can be found in Chapter 5.

37

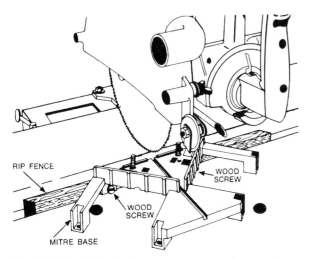

Illus. 98. The mitring jig is an accessory used to cut mitres without turning the blade or arm of the saw. It is screwed to an auxiliary fence, which clamps between the table boards.

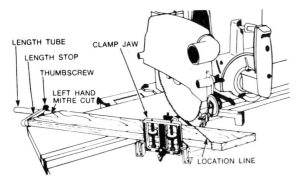

Illus. 99. The mitring jig is equipped with a stop rod and clamp to increase its accuracy.

Illus. 100. This scrolling attachment is mounted on the saw arbor. It allows you to make irregular cuts in wood.

Router Attachment The router attachment is simply a bracket. It attaches to the motor of your saw (Illus. 101). A portable router is then mounted in the bracket (Illus. 102). The table of the radial arm saw is used in conjunction with the router. The fence may also be used in conjunction with the router. The motor on the radial arm saw has no effect on the operation. In fact, those who manufacture the router attachment recommend that the radial arm saw be disconnected from its power source before mounting the attachment.

With the router attachment, the radial arm saw can be used as an overarm router. It will perform many routing operations. A complete discussion of routing on the radial arm saw can be found in Chapter 6.

Illus. 101. The router bracket bolts to or around the saw arbor. The saw is disconnected when the router is set up.

Illus. 102. The router is bolted to the bracket. It is now ready for routing. The radial-arm-saw table supports the work and the fence can control it.

3

Radial-Arm-Saw Blades and Attachments

Wood is a stringy material. If you break a piece of it, the stringy fibres make it difficult to get a clean break. If a piece of wood is split, the split is clean because the fibres run parallel to the separation. When wood is crosscut (cut across the grain or fibres), a crosscut blade is used (Illus. 103). The teeth are designed for crosscutting. Rip blades (for cutting with the grain or fibres) are designed for ripping only (Illus. 104) and they do not crosscut efficiently.

The blade on a radial arm saw is the most important link in the sawing process. Check the blades frequently to make sure they are sharp and true.

A saw blade is subjected to extreme forces. Imagine a thin disc with the force of 1½ hp at 3,450 rpm applied at the center, and the resistance of 2″ oak applied at the periphery. There is great power at the center and great resistance at the outer edge. This generates the stress, heat, and vibration that dull the blade. This is why many blades have small slots at the outer edge. These slots are called expansion slots. They allow the blade to expand as the edge heats up and prevent possible blade warpage.

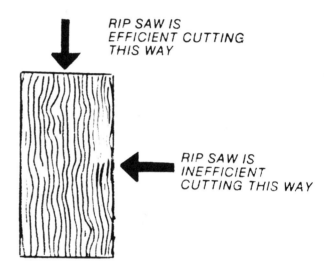

Illus. 104. Ripping is done with the grain or stringy fibres. A rip blade with chisel-shaped teeth works best for this operation.

Circular Saw Terms

The cut made by a circular saw blade is called the *kerf* (Illus. 105). The kerf must be slightly larger than the saw blade thickness. The *tooth set* or *offset* is the bend in the tooth (Illus. 106). This set allows the blade to cut a kerf that is larger than the blade's thickness. The teeth on a circular saw blade are set in alternate directions.

The *gullet* is the area behind the cutting edge of the tooth (Illus. 107). It carries away the sawdust cut by the tooth. The larger the tooth, the larger the gullet.

The *hook angle* is the angle of the tooth's cutting edge as it relates to the center line of the blade (Illus. 108). Rip blades used on table saws usually have a hook angle of about 30° (Illus. 109). This hook is too large for a radial arm saw. On a table saw, the 30° hook forces the work down on the table, but it does just the opposite on a radial arm saw. The hook lifts the work off the table and kicks it back towards the operator.

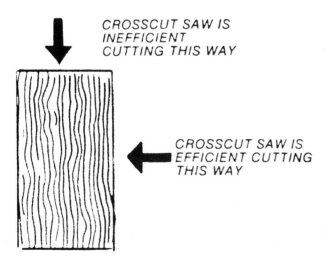

Illus. 103. Crosscutting is done across the grain of stringy fibres. A crosscut blade with pointed teeth works best for this operation.

Illus. 105. The cut made by the blade is called the kerf. The kerf is slightly larger than the blade thickness due to the set of the teeth.

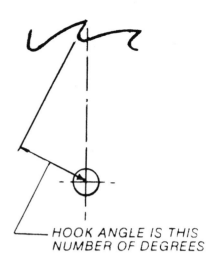

HOOK ANGLE IS THIS NUMBER OF DEGREES

Illus. 108. A rip tooth has a hook angle of about 30°. This angle is measured between the center line of the blade and the face of the tooth. This hook is too great for radial-arm-saw use.

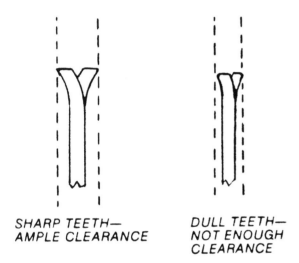

SHARP TEETH—
AMPLE CLEARANCE

DULL TEETH—
NOT ENOUGH
CLEARANCE

Illus. 106. The bend in the teeth is the set. Sharp teeth have more set than dull teeth. Set allows clearance for the blade as it travels through the kerf.

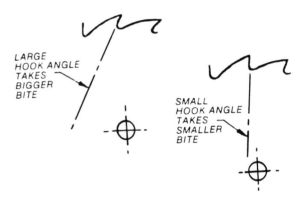

LARGE HOOK ANGLE TAKES BIGGER BITE

SMALL HOOK ANGLE TAKES SMALLER BITE

Illus. 109. The greater the hook angle, the bigger the tooth's bite. The larger the bite, the larger the gullet must be to clear the chips or sawdust.

When selecting a rip blade for use on the radial arm saw, select one with a hook less than 15° (Illus. 110). In fact, the closer the hook is to 0°, the less chance there will be of lifting or a kickback. Chapter 5 discusses blade selection for ripping and suggests some blades.

Crosscut blades used on a table saw usually have a hook of about 15°. These blades also work well on a radial arm saw. The greater the hook angle, the bigger the tooth's bite. Too large a hook angle on a crosscut blade can cause the saw blade to climb the work and jam. This is one of the most common ways of throwing a radial arm saw out of alignment.

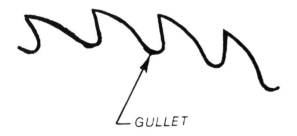

GULLET

Illus. 107. The gullet is the area behind the cutting edge of the tooth. It is curved to reduce strain on the blade as it removes the chips or sawdust.

Negative hook angles (Illus. 111) are sometimes used on blades intended for tough cutting jobs. Some circular saw blades designed to cut used lumber have a negative hook angle. This allows them to cut nails or other metal in wood. Be careful when cutting used lumber. Observe all safety procedures and protect your eyes. Pieces of metal can be thrown at you by the blade.

Top clearance (Illus. 112) is the downwards slope of the back of the tooth. This slope keeps the back of the tooth from rubbing on the wood. Without top clearance, the blade cannot cut.

Illus. 110. Notice the difference between the hook angle on these two blades. The Woodworker I (front) is designed for radial arm or table saw use. The Woodworker II is designed strictly for table saw use.

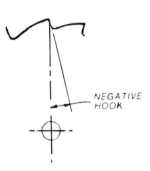

Illus. 111. Negative hook angles are sometimes used on blades that are used for tough cutting jobs.

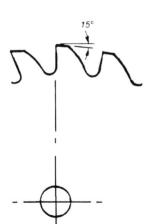

Illus. 112. Top clearance is the downwards slope of the back of the tooth. This clearance angle keeps the back of the tooth from rubbing or pounding on the wood as the cut is made.

Common Blade Types

Rip Blades Rip blades have deep gullets and a large hook angle (Illus. 113). They have a straight cutting edge designed to cut with the grain. This cutting edge looks like a chisel. Rip teeth are usually quite large.

Illus. 113. Shown from left to right are the rip, crosscut, and combination blades. Study the tooth shape so that you can identify common saw blades. Notice the plastic coating on the combination blade. Its purpose is to minimize pitch buildup.

Crosscut Blades Crosscut blades have smaller teeth than rip blades (Illus. 113). The teeth on a crosscut blade come to a point, not an edge. This allows them to cut the stringy fibres in wood with little pounding or tearing. A rip blade would pound and tear the fibres if it were used for crosscutting.

Combination Blades Combination blades (Illus. 114) are designed for both ripping and crosscutting. They work very well for cutting wood fibres at an angle (mitre joints). Some combination blades have teeth that come to a point, but have a rip-tooth profile. Others have a chisel edge and a smaller hook angle. These blades do not produce smooth cuts, but they are well-suited for general carpentry or rough construction.

Smooth-cutting combination blades are sometimes called novelty combination blades. These blades have both rip and crosscut teeth. Novelty combination blades (Illus. 114) are preferred for cabinet and furniture work because they cut smoothly with little tear-out.

There are some hybrid combination blades being marketed today. These blades proclaim their ability to do all jobs. Those marketing the blade claim that they are the only blade needed. Most of these blades have been made to industrial standards, and are very high in quality. They will do 90% of the work, but there are some jobs they cannot do. There are too many compromises in the design of a saw blade to expect it to do all jobs well.

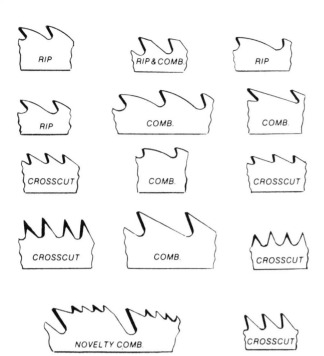

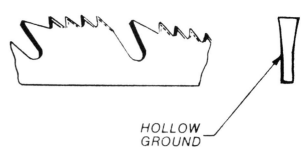

HOLLOW
GROUND

Illus. 115 (left) and 116 (right). Hollow-ground blades have sides that are relieved or ground thinner than the teeth. The thinner sides provide clearance in the kerf. The teeth have no set and there is less tear-out.

Illus. 114. Not all tooth shapes are as easy to identify as those in Illus. 113. Compare other blade profiles with the ones in this drawing for identification.

Illus. 117. This hollow-ground blade is ground back to the hub. It will cut through thick stock.

Hollow-Ground Blades Hollow-ground blades (Illus. 115 and 116) are blades with no set. The sides of the blade are recessed for clearance in the kerf. Some hollow-ground blades have sides that are recessed all the way to the hub (Illus 117). Others are recessed only part of the way (Illus. 118). Blades with partially recessed sides cannot cut thick stock, but are more rigid.

Hollow-ground blades cause less splintering and tear-out in the wood they cut. The sides of the blade may burn and accumulate pitch (wood residue) if they are used for heavy cutting instead of finish cutting. Hollow-ground blades work best with very true stock. Use them to cut mitres and compound mitres. Avoid using them for heavy ripping.

Most hollow-ground blades have novelty combination teeth. Hollow-ground blades are sometimes called *planer* blades. This is because the wood is so smooth after being cut that it appears to have been planed. There are also blades with abrasives attached to each side. These blades sand the sides of the kerf after the blade cuts the wood.

Plywood Blades Plywood blades, sometimes called panelling or veneer blades, are designed to cut hardwood plywood with cabinet-grade or furniture-grade outer veneers. These blades have very fine crosscut teeth with little set (Illus. 119). Some of these blades are hollow-ground. The fine teeth and small amount of set allow very

Illus. 118. This hollow-ground blade is only ground part of the way back to the hub. It is designed to cut through sheet stock and solid stock less than 1¼". This blade has greater rigidity than those ground all the way to the hub.

smooth splinter-free cuts. These blades should be used only when appropriate. Using them for other purposes can ruin them quickly. Certain types of plywood cores (particle or fibre) can dull these blades quickly. Carbide-tipped blades would be a better choice for particle or fibre-core plywood or other sheet stock.

Carbide-Tipped Blades Carbide-tipped blades have teeth made from small pieces of carbide. The carbide is brazed onto the circular blade (Illus. 120). Usually there is a little seat cut in the blade. This is where the carbide is brazed. Most carbide tips are wider than the metal blade, so no set is required. Carbide-tipped blades stay sharp 5 to 10 times longer than conventional blades.

Carbide is much harder than the steel used for conventional blades. Because of its hardness, carbide is also quite brittle; it will fracture easily if struck against a hard object. Carbide-tipped blades must be handled with care.

Carbide-tipped blades are more expensive than steel blades, but they require much less maintenance. Carbide-tipped blades are preferred for tough materials such as hardboard, plastic laminates, and particle board.

Carbide-tipped blades come in rip, crosscut, combination, hollow-ground, and plywood categories. They do not always resemble their steel counterparts (Illus. 121–124). Usually the type of teeth, the number of teeth, and the hook angle determine the blade's function. The teeth may be alternate top bevel, triple chip, rip, cutoff, or combination (Illus. 125).

Some carbide blades are called *control-cut* blades. These blades have 8–12 teeth, which are set slightly above the blade's periphery. These teeth minimize the chance of a kickback or severe cut. Consult a manufacturer's catalogue for specifics and blade function. Some manufacturers now sell blades designed specifically for the radial arm saw; these blades should do the best job.

Illus. 119. This plywood blade has fine teeth and very little set. Use these blades for finish cuts only. General use will dull the teeth quickly.

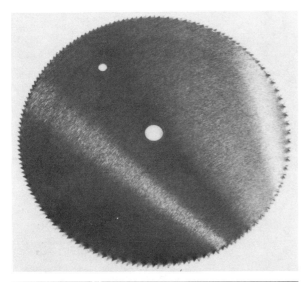

Illus. 120. Carbide-tipped blades have small pieces of carbide brazed to a steel rim. The carbide is located in an L-shaped seat. The carbide-tipped blade stays sharp much longer than a steel blade.

Illus. 121. The carbide-tipped blade shown here is a rip blade. It works well for a table saw ripping stock 1" or thinner. It has too many teeth (30) to rip 2" stock easily. Note the hook angle. When used on a radial arm saw, it tends to lift the work.

Illus. 122. This 40-tooth carbide-tipped combination blade is well suited to general cutting in stock to 2" thick.

Illus. 123. This 48-tooth, carbide-tipped blade is designed for crosscutting and trimming plastic laminates.

Illus. 124. This 60-tooth, thin-rim, carbide-tipped blade is designed for very fine cutting in sheet stock, plastic laminates, and hardwood. Depth of cut is limited by the hub just below the expansion slots.

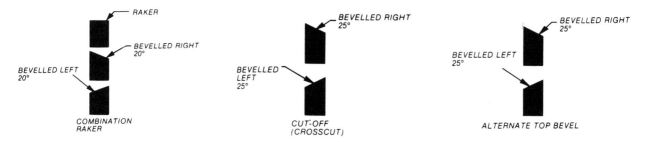

Illus. 125. Some common carbide tooth shapes and groupings. Tip blades have flat raker teeth only. Combination blades have rakers ground slightly lower than the other teeth. This allows them to clean out the kerf. Cutoff blades are used for cross-grain trimming. Alternate top bevel blades are used for fine cutting of veneers where tear-out could be a problem.

Evaluating Carbide Blades. Not all carbide blades do the job equally well. Before buying any, look them over and evaluate them carefully. The size of the carbide tips is important (Illus. 126). The larger the tips, the more times the blade can be sharpened. Look at the braze joint between the blade and the carbide tip. It often indicates blade quality. There should be no pits in the braze.

Inspect the teeth. They should be ground smooth. The smoother the surface of the carbide, the better the cut (Illus. 127). Keep the carbide blade sharp. Use a reliable sharpening service that polishes the teeth and leaves no coarse grinding marks. Blades that are ground using a coolant will usually be smoother and sharper than those which are ground dry (Illus. 128).

Selecting Blades

One blade cannot perform all sawing operations. About 3 blades are needed for general sawing. For a 10″ saw, select a rip blade with about 24 teeth. This will be coarse enough to handle any thickness the saw will accommodate. Choose a crosscut or cutoff blade with about 40 teeth. This blade will handle most general cutoff work. A finer-cutting hollow-ground blade with 60 to 80 teeth will complete the selection. Use it to cut finished pieces to length and to cut plastic laminates.

Select additional blades as needed. A general rule is that 3 teeth should be engaged with the work at any given time. Thicker pieces require less teeth than thinner ones. Consider what you are cutting, the desired finish, and whether you are ripping or crosscutting before selecting a blade.

Illus. 126. Can you see a difference in the size of the carbide tips? How many sharpenings could you get out of the one on the left?

Illus. 127. Notice the difference in grinding quality from rough surface (left) to smooth surface (right). Smoother surfaces mean sharper teeth and greater longevity.

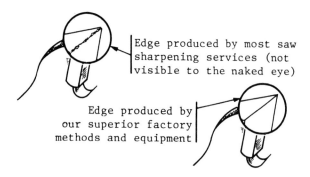

Edge produced by most saw sharpening services (not visible to the naked eye)

Edge produced by our superior factory methods and equipment

Illus. 128. Coolant and industrial equipment will produce an edge that will stay sharp longer.

Blade Collars Blade collars or stabilizers are used to increase saw blade rigidity. Some collars go on one side of the blade (Illus. 129), while others go on both sides of the saw blade (Illus. 130). The blade collars go between the arbor washers, with the blade in the middle. The concave sides go against the blade.

Illus. 129. This blade collar can be mounted on either side of the blade. Either side of this collar may touch the blade. It has been ground perfectly true.

Illus. 130. These collars are mounted on both sides of the blade. The concave side goes against the blade.

By reducing vibration, circular saw blades stay sharp longer. True-running carbide-tipped blades have less stress on the sides, which reduces tip breakage and improves cutting. Reduced vibration also means reduced noise. The vibration causes resonant noise (singing or screaming) or pounding as the blade cuts the wood. Resonant noise or pounding causes an increase in the noise level that is quite noticeable. The excess noise increases operator fatigue and is distracting.

If you install blade collars, some readjustment of the saw will be necessary. Blade collars change the relative position of the blade on the arbor. This requires readjustment of the splitter, and will enlarge the kerf cut made in the fence and table (Illus. 131).

Illus. 131. Installation of blade collars will enlarge the kerf cut made in the table and fence.

Blade Maintenance

Blades should be protected from damage when not in use. The teeth of blades in storage should not touch. Such contact can dull or break carbide teeth, and will dull steel blades. Hang blades individually or with spacers between them. This will keep them sharp. Protect blades from corrosion. Corrosion will deteriorate a sharp cutting edge.

Handle circular saw blades carefully. A sharp (or dull) blade can cut you. Never lay a blade on a metal surface. The set of the teeth wears against the metal and becomes dull.

Pitch When a circular saw blade becomes hot, pitch will accumulate on it. Pitch is a brown, sticky substance (wood resin) that looks like varnish (Illus. 132). As pitch accumulates on the blade, it acts as an insulator. This keeps the blade from dissipating heat and causes it to become dull faster.

Pitch is usually a sign of a blade with too little set for the job. It can also mean that the blade is too dull to cut. In some cases, the blade accumulates pitch and smokes when it is installed backwards (teeth pointing the wrong way). Some blades are Teflon™-coated to resist pitch accumulation, but the Teflon™ may wear off after 2 or 3 resharpenings.

Commercial pitch removers can be used to clean blades. Kerosene, liquid hand cleaners, hot water, and oven cleaners also work well. Avoid using abrasives to remove pitch. Abrasives leave scratches that make it easier for pitch to anchor itself to the blade.

Pitch accumulation does not always mean the blade is dull. A sharp hollow-ground blade will accumulate pitch quickly when used for heavy ripping.

Illus. 132. Pitch is a brown, sticky substance that looks like varnish. Pitch is accumulating behind the carbide tips on this blade.

Dull Blades Some indications of a dull blade include the following: 1. the blade tends to bind in the cut; 2. blade smokes or gives off a burnt odor; 3. increased effort is needed to feed the stock into the blade; 4. the saw no longer cuts a straight line.

Dull blades can also be identified by visual inspection. Look at the teeth. Rip teeth should come to an edge (Illus. 133). The edge should be a straight line and not rounded. Crosscut teeth should come to a point. The 2 cutting angles should form a straight line to the point of the tooth (Illus. 134).

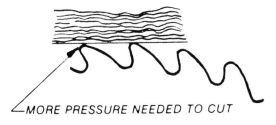

MORE PRESSURE NEEDED TO CUT

Illus. 133. The rip teeth shown here have rounded ends. This means they are dull. They should form a straight line or edge. More energy and feed pressure is needed to make a rip with a dull blade.

SHARP   DULL

Illus. 134. Crosscut teeth also become rounded or flat on the end. Sharp teeth come to a point.

Carbide teeth stay sharp longer than steel teeth, but they also become dull. If a dull carbide blade is left on the saw, the brittle teeth will crack or shatter. Drag your fingernail across the carbide tip (Illus. 135). It should cut a chip (remove a curl from your fingernail). If it does not (fingernail slides across the tip), it is too dull to cut properly. Disconnect the saw to check a blade that is mounted. Replacing broken carbide tips is much more expensive than sharpening. Keep carbide blades sharp, and broken tips will not be a problem.

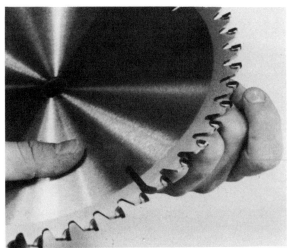

Illus. 135. If a carbide-tipped blade is sharp, it will raise a chip on your finger (you can see one on my index finger). If it is dull, your fingernail will slide across the tip.

Getting Blades Sharpened It is best to have your blades sharpened by a professional. The equipment they use is very accurate, but very expensive (Illus. 136). Find a reliable service and develop a good working relationship.

Not all sharpening services are equal. Some do better work than others. When trying a new service, do not send them your best blades. Have them sharpen one or 2 general-duty blades first. Inspect the blades carefully (Illus. 137). If the results are not satisfactory, try another sharpening service.

Make a board for transporting blades (Illus. 138). Put cardboard spacers between the blades. This will make the blades safer and easier to transport. It will also keep them well-protected and sharp.

Illus. 136. Professional sharpening equipment is very accurate, but too expensive for the average woodworker. A quality sharpening job is a bargain.

Illus. 137. Inspect blades after sharpening. Carbide-tipped blades ground as smoothly as the one shown here will stay sharp a long time.

Illus. 138. A sharpening or transportation board like this will keep blades sharp. Use a cardboard spacer between the blades to keep them separated and sharp.

Selecting the Correct Blade for the Job Blade performance is best when the blade is matched to the job. The following general rules will help you select the correct blade:

1. Three teeth should be in the work at all times.
2. Larger teeth are best for ripping.
3. Use a rip blade when the job is strictly ripping.
4. Small teeth mean a smoother cut and a slower feed rate.
5. Use the largest tooth blade that will produce satisfactory results.
6. Smaller diameter blades have more power because less energy is required to turn them.
7. The thinner the kerf, the less energy needed, but there is increased chance of blade flutter.
8. Hollow-ground blades and panelling blades should be used only for true, dry cabinet-grade lumber.
9. Remove high-quality or specialty blades as soon as the job is done.
10. Green lumber and construction lumber require blades with more set than dry hardwood lumber. This is due to the increased moisture content.
11. Never use a dull blade. It is unsafe and produces poor results.

Always analyze the job using the general rules listed and any other information you may have. The time spent changing blades is time well spent. The correct blade does the most efficient and safest job. Dull blades waste time and energy.

Trial-and-error experience will help you select the best blade for every job you do. Make note of which blade does the best job. This provides a ready reference for future use.

Some blades have a knockout arbor hole so that they may be used with more than one size of arbor. Be sure the knockout is in securely when it must be used. The blade's arbor hole should just fit the arbor. A sloppy fit means the blade is incorrect for the arbor. Extra knockouts or spacers can be purchased at most hardware stores (Illus. 139).

A prick punch can be used to offset metal around the arbor hole (Illus. 140). This holds the knockout in more securely. Knockouts are frequently removed when the blade is sharpened. Always check the arbor hole after your blades have been sharpened.

When selecting new blades, try to buy blades that have no knockouts. Blades designed to fit the arbor will do a better job and run truer. The knockouts tend to wear quickly. This causes the blade to turn in an irregular or eccentric manner.

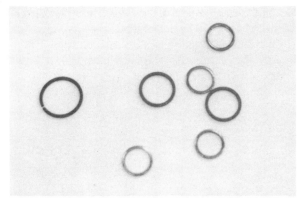

Illus. 139. Extra knockouts or arbor spacers are available at most hardware dealers. They are used to reduce the size of the arbor hole.

Illus. 141. This sanding disc allows complete use of the abrasive since the arbor does not protrude through the front.

Illus. 140. A prick punch can be used to offset metal around the arbor hole. This holds the knockout in more securely.

Sanding Discs

Sanding discs for radial arm saws are made from tempered steel or cast aluminum. They vary in size from about 6 to 10″ in diameter. When a sanding disc is mounted on the arbor, the radial arm saw can be used to disc-sand outside curves and straight edges. The disc can be tilted to sand chamfers and bevels. Some discs are designed to be used in conjunction with the fence. They have a 2° bevel on the face. When they are used to sand edges of stock fed between the disc and the fence, they leave sanding marks that are parallel with the grain.

Some discs have a hole bored through them. These discs are bolted to the saw arbor. Others have a blind hole on the back of the disc. They too are mounted on the saw arbor. The difference is that the arbor does not come through the disc. This allows complete use of the sanding disc (Illus. 141 and 142) since there is no arbor to interfere with the work. Discs with through holes also have an advantage. Abrasives can be glued to both sides, which allows the operator to switch quickly to the abrasive he wants to use.

Illus. 142. There is a slight chamfer on this disc. This allows you to feed under it when it is in the horizontal position. Note how clean the disc is. Certain contact glues allow easy removal of the disc.

The most common mistake made when disc-sanding is using too fine an abrasive. Because of the high rpms of the disc, fine abrasives cannot clear the wood chips fast enough. This causes heat and ultimately burns the abrasive. For general-duty sanding, 60-grit or 80-grit abrasives work best. Rougher work can be done with 40-grit abrasives, and finer work can be done with 100-grit or 120-grit abrasives. Avoid heavy feed or large cuts when using fine abrasives. Remove most of the stock with coarse abrasives. Then progress to a finer abrasive. Use an abrasive cleaner such as the Pro-Stik™ to keep your abrasives clean and make them last longer.

When abrasives wear out (Illus. 143), they must be replaced. If contact-type cement is used, the abrasive sheet peels off easily. Other disc cements make disc removal more difficult. If residue remains on the disc, it can be removed with a sharpened piece of hardwood (Illus. 144).

Mount the disc on the radial arm saw. Turn the saw on and use the sharpened piece of hardwood to scrape the disc. Press the wood lightly against the disc (Illus. 145). Work from the outside edge towards the middle. Repeat the process until the disc is clean. Attach the new disc according to the directions furnished with the disc cement (Illus. 146–148). Cement and precut discs are avail-

Illus. 143. When abrasives become worn or burned, they must be replaced.

Illus. 146. Apply the contact cement liberally to the surface.

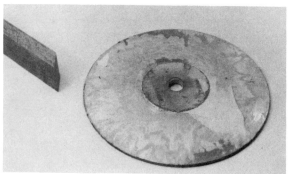

Illus. 144. Residue left on this disc can be removed with the sharpened piece of stock shown behind the disc.

Illus. 147. Press the disc into the cement and lift up to allow the solvents to evaporate.

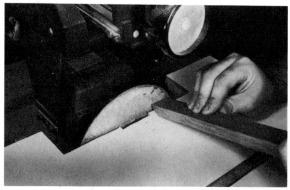

Illus. 145. Press the piece of stock against the turning disc. Work from the outside towards the center. The disc should be completely clean before new abrasives are applied.

Illus. 148. After 30 seconds, lay the abrasive down on the disc and smooth out any bubbles.

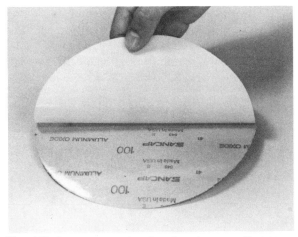

Illus. 149. Some precut abrasive discs have a self-sticking back. The protective paper is removed and the abrasive is bonded to the disc.

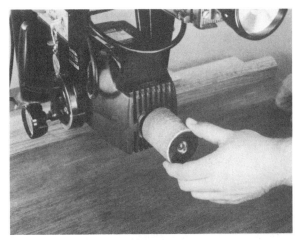

Illus. 151. This sanding spindle mounts on the auxiliary arbor opposite the saw arbor. The saw-blade arbor washers, arbor nut, and guard are all removed when using the auxiliary arbor.

able from most hardware dealers (Illus. 149). Discs can also be made from heavyweight abrasive paper.

Sanding Spindles Spindle-sanding attachments are available for radial arm saws. Some mount directly to the saw arbor (Illus. 150). Others mount on the auxiliary arbor opposite the saw arbor (Illus. 151).

Abrasives can be changed while spindles are mounted

on the arbor. This technique and sanding techniques are discussed in Chapter 5.

Stroke Sander A stroke-sanding attachment can also be mounted on the radial arm saw (Illus. 152). Complete mounting and operating techniques are discussed in Chapter 5.

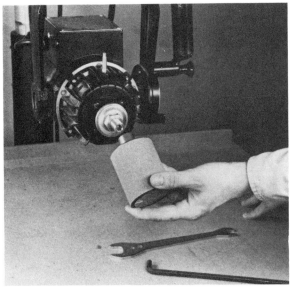

Illus. 150. This sanding spindle mounts directly to the saw arbor. Sanding spindles are available in a number of diameters.

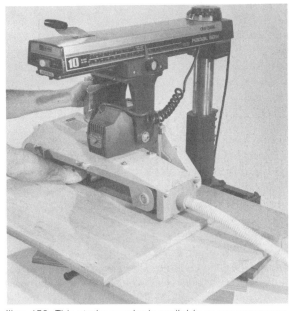

Illus. 152. This stroke sander is available as an accessory for radial arm saws. It will accommodate work 30" wide.

Dado Heads

A dado head is used to cut dadoes and rabbets. Dadoes are square or rectangular channels in wood (Illus. 153). Rabbets are L-shaped cuts along the edge of a piece of stock. The dado head is used for joinery cuts. There are 3 types of dado heads: the wobble type, the blade and chipper type, and the twin-blade adjustable type. When used in the horizontal position, the moulding guard replaces the standard guard.

Illus. 154. This pair of dado or wobble washers are used with a conventional saw blade. By turning the washers on the arbor, various dado widths can be cut.

Illus. 153. The dado head cuts a square or rectangular channel in wood. It will also cut an L-shaped channel in wood, known as a rabbet. See left end of the work.

Wobble Types Wobble-type dado heads form a dado with a single wobbling (oscillating) blade. The oscillation of the blade causes it to cut a dado of the desired shape. Offset washers make the blade oscillate. One is mounted on either side of the blade. Both washers have registration marks. These marks serve as guides to the width of dado that will be cut at that setting.

Some wobble dado heads consist only of a pair of offset washers (Illus. 154). These washers are then used with a circular saw blade that fits the saw. Most blades will work with these washers. Experimenting with various blades on scraps will determine which blade is best for cutting dadoes. Usually, the thicker the blade, the better it will

work. Blades with very little hook will cut better and will have less chance of kickback.

Other wobble dado heads consist of a heavy carbide-tipped blade and a pair of offset washers (Illus. 155). This wobble dado works only as a unit. The heavy carbide-tipped blade makes this unit suitable for particle board and other wood-composition products. This wobble dado set (blade and washers) is available with a varying number of carbide tips on the blade. The one with the largest number of carbide tips cuts the smoothest dado. It also is less likely to tear out the wood next to the dado. It is good practice to mark the "high" and "low" tooth with a scriber (Illus. 156). This makes measuring between the fence and blade easier when setting up the dado head.

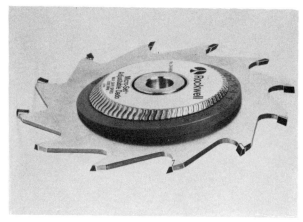

Illus. 155. This wobble dado is sold as a set. The washers and blade work as a unit to cut dadoes. This blade has carbide-tipped teeth, which makes it suitable for cutting particle board and plywood.

Illus. 156. The "high" and "low" tooth on this wobble dado have been marked with a scriber. This helps determine the position of the blade relative to the work. Use the "high" or "low" tooth to decide where the work or fence should be positioned.

Illus. 158. This carbide-tipped cutter (right) and chipper (left) are best suited to particle board and plywood. The 2 missing teeth on the cutter make room for the chipper when it is mounted between 2 cutters.

Blade and Chipper Types Blade and chipper dado heads come as a complete set. The 2 blades or cutters resemble a combination blade (Illus. 157). Each blade or cutter is designed to cut a ⅛" kerf. The chippers have 2 cutting edges. They are mounted between the blades. Chippers are designed for ⅛ or ¹⁄₁₆" spacing. Blade and chipper dado sets may be carbide-tipped (Illus. 158) or tool steel.

Some carbide-tipped dado heads have chippers with more than 2 cutting faces. The chipper shown in Illus. 159 has 8 cutting faces. It cuts much smoother than chippers with only 2 cutting faces. The cutting faces on this

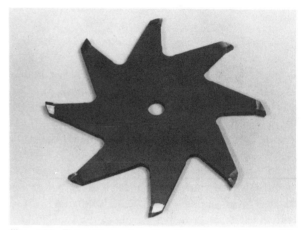

Illus. 159. This chipper has 8 cutting faces with special grinding. This chipper cuts much smoother than a chipper with only two cutting faces.

Illus. 157. This steel cutter (right) and chipper (left) are the two components of a dado head. Chippers are used with the cutters to make dadoes over ¼" wide.

chipper have special cutting angles ground on them to make the cut smoother.

A complete dado set will cut dadoes from ⅛ or ¼" or to ¹³⁄₁₆" by varying the number of chippers between the blades. Two blades or cutters must be used for all dadoes except those ⅛", which require one cutter. A ¼" dado is made with 2 blades. A ⅜" dado is cut with the two ⅛" blades and one ⅛" chipper.

A blade and chipper type of dado head cannot be adjusted to odd-sized dadoes as easily as a wobble type. With the use of plastic, paper, or cardboard rings (Illus. 160), the dado head can be adjusted somewhat. The rings are slipped over the arbor between the cutters and chippers. This allows extended spacing and an oversized cut. As the dado becomes dull, some paper spacing is needed to compensate for wear.

Illus. 160. These plastic washers can be used to space the cutter and chipper dado to an odd size.

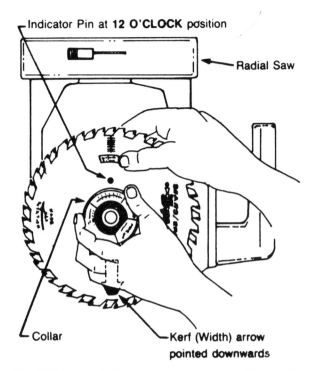

Indicator Pin at **12 O'CLOCK** position

Radial Saw

Collar

Kerf (Width) arrow
pointed **downwards**

Illus. 162. The adjusting collar at the center of the dado head gives you the approximate dado width.

Twin-Blade Adjustable Dado   The twin-blade adjustable dado has two blades similar to the cutters in a cutter-and-chipper dado head. The blades are held together at the center. The center is turned the same way for adjustment as the center of a wobble dado. When the dado opens up, the blades spread at only one end (Illus. 161). The adjustment collar at the center tells you the approximate dado width (Illus. 162). The blade is marked at the widest point to simplify setup. It is also marked with a depth-of-cut scale to help set dado depth quickly and accurately (Illus. 163). The twin-blade adjustable dado is carbide-tipped and has 24 teeth on each cutter.

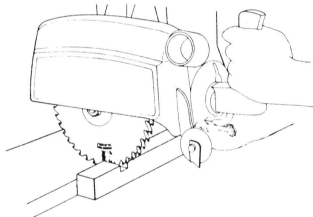

Illus. 163. The depth of cut scale is stencilled onto the blade. This scale helps you set dado depth quickly and accurately.

Moulding Heads

Moulding heads (Illus. 164) are used to shape stock on the radial arm saw. Stock can be shaped into moulding, lipped doors, and joinery. The moulding head mounts on the saw arbor. It has slots into which the moulding cutters are fastened. A special throat plate is used with the moulding head. Some moulding heads have only 1 or 2 cutters, but most have a set of 3 cutters for each shape that is cut. The moulding heads that use a set of 3 cutters are safer and cut smoother moulding.

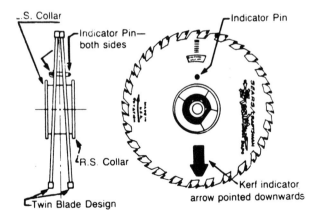

L.S. Collar

Indicator Pin—
both sides

Indicator Pin

R.S. Collar

Twin Blade Design

Kerf indicator
arrow pointed downwards

Illus. 161. When this dado head is adjusted, the blades spread at only one end.

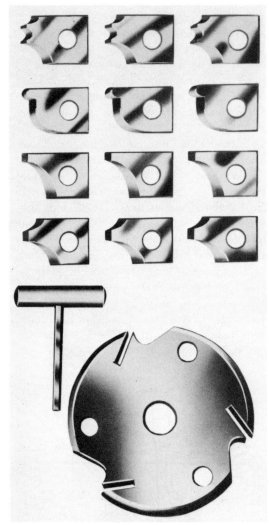

Illus. 164. The moulding or shaper head is used to shape stock. There are many different cutters that can be used in the moulding head.

on the cutters. This could change the shape of the cut. If cutters have large nicks, discard them and buy a new set. It is important to keep shaper cutters sharp. Dull cutters tend to tear the wood and may cause a kickback.

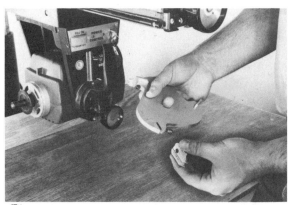

Illus. 165. Most shaper cutters have a hole in them that is used to lock them to the cutterhead.

Illus. 166. Follow the manufacturer's directions for mounting moulding cutters. Check them periodically during operation to make sure they are tight.

There are many moulding cutter types and shapes. They are ground from flat steel and usually have a mounting hole. The mounting hole is used to attach them to the moulding head (Illus. 165). Moulding cutter manufacturers have their own mounting designs. This means that cutters of different brands are not interchangeable. Follow the manufacturer's directions for mounting moulding cutters in the moulding head (Illus. 166). Check them periodically during operation to be sure they are tight. Be sure the cutters all face forward. The flat side of the cutter does the cutting. Stock is fed against the flat face of the cutter.

When the cutters become dull, the flat side can be honed on an oilstone or waterstone (Illus. 167). Honing the flat side will cause the clearance angles to form an edge with the flat side. Never hone the clearance angles

Illus. 167. Dull cutters can be honed on an oilstone or waterstone. Hone the flat side only. Keep the cutters sharp and free of rust. Discard cutters that are chipped or damaged.

Chucks and Collets

Most radial arm saws have an accessory shaft on the end of the motor opposite the saw blade arbor. This shaft was designed for devices that make the radial arm saw more versatile. Chucks and collets are such devices.

Chuck   The chuck (Illus. 168) is a device used to hold specialty tools, router bits, drill bits, and other boring tools. The chuck is similar to the one found on a drill press. It has threads that match those on the accessory shaft or arbor. Install it carefully so that the threads do not bind. Tools may then be mounted in the chuck. Be sure to remove the chuck key after installation (Illus. 169).

Illus. 168. This chuck is mounted on the auxiliary arbor. It can be used to hold sanding devices, drill or router bits.

Illus. 169. The bit is chucked and work can begin. Remember to remove the chuck key before work begins. Note that everything has been removed from the saw arbor prior to mounting the chuck.

Collet   The collet or ¼″ adapter is used to mount router bits with a ¼″ shank. Other tools with a ¼″ shank may also be mounted in this collet. The collet has a tapered sleeve that tightens around the tool's shank for positive seating. A bit is less likely to slip in the collet than in the chuck. For that reason, a collet is used for routing operations.

The collet is mounted on the accessory shaft in the same way as the chuck (Illus. 170). Bits may then be mounted in the collet. Make sure that at least ½″ of tool shank is inserted into the collet. The collet may then be tightened (or loosened) with 2 wrenches. One holds the collet stationary while the other wrench tightens (or loosens) the tapered sleeve in the collet. Tighten the collet securely, but do not overtighten. This makes bit removal difficult and can damage the tapered sleeve.

Keep all chucks and collets lightly oiled when not in use. This will minimize rusting. It will also make them easier to install and use. Note: The accessory shaft turns at a very high speed. For this reason, not all drilling and boring tools may be used in a chuck or collet. Be sure to read Chapters 4 and 6 before using a chuck or collet on the accessory shaft.

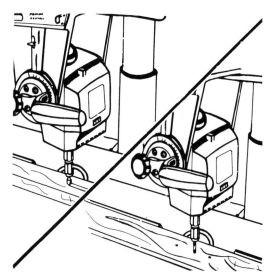

Illus. 170. The collet is mounted in the same way as the chuck. The collet only accommodates tools with a ¼″ shank.

Planing Head

The planing head (also known as a Safe-T-Planer™ or rotary planer) is an accessory that can perform many functions. Most frequently, it is used to surface-plane rough stock, but it can also be used to make raised panels and cut rabbets. The actual operation of the planing head is discussed in Chapter 6.

The planing head is mounted on the saw arbor (Illus. 171). It is a round device approximately 3 to 5" in diameter. On the underside, 3 cutters are mounted. These cutters may be carbide or tool steel. The cutters are set in relation to the bottom of the planer head (Illus. 172). When the tool steel cutters become dull, they can be removed and resharpened. Carbide cutters may also be resharpened if the correct grinding equipment is available. If not, they may be replaced. Be sure the cutters are aligned correctly and tightened securely when they are replaced. The planing head is usually used in the horizontal position. The shaper guard is used with it (Illus. 173) in most cases.

Illus. 171. The planer head is mounted on the saw arbor. The arbor nut is housed inside the casting.

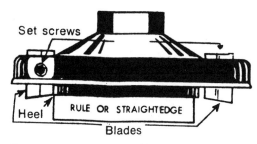

Illus. 172. The cutters are set in relation to the bottom of the cutter.

Illus. 173. The shaper guard is usually used when the planing head is mounted on the saw arbor.

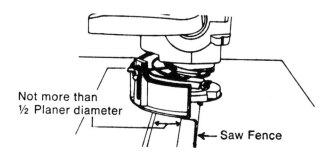

Not more than ½ Planer diameter

Saw Fence

4

Safety Procedures

Both the novice and experienced operator can have accidents with the radial arm saw. The novice operator's accident is usually caused by a lack of knowledge of radial-arm-saw safety procedures. He is not able to foresee a hazard or identify an accident-producing situation. The experienced operator's accident is usually caused by carelessness, a shortcut, or an outright violation of the safety rules. When an experienced operator attempts and gets away with safety rule violations, they soon become common practice. This is when an accident is likely to occur.

The radial arm saw has many locks, clamps, jigs, and devices that must be considered when it is set up for any job. Operators frequently forget to check *every* aspect of the setup before they begin (Illus. 174). This can produce a hazardous condition or accident. It can also waste time and material. Rushing into the operation can cause problems. Double-check every setting and adjustment before beginning. Check them periodically as you work.

Remember, the radial arm saw is capable of doing many jobs without a saw blade. When you are working without a saw blade there is just as much chance of an accident occurring. These accidents could be as severe as those caused by a saw blade. In fact, in the case of shaping, the accident could be of greater severity (Illus. 175). Whatever attachment or jig you use, read the manufacturer's directions and safety precautions. Consult the text in this book also. Safety rules for various operations are discussed when the operation is first presented.

Illus. 174. Check every lock and clamp before you begin working. Make sure any stops, jigs, or fixtures are secured correctly. Most problems are eliminated by these routine checks.

Illus. 175. Shaping and other operations that do not require a blade can be just as dangerous as operations using a saw blade. Approach all setups and operations with caution.

All accidents have contributing factors, among which are the following:

1. *Working while tired or taking medication.* Accidents are most likely to happen when you are tired. Whenever you are tired, stop or take a break. Medication and alcohol can affect your perception or reaction time.

2. *Rushing the job.* Trying to finish a job in a hurry leads to errors and accidents. The stress of rushing the job also leads to early fatigue. If you injure yourself or make a mistake while rushing the job, the job will take far longer than it would working at a normal pace.

3. *Inattention to the job.* Daydreaming or thinking about another job while working with the radial arm saw can lead to accidents. Be doubly careful when making repetitive cuts (Illus. 176), for they can lead to daydreaming.

4. *Distractions.* Conversing with others, telephone calls, unfamiliar noises, and doors opening and closing are all distractions in the shop. Shut off the radial arm before conversing, answering the phone, or investigating an unfamiliar noise.

5. *General Housekeeping.* A dirty or cluttered work area provides tripping hazards and excess dust that can be a breathing hazard. Keep the shop and your radial arm saw neat (Illus. 177). Contain, collect, and dispose of the dust to control the airborne breathing hazard. It is more pleasant and safer to work in a clean area.

Know Your Saw

Complex operations require several adjustments of the radial arm saw. To work safely, you must know what the adjustments are and how to make them in the correct sequence. Chapters 1 and 2 help you become acquainted with the radial arm saw. The owner's manual also helps you understand the radial arm saw.

Many radial-arm-saw manufacturers offer general lists of safety precautions (Figs. 1–3). Study these lists. Not all will pertain to your saw, but they will help you work safely with other tools or radial arm saws.

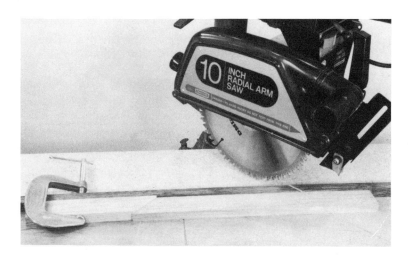

Illus. 176. Repetitive cuts can lead to day-dreaming or inattention. If you lose your concentration, take a break and come back to the job later.

Illus. 177. Keep the radial arm saw and your work area neat. Always shut the saw off before clearing scrap from it.

1. **FOR YOUR OWN SAFETY, READ INSTRUCTION MANUAL BEFORE OPERATING THE TOOL.** Learn the tool's application and limitations as well as the specific hazards peculiar to it.

2. **KEEP GUARDS IN PLACE** and in working order.

3. **GROUND ALL TOOLS.** If tool is equipped with three-prong plug, it should be plugged into a three-hole electrical receptacle. If an adapter is used to accommodate a two-prong receptacle, the adapter lug must be attached to a known ground. Never remove the third prong.

4. **REMOVE ADJUSTING KEYS AND WRENCHES.** Form habit of checking to see that keys and adjusting wrenches are removed from tool before turning it "ON."

5. **KEEP WORK AREA CLEAN.** Cluttered areas and benches invite accidents.

6. **DON'T USE IN DANGEROUS ENVIRONMENT.** Don't use power tools in damp or wet locations, or expose them to rain. Keep work area well lighted.

7. **KEEP CHILDREN AND VISITORS AWAY.** All children and visitors should be kept a safe distance from work area.

8. **MAKE WORKSHOP CHILDPROOF**—with padlocks, master switches, or by removing starter keys.

9. **DON'T FORCE TOOL.** It will do the job better and be safer at the rate for which it was designed.

10. **USE RIGHT TOOL.** Don't force tool or attachment to do a job for which it was not designed.

11. **WEAR PROPER APPAREL.** No loose clothing, gloves, neckties, rings, bracelets, or other jewelry that can get caught in moving parts. Nonslip footwear is recommended. Wear protective hair covering to contain long hair.

12. **ALWAYS USE SAFETY GLASSES.** Also use face or dust mask if cutting operations are dusty. Everyday eyeglasses only have impact-resistant lenses; they are NOT safety glasses.

13. **SECURE WORK.** Use clamps or a vise to hold work when practical. It's safer than using your hand and frees both hands to operate tool.

14. **DON'T OVERREACH.** Keep proper footing and balance at all times.

15. **MAINTAIN TOOLS IN TOP CONDITION.** Keep tools sharp and clean for best and safest performance. Follow instructions for lubricating and changing accessories.

16. **DISCONNECT TOOLS** before servicing and when changing accessories such as blades, bits, cutters, etc.

17. **USE RECOMMENDED ACCESSORIES.** Consult the owner's manual for recommended accessories. The use of improper accessories may cause hazards.

18. **AVOID ACCIDENTAL STARTING.** Make sure switch is in "OFF" position before plugging in power cord.

19. **NEVER STAND ON TOOL.** Serious injury could occur if the tool is tipped or if the cutting tool is accidentally contacted.

20. **CHECK DAMAGED PARTS.** Before further use of the tool, a guard or other part that is damaged should be carefully checked to ensure that it will operate properly and perform its intended function—check for alignment of moving parts, binding of moving parts, breakage of parts, mounting, and any other conditions that may affect its operation. A guard or other part that is damaged should be properly repaired or replaced.

21. **DIRECTION OF FEED.** Feed work into a blade or cutter against the direction of rotation of the blade or cutter only.

22. **NEVER LEAVE TOOL RUNNING UNATTENDED. TURN POWER OFF.** Don't leave tool until it comes to a complete stop.

23. **DRUGS, ALCOHOL, MEDICATION.** Do not operate tool while under the influence of drugs, alcohol or any medication.

24. **MAKE SURE TOOL IS DISCONNECTED FROM POWER SUPPLY** while motor is being mounted, connected or reconnected.

Fig. 1. Study the safety practices listed by radial-arm-saw manufacturers, like the ones shown here and on pages 61 and 62. They will help you work safely around any radial arm saw. The safety practices listed above are put out by Delta for the operation of all tools. On the following page is a list of safety practices for the DeWalt radial arm saw. On page 62 is a list of safety procedures for the operation of the Uni-Point radial arm saw put out by Northfield Foundry and Machine Co.

DeWALT SAFETY CHECKLIST

DISPLAY NEAR SAW

1. *HAVE YOU BEEN SHOWN A SAFE METHOD FOR PROPERLY PERFORMING THIS OPERATION?*

2. *REVIEWED YOUR OWNER'S MANUAL?*

3. *WHAT PATH WILL BLADE FOLLOW? KEEP HANDS AWAY!*

4. *WEARING LOOSE CLOTHING, TIES, GLOVES, JEWELRY? DON'T!*

5. *UPPER & LOWER GUARDS IN PLACE?*

6. *ANTI-KICKBACK IN PLACE?*

7. *ALL CLAMPS TIGHT? YOKE? BEVEL? ARM?*

8. *BLADE RIGHT SIZE? CORRECTLY MOUNTED? SHARP?*

9. *WEARING SAFETY GLASSES?*

10. *ROLLER HEAD RETRACTING AFTER CUT?*

11. *PUSHER STICK FOR RIPPING OR PLOUGHING?*

12. *DON'T REMOVE SMALL SCRAPS WITH FINGERS.*

CONCENTRATE—AVOID DISTRACTION—
SAWS CAN'T THINK—YOU MUST!

Fig. 2.

The safety rules contained herein are printed for your protection and well-being. Read them carefully and observe them strictly. If there are any portions of this manual that you do not understand completely, do not hesitate to contact your supervisor for clarification.

Your undivided attention is required when operating this machine. Concentrate fully on the task at hand and accord the Uni-Point the respect a machine of this type is due. Usage of your good common sense is essential for safe, efficient operation. The following list of safety instructions are general in nature and you will want to incorporate specific rules related to your application.

GENERAL SAFETY INSTRUCTIONS FOR UNI-POINT

1. Familiarize yourself with all machine controls. Pay particular attention to the location of the Stop-Start control.
2. Ground the machine properly.
3. Check the saw blade guard to see that it is mounted tightly and functioning properly.
4. Do not wear loose clothing while operating this machinery.
5. Always wear proper eye and ear protection around machinery.
6. Check saw blade to see that it is not warped or cracked. Use only blades that are sharp and properly set.
7. Be sure that the saw blade is positioned correctly on the arbor and that the arbor nut is tight. Use wrench provided to tighten arbor nut.
8. Make all necessary adjustments before turning on the machine. Be sure that all clamping devices and locks are tight and the depth of cut is correct.
9. Allow the motor to reach its full operating speed before starting cut.
10. Maintain a 6″ margin of safety. To do this you must keep your hands this distance away from the path of the saw blade.
11. Check stock for nails, staples, etc. before cutting.
12. Make sure the wedges are holding the fence tight to the table.
13. Stock must be held firmly on the table and against the fence for all crosscutting operations. The ends of long boards must be supported level with the table.
14. Always return the saw to the rear of the table after completing a crosscut or a mitre cut. Never remove the stock from the table until the saw has been returned to the rear of the table.
15. When ripping, feed stock into side opposite splitter and anti-kickback dogs. Be sure the splitter and anti-kickback dogs are engaged.
16. Stock to be ripped should be flat and have one straight side to hold against the fence.
17. Never stand directly behind material being ripped.
18. An offbearer should be used during the ripping operation.
19. Feed the material carefully and only as fast as the machine will cut it easily.
20. Upon completion of an operation, shut off the power and wait until the blade stops before leaving machine or setting up another cut. Never leave the machine running and unattended.
21. Make sure all electrical power is turned off and cannot be accidentally restarted before making any adjustments, repairs, replacements or lubricating machine.
22. Keep the table clean and free of scrap pieces and excessive amounts of sawdust. Keep the floor around the machine clean.

Fig. 3. Safety instructions for the Uni-Point radial arm saw put out by Northfield Foundry and Machine Co.

OSHA Regulations

Radial arm saws used in industry are covered by OSHA (the Occupational Safety and Health Act). This act regulates the setup and use of industrial equipment, and is enforced by the Occupational Safety and Health Administration, which is part of the U.S. Government. OSHA lists specific requirements for radial arm saws. In addition, there are some general requirements for all woodworking shops.

Some of the requirements listed by OSHA for radial-arm-saw use are as follows:

1. The upper hood shall completely enclose the upper portion of the blade down to a point that will include the end of the saw arbor. The upper hood shall be constructed in such a manner and of such material that it will protect the operator from flying splinters, broken saw teeth, etc., and will deflect sawdust away from the operator. The sides of the lower exposed portion of the blade shall be guarded to the full diameter of the blade by a device that will automatically adjust itself to the thickness of the stock and remain in contact with stock being cut to give maximum protection possible for the operation being performed.

2. Each radial arm saw used for ripping shall be provided with nonkickback fingers or dogs located on both sides of the saw so as to oppose the thrust or tendency of the saw to pick up the material or to throw it back toward the operator. They shall be designed to provide adequate holding power for all the thicknesses of material being cut.

3. An adjustable stop shall be provided to prevent the forward travel of the blade beyond the position necessary to complete the cut in repetitive operations.

4. Installation shall be in such a manner that the front end of the unit will be slightly higher than the rear, so as to cause the cutting head to return gently to the starting position when released by the operator.

5. Ripping and ploughing shall be against the direction in which the saw turns. The direction of the saw rotation shall be conspicuously marked on the hood. In addition, a permanent label not less than 1½ inches by ¾ inch shall be affixed to the rear of the guard at approximately the level of the arbor, reading as follows: "Danger: Do Not Rip or Plough from This End."

The radial-arm-saw requirements developed by OSHA do not apply to small private shops, but they can make your shop a safer place to work. All of the OSHA requirements have been incorporated into this book wherever possible.

Crosscutting Safety

Crosscutting is the most common operation performed on radial arm saws. Although it is not hazardous, it is the most likely to cause an accident simply because of frequency of use. Stock should always be butted against the fence (Illus. 178). When stock is not in contact with the fence, it will slam into the fence when the blade touches it. Anything between the work and the fence will be pinched. This may also throw the radial arm saw out of adjustment. Stacking pieces can cause this slamming between any 2 pieces. It is safest to cut pieces one at a

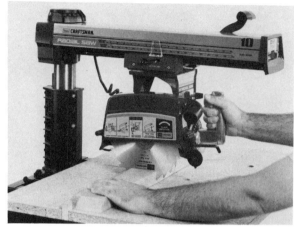

Illus. 178. When crosscutting always butt your work against the fence. Keep hands well away from the blade when crosscutting.

Illus. 179. Round stock should be clamped when crosscutting. The clamp keeps it from rolling into the blade.

time. If the pieces have to be stacked, clamp them to the fence.

When crosscutting round stock, be sure to clamp it to the fence or table (Illus. 179). The stock has a tendency to turn when the blade touches it, which can cause the blade to climb the work. Climbing can ruin the work, damage the blade, or throw the saw out of adjustment.

When crosscutting, one hand usually holds the work against the fence and the other pulls the carriage. After the cut, the carriage is returned to the column and locked in position. A carriage-return spring pulls the carriage back to the column (Illus. 180). Whenever you make a

Illus. 180. The carriage return spring pulls the carriage towards the column when released.

crosscut, your arms should be parallel to the blade. Never cross your arms. This will put one arm in the blade's path. When crosscutting, keep your hands 6 to 8″ away from the blade at all times.

When working with small stock, use a table clamp or other hold-down to position your work (Illus. 181). This will keep your hand well away from the blade. When working with large stock, make sure the ends are supported. When the piece is cut, the end could lift. This could put your hand dangerously close to the blade.

Illus. 181. A table clamp makes working with small pieces much safer. Always keep your hands well away from the saw blade.

When doing repetitive crosscutting, keep the table free of scrap. If scrap from any operation accumulates on the saw, stop cutting, shut off the saw, and clear the table. Clear the table only when the saw is turned off. Use a fence that is in good shape. A fence with several cuts in it can cause little scraps to pinch and be thrown away from the machine. Repetitive crosscutting is also safer when an arm clamp or stop limits carriage travel (Illus. 182).

When trimming several parts, replace the fence. The new fence will keep scraps from being pinched between the blade and the opening in the fence. Support the ends of long pieces when crosscutting. Unsupported ends may cause the work to lift after it is cut. If your reaction is to grab the work as it lifts, you will have your hand in motion dangerously close to the blade. Think before you work!

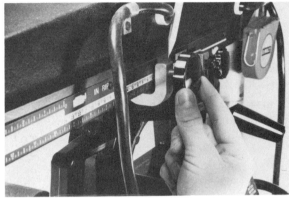

Illus. 182. Use an arm clamp to limit carriage travel when making repetitive cuts.

Ripping Safety

Ripping is the most dangerous of the common radial-arm-saw operations. There must be absolute control over the work during the entire ripping operation.

The blade orientation during ripping causes lifting and kickback problems. (Study the section on kickbacks on page 66 for specific practices.) Commercial hold-downs can help keep your hands clear of the blade. These hold-downs hold the stock down on the table and in against the fence (Illus. 183 and 184). They are used in addition to the guard and splitter. A cleat can also be clamped to the fence to control lifting (Illus. 185). This does not hold stock in against the fence, but a featherboard can also be used.

Keep your hands 6 to 8″ from the blade when ripping. Use push sticks to feed stock at the end of each cut. Avoid ripping pieces shorter than 18″. These pieces are harder to control and bring your hands too close to the blade.

The direction of feed is an important safety factor. When in-ripping (see page 73), feed from the right side of the saw (as you face the front of the saw). Feed from the left side of the saw for out-ripping (see page 73). When in doubt, check the arrow on the guard. It will tell you which way the blade is turning.

Blade selection is important. Blades favored for ripping on the table saw have too much hook angle for ripping on the radial arm saw. Table saw rip blades have hook angles of 15 to 25°. Radial-arm-saw rip blades should have less hook than this (large hook angles contribute to the lifting

Illus. 183. These Shophelper hold-downs keep stock on the table and against the fence. They only turn one way, so the chance of a kickback is minimized.

Illus. 184. These commercial hold-downs keep stock on the table against the fence.

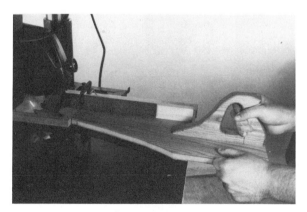

Illus. 185. A cleat clamped to the fence controls stock lifting during all rip and some shaping operations.

and kickback problem). An angle of 0 to 15° (the lower the better) is best.

It has been my experience when ripping on the radial arm saw that any of the following blades will make the job safer: Mr. Sawdust 1™, Forrest Saw Woodworker I™, DML Inc. Radi-All Blade™, Freud LU70M, and Wisconsin Knife Nos. 08074 and 08502. All blades are of high quality and produce excellent results on a radial arm saw that has been set up correctly. The hook angle on these blades ranges from −6 to +15°.

To set up the radial arm saw safely for ripping, position the nose of the guard no more than ¼" above the workpiece (Illus. 186). Most guards have a warning that specifies which end of the guard *not* to rip from. Look for it on your saw. Feed towards the face of the tooth. Think before you cut. Efficiency is not attained by hurrying.

Illus. 186. When ripping, the nose of the guard should be no more than ¼" above the blade. This minimizes the chance of stock lifting when ripping.

The splitter should be adjusted for proper alignment with the blade, and the anti-kickback pawls should be riding on the wood. The pawls should be sharp so that they will dig into the wood in the event of a kickback (Illus. 187). Remember that any adjustment of the guard or blade height usually affects the position of the pawls and splitter. If you adjust the guard, check the splitter and pawls before making a cut.

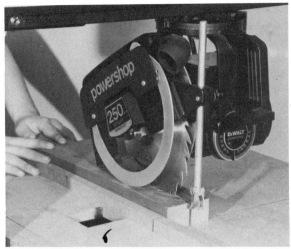

Illus. 187. The pawls should ride on the work while ripping. A sharp pawl will dig into the work and stop a kickback before any injury occurs.

Keep your hands clear of the kickback zone both in front and back of the blade. If you are holding stock after it has been cut (behind the blade) and it kicks back, your hand could follow the wood directly into the blade. Always use the splitter and anti-kickback pawls when ripping. Lengths of stock over 24″ are safest.

Ripping requires your full attention. Study the ripping practices presented in Illus. 208–229 in Chapter 5. Plan your ripping setups with these practices or similar ones. Remember, the time put into a safe setup is time well-invested.

Kickbacks

A kickback occurs when a piece of stock is forced towards the operator at great speed. Usually the stock becomes trapped between a rotating blade and a stationary object such as the fence or guard. In some cases, stress in the wood causes the saw kerf to close around the blade. This traps the blade and may cause a kickback. The splitter is designed to keep the wood from closing around the blade.

Stock that is kicked back can have the velocity of an arrow. This is a serious hazard. Another hazard of the kickback is that the operator's hand can be pulled back into the blade during a kickback if it is on the outfeed side of the blade.

Kickback hazards can be minimized by observing the following precautions:

1. Cut only true, smooth stock that will not become twisted and pinched in the blade. Avoid stock with loose knots; the knots can be ejected from the wood in the same manner as a kickback.
2. Use a guard that is equipped with a splitter and anti-kickback pawls. The splitter will keep the kerf open and the pawls will stop the work if a kickback begins.
3. Keep the anti-kickback pawls sharp. To be effective, they must dig into the wood if a kickback begins.
4. Use only sharp, true blades. Dull or pitch-loaded blades can cause kickbacks. Warped blades also tend to pinch in the kerf and cause kickbacks.
5. When ripping, select a blade with a hook angle under 15°. Too much hook angle can cause the stock to lift or kick back.
6. Control all cuts with the fence. Never try to rip freehand or without support.
7. Avoid using the rip setup for crosscutting. Stock can get trapped between the blade and fence, and will kick back or kick up when the cut is completed.
8. Make sure the rip fence is parallel to the blade (Illus. 188). When the fence is not parallel, stock may be pinched.
9. Always feed the piece being cut completely through and past the blade when ripping. Never release the stock while it is still touching the blade and fence. A kickback may result. Use a push stick or push block for thin rips. Retract the stick or block carefully after the cut has been made.
10. Stand to the side of the saw when ripping. If you stand behind the piece being ripped, you will become the target of a kickback.

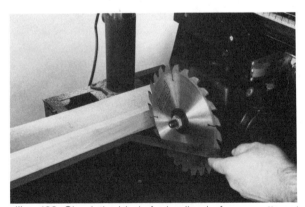

Illus. 188. Check the blade for heeling before you attempt to rip. Eliminate the heeling condition (blade is not perpendicular to fence) or a kickback could occur.

General Working Environment

The working environment can also be a factor in the safe operation of the radial arm saw. The saw should be set at a comfortable height. Most radial arm saws have a table height of 30 to 40". The lower tables are preferred for heavy crosscuts because less lifting is required. Make sure the saw has been properly levelled and does not rock before you begin working. When possible, anchor the saw to the floor.

Make sure a grounded outlet of the proper voltage and correct amperage is close by (Illus. 189). The outlet should be below the saw so that the cord does not interfere with the stock when it is cut or handled. Adequate lighting makes the operation of the saw much safer. Shadows and dim lighting increase operator fatigue and measurement errors.

The area surrounding the radial arm saw should be large enough to handle large pieces of stock. If space is at a premium, folding tables or a dead man can be used for support. Traffic should be routed away from the saw, especially when ripping. In the event of a kickback, traffic around the radial arm saw could increase the chance of injury. Keep the floor around the radial arm saw free of cutoffs and debris. Cutoffs and debris can cause tripping or slipping. A box for cutoffs can be made to fit under the saw.

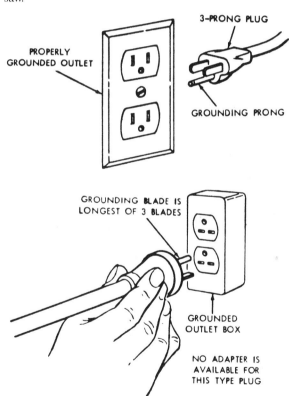

Illus. 189. Make sure the outlet is grounded and the circuit is of the correct amperage.

Radial-Arm-Saw Operating Rules

1. *Protect Yourself*. Always wear protective glasses when operating the radial arm saw. If the area is noisy,

wear ear plugs or muffs to preserve your hearing and minimize fatigue (Illus. 190). Gloves are alright for handling rough lumber, but never wear gloves (or other loose clothing) when operating the radial arm saw. Your hand could easily be pulled into the blade if the blade caught the glove (or other loose clothing). Also, remove rings and other jewelry.

Illus. 190. Ear muffs or ear plugs can preserve your hearing and minimize fatigue. Wear them whenever you operate the saw for an extended period of time.

When using a fine-tooth blade, wear a dust mask or use a dust collction system (Illus. 191). Studies have found a high incidence of nasal cancer in woodworkers. This incidence among woodworkers is *far* higher than that of the normal population. Dust masks or collection systems are even more important when machining treated timbers or composition boards.

Illus. 191. Dust masks or other dust-collection devices should be used for all radial-arm-saw operations.

2. *Use the Guards.* Use either the upper guard or shaper guard for all operations. Never work without one of them. In addition, whenever possible use the lower guard in conjunction with the upper guard (Illus. 192). The lower guard makes contact with the blade almost impossible. The splitter and anti-kickback pawls on the upper guard minimize the chance of kickbacks when ripping. These should always be engaged when ripping.

Illus. 192. The lower guard prevents contact with the blade when cutting. Use it whenever possible.

3. *Keep the Blade Sharp.* A sharp blade makes the radial arm saw much safer to use. A dull blade or the incorrect blade increases the chance of kickback or climbing. Dull blades also require more cutting force. This excess force can throw the operator off balance and lead to an accident. It also wastes electrical energy (Illus. 193).

4. *Inspect Your Stock.* Before sawing any stock, look it over. Loose knots, nails, twists, cupping, and rough or wet lumber can mean trouble. Loose knots can be ejected by the saw blade. Rough, warped, or wet lumber can cause kickbacks. Small pieces can also mean trouble. Machining them puts your hands too close to the blade. If possible, machine large pieces and cut them into smaller pieces.

5. *Position Yourself.* Stand to the side of the blade to avoid kickbacks when ripping. When crosscutting, the arm that pulls the carriage should be slightly stiff. This will resist the climbing tendency the saw may have. Make sure you have firm footing and balance when operating the radial arm saw. Avoid overreaching, crossing your hands, or reaching under the blade.

Illus. 193. A sharp blade does a better job and requires less force. Less force makes the job safer and requires less energy.

6. *Guard Against Accidental Starting.* When making adjustments to the radial arm saw, do so with the power off. It is too easy to make an adjustment error that could cause an accident when the power is on. Make repairs, perform maintenance, make setups, and install dado heads or moulding heads with the power disconnected (Illus. 194). Otherwise, a serious accident could occur.

Illus. 194. Install blades and cutters with the power disconnected. This will eliminate the chance of accidental starting.

7. *Use Control Devices.* Devices like push sticks, hold-downs, and featherboards make handling stock safer. These devices get in close and control the stock. Your hands are well away from the blade in a safe position. Keep the control devices near the saw at all times. Patterns for push sticks can be found in Chapter 2.

8. *Keep a Safe Margin.* By keeping your hands a safe distance (6 to 8″) from the blade, you allow a margin for error. When your hands are a safe distance from

the blade, there is always time to react to a hazardous situation.

9. *Know Your Saw*. Read the owner's manual and understand it before operating the radial arm saw. All saws are different; make sure you understand the one you are using (Illus. 195). Make sure all adjustments are made, all locks and clamps secured, and that the fence is clamped securely before making any cut. Keep the carriage locked at the column when the saw is not in use (Illus. 196).

10. *Think About the Job*. When performing a new operation, think about the job before beginning. Ask yourself, "What could happen when I . . .?" Questions of this nature help you identify and avoid an accident-producing situation (Illus. 197). If you have a premonition of trouble, *stop*. Avoid any job that gives you a bad feeling. Try setting the job up in another way, or ask some other experienced operator for an opinion.

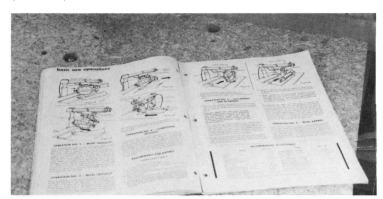

Illus. 195. Read the owner's manual. This will help you know the radial arm saw and its particular setup and adjusting features.

Illus. 196. The carriage belongs clamped next to the column when not in use. This prevents accidental movement.

Illus. 197. When you start any job try to foresee the hazard. Ask yourself, "What could happen when I . . . ?" or "What if I . . . ?" Questions of this nature could make the job safer.

5

Basic Operations

Basic operations include common radial-arm-saw cuts and maintenance procedures. Careful planning and accurate measurement are a part of every radial-arm-saw operation. Always plan ahead. Think about the job before beginning. Try to anticipate any hazards or problems before you turn on the saw. The job will be safer, and the results better.

Changing the Blade

Changing the blade is one of the most common radial-arm-saw operations. Select the correct blade (diameter and tooth style) for the job you are doing. Before changing the blade, disconnect the power. Unplug the saw, or shut off the power at the main junction box.

Raise the blade so that it clears the table and pull the carriage towards you. Lock the carriage near the end of the stroke (Illus. 198). This brings the blade closer to you and makes blade removal less cumbersome. Release the guard's(s') clamping mechanism(s) and remove the guard(s) (Illus. 199). There may be 2 guards (an upper and lower) or only one (an upper).

Look at the threads on the arbor. If they are right-hand threads, remove the arbor nut by turning it counterclockwise. Remove a left-hand arbor nut by turning clockwise. Radial arm saws with a brass arbor nut have left-hand

Illus. 199. Remove the guard for access to the arbor nut. Note that the saw has been unplugged before removing the guard.

threads. The nut was machined out of brass, so that it would be the weakest part. It is cheaper to replace an arbor nut than to replace the arbor. However, if it is turned the wrong way, the threads will strip.

Most radial arm saws require 2 wrenches to remove the arbor nut. One wrench holds the arbor stationary while the other turns the arbor nut (Illus. 200). Note: Some radial arm saws need only one wrench to turn the arbor nut. The arbor is held stationary with a lock pin that is mounted on the motor. This spring-loaded pin is pushed down against the arbor to hold it in place. Your owner's manual can provide more specific information.

After the arbor nut is removed, pull the arbor washer (and blade stabilizers, if used) off the arbor. Inspect the arbor washers (Illus. 201) and blade stabilizers for pitch, wood chips, nicks, or dents. Remove any irregularity from the washers (and stabilizers). They should bear against the saw blade uniformly at their outer edge.

Replace the inner blade washer (and blade stabilizer) (Illus. 202). Install the desired blade over the arbor (Illus. 203). The blade's teeth should point towards the table at the front (operator's side) of the table. Note: If the replacement blade is larger than the one removed, it may be necessary to raise the motor using the blade-elevating crank.

Illus. 198. Move the carriage closer to you and lock it before changing the blade. This makes the task much easier.

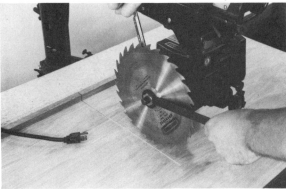

Illus. 200. Two wrenches are used to remove the blade. One holds the arbor stationary while the other removes the nut. Check the threads to be sure you are loosening (not tightening) the arbor nut.

Illus. 203. Mount the blade on the arbor. Wipe it with a clean cloth to remove any dirt from the contact surface. Be sure the teeth are pointing towards the table at the operator's side of the saw.

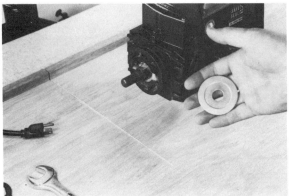

Illus. 201. Always inspect the arbor washers and blade stabilizers when changing the blade; any irregularities can affect the quality of the cut.

Now place the outer arbor washer (and blade stabilizer) on the arbor (Illus. 204). Replace the arbor nut. Tighten it snugly against the blade, but do not overtighten it (Illus. 205). This can make removal very difficult. Machines that have an electronic brake put more strain on the arbor nut and should be tightened with increased force. Otherwise, the nut could loosen when braking occurs.

Replace the guard(s) (Illus. 206). Be sure the guard(s) is clamped securely and adjusted correctly. Release the carriage and move it to the column. Lower the blade so that it is just above the table. Plug in the saw and turn it on. Lock the carriage to the arm, and lower the blade slowly into the table. Release the clamp and pull the carriage through its complete stroke. There should be a cut in the table 1/16 to 1/8″ deep (Illus. 207).

It may not be necessary to kerf the table. If the new blade fits in the kerf cut by the previous blade, then cross-

Illus. 202. Replace the inner washer and blade stabilizer. Wipe them with a clean cloth to be sure there is no dust or dirt on the contact surfaces.

Illus. 204. Wipe the arbor washer with a clean cloth and place it against the blade.

Illus. 205. Tighten the arbor nut snugly. Saws with an electronic braking system must be tightened more than other saws. The braking mechanism tends to loosen the arbor nut as it slows the blade down.

Illus. 206. Replace the guard or guards. it is good practice to turn the blade over by hand to make sure it does not hit the guard. Do this with the power disconnected.

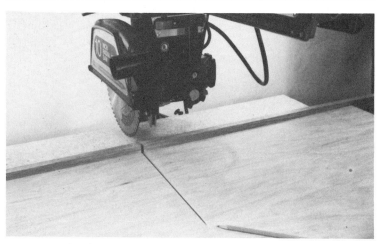

Illus. 207. Make a cut in the table and fence. The kerf in the table should be about ⅛" deep.

cutting can begin right away. Pull the carriage through its stroke before sawing. Do this with the power off. Make sure that everything is aligned before you begin sawing.

If you put a blade smaller than the maximum diameter on the radial arm saw, there are certain advantages and disadvantages. The advantages include:

    A. More power at the tooth. Less energy is needed to turn a smaller diameter blade, so increased power is available at the cut.

    B. Less flutter. Since the blade is smaller, maximum runout (blade deviation at its periphery) is decreased. This increases blade life and improves the cut.

The disadvantages include:

    A. Less depth of cut. The smaller diameter blade cannot cut thicker stock. To crosscut or rip thicker stock, you will have to place a larger diameter blade on the saw.

B. Sawdust will not collect, and will not be ejected as well. The upper guard is designed to eject sawdust away from the cutting area. The design works best with a blade of maximum diameter. When smaller blades are used, the chips tend to fall on the work. This can sometimes damage stock that has been finish-sanded.

If you use a smaller diameter blade, be cautious. Make sure the rpm rating for the blade is correct for your saw. Also, when a smaller blade is tilted, it will not follow the same path as a larger blade. Make sure its path does not go through a table clamp or table fastener. This could damage the blade or table.

Keep in mind that a smaller blade has a different relationship to the guard than a larger one. This can alter your perception of blade position and cause an error or mishap. When a smaller blade is used, some operations do not return the carriage completely to the column. This has caused the blade to engage with the work before it was intended to. When this happens, the blade tends to climb the work and may throw the saw out of alignment.

Try to anticipate the hazard. Ask yourself "What if . . .?" and "What will happen when I . . .?" before beginning an operation. If it doesn't look or feel safe, try an alternate approach or ask an experienced operator for advice.

Ripping

Ripping is one of the 2 most common radial-arm-saw operations (crosscutting is the other). In ripping, the cut is made *with or along* the grain. The yoke is turned 90° so that the blade is parallel with the fence. The yoke can be turned 90° in either direction. The wood is then fed against the cutting rotation.

When the blade is closest to the fence, it is known as "in-ripping." When the motor is closest to the fence, it is known as "out-ripping." In-ripping is usually set up for cutting narrow strips. Out-ripping is the favored setup for cutting wide parts. It allows you to make the very widest cut on your radial arm saw.

Review the safety procedures for ripping in Chapter 4 (page 64) before beginning. Begin the ripping operation by checking the blade for heel while it is in the crosscut position (Illus. 208). Remove any heel before proceeding. (This procedure is discussed in Chapter 7.) Next turn the yoke 90° and cut your rip through. (This procedure is discussed in Chapter 2.) An auxiliary table can be placed on your saw to protect the saw table.

When a special rip setup for precise cuts is made, an auxiliary table without a rip trough should be used (Illus. 209 and 210). In this case, the blade is adjusted for rip width while it is above the table, then it is turned on and lowered into the table about ⅛". This helps minimize blade deflection as the cut is made. For best results, a new fence should also be installed (Illus. 211). A fence with many cuts in it can catch on the work as it moves past. This can damage your work, and may cause a kickback.

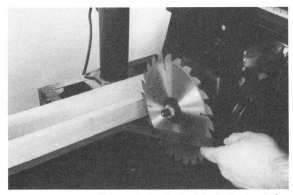

Illus. 208. Before ripping, check the blade for heel. See Chapter 7 for a discussion of heel. Heel should be removed before any rip operation is performed.

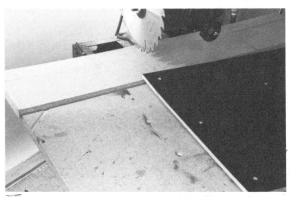

Illus. 209. This laminate-covered table will cover the saw's table. It is smoother and has no kerfs in it. Kerfs can catch or turn the stock as it is ripped.

Illus. 210. The auxiliary table is screwed to the saw table. Keep screws away from the blade's rip path.

Illus. 211. A true uncut fence replaces the original. Kerfs in the fence can catch the work while it is being ripped.

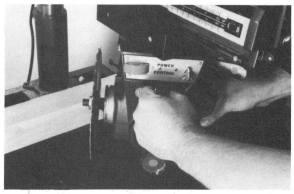

Illus. 212. The yoke is being turned to the in-rip position. Raise the blade above the table to turn the yoke.

Turn the yoke to the rip position (Illus. 212). Lock it in position (Illus. 213). Move the carriage and set the distance between the blade and fence to the desired width. Set this distance from a tooth that points towards the fence (Illus. 214). This gives the most accurate setting. Carriage clamps can be attached to the arm to eliminate creeping. Move the upper blade guard down so that it just clears the stock (Illus. 215 and 216). Clamp a cleat on the fence (Illus. 217–219) and/or use a commercial hold-down (Illus. 220) to keep the stock from lifting during the cut.

Drop the splitter and anti-kickback pawls into position (Illus. 221). Use a piece of stock to position them. Clamp the splitter and pawls securely in position. The splitter and pawls help control the stock and guard against a kickback.

Turn on the saw, and feed the stock against cutter rotation (Illus. 222). When in-ripping, feed the stock from the right side of the saw (as you face the front of the saw). When out-ripping, feed the stock from the left side. Guide the stock into the blade at a uniform speed. Stand to the side of the stock so that you are clear of the kickback zone. If the blade slows down, either you are feeding too fast or the blade has teeth that are too fine for the stock thickness. If the edges of the saw kerf appear burned, you may be feeding too slowly. This may also indicate a dull blade or blade binding. If the work tends to pull away from the fence, there may be heel in the blade. Check the blade to be sure it is parallel to the fence. (This procedure is discussed in Chapter 7.)

Guide the entire length of the work through the blade (Illus. 223). Use a push stick to keep your hand clear of the blade (Illus. 224). Do not stop feeding until the entire piece is past the blade (Illus. 225). If the piece stops while in contact with the blade and fence, a kickback could occur.

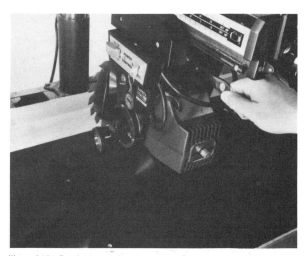

Illus. 213. Push the yoke pin into position and tighten the yoke clamp.

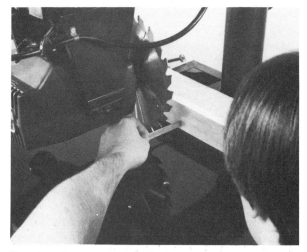

Illus. 214. Set the distance from the fence to the blade to desired rip width. Use a tooth that points towards the fence when making the setup. Clamp the carriage in position. Carriage clamps may be attached to the arm to eliminate creeping.

Illus. 215. Replace the guard and lock it securely in position.

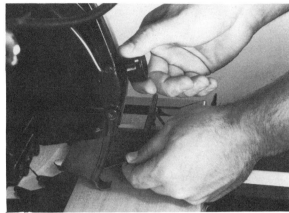

Illus. 216. Adjust the front of the guard so that it just clears the work. Lock it in position.

Illus. 217. Use a piece of stock the same thickness as you are ripping to position the cleat.

Illus. 218. Clamp the cleat securely to the fence. Keep the clamps clear of the guard so that it may be adjusted easily.

Illus. 219. Make sure the cleat is even or parallel to the table. A slight clearance is allowed for twist or bow in the stock being ripped.

Illus. 220. Commercial hold-downs may be used instead of a cleat. Hold-downs like this one make ripping much safer. The wheels turn only in the direction of feed, so they help resist kickback forces.

Illus. 221. The splitter and anti-kickback pawls are adjusted after the front of the guard is positioned. On some guards these two adjustments are related. Notice how the pawls point in the direction of feed.

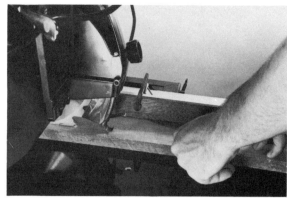

Illus. 222. The stock is fed against cutter rotation. Keep the work against the fence and table.

Illus. 223. The kerf will be wider than the splitter and will pass through it. The anti-kickback pawls will ride on the work. If the work kicks back, then the pawls will dig into the wood.

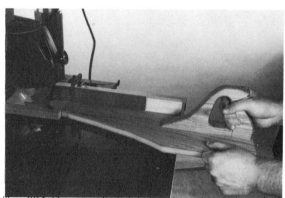

Illus. 224. Use a push stick to keep your hand clear of the blade. The push stick goes under the fence, just like the workpiece.

Illus. 225. The push stick feeds the work well beyond the blade before it is retracted. Do not allow the push stick to engage the anti-kickback pawls. It will be impossible to retract it. Retract the push stick carefully. If you twist or turn it, it could kick back.

When ripping long pieces, use a dead man or other device to support the wood (Illus. 226). Large, heavy pieces may require an extra person to handle and guide them safely. Never try to rip stock that is too heavy for you to handle. When ripping strips off a piece of sheet stock, make the widest rip first (Illus. 227). This puts most of the panel's weight on the radial arm saw. It also minimizes flexing in thin, lighter sheets, and gives truer cuts. It may also be beneficial to cut the length of the panel in half before ripping.

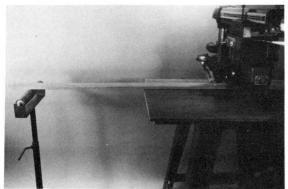

Illus. 226. A dead man should be used to support long rips. Extra help should be used when ripping large heavy pieces.

Illus. 227. When ripping sheet stock, make the widest rip first. This puts most of the weight on the saw and makes control much easier.

A stock-cutting sheet allows you to plan your cuts before doing any cutting. Graph paper makes the layout simple. Mark off an area 4 squares by 8 squares. Sketch in the grain direction if your stock has a grain direction. Draw all the needed parts onto the graph paper, so that all cuts are organized. Number the cuts for more efficient cutting. Remember, the outer edges of the sheet stock are true and square. These edges can always be used as control surfaces for accurate cutting.

Ripping Narrow Pieces Ripping narrow pieces can be dangerous if not performed correctly. Narrow pieces tend to vibrate and flutter as they are cut. These pieces can snap in half, shatter, or kick back. It is important that appropriate hold-downs be used to prevent vibration and fluttering. A push stick should also be used.

A blade with finer teeth should be used for ripping thin, narrow strips. The finer teeth cause less vibration and fluttering. They also reduce the problem of stock lifting (raising off the table) during the cut.

Avoid ripping thin strips off pieces less than 18″ long. Select an alternative method of cutting the strips. If the pieces are quite long, make sure you have a helper to pull the thin strips through. Use a push block to feed the strip beyond the saw blade. However, with certain holding devices, this is not necessary (Illus. 228 and 229).

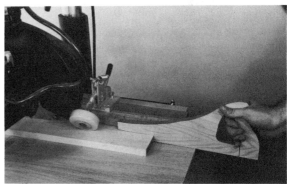

Illus. 228. The rollers make it difficult to feed stock with a push stick, but they hold the stock well enough so that one is not needed.

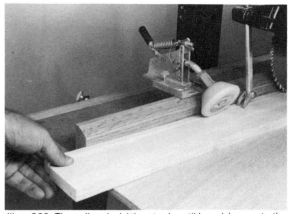

Illus. 229. The rollers held the stock until I could move to the other end of the saw. I pulled both the strip and the workpiece through the final inches of this rip operation.

When retracing the push block, pull it back carefully. If you twist it, the end may be torn up by the blade. The thin strip that does the pushing will be removed. Replace the push block if this occurs.

Crosscutting

Crosscutting is the most common cut done with the radial arm saw. In fact, some people limit their use of the tool to crosscutting. This is using the saw at about 10% of its potential.

Before beginning, carefully review the safety procedures for crosscutting discussed on page 63. Crosscutting is done by putting the edge of the work against the fence and pulling the carriage (and blade) across it. To ensure a square cut, make sure the arm and blade are perpendicular to the fence, and the blade is perpendicular to the table. To prevent tear-out, make sure the blade does not heel. Make these checks before crosscutting. First check the blade. It should be square with the fence (Illus. 230) and the table (Illus. 231). Keep the square off the blade's teeth. Then check for heel (Illus. 208). Make any necessary adjustments. Saw alignment is discussed in Chapter 7.

Check arm tracking by placing a framing square against the fence (Illus. 232). Line the other leg of the square up with the blade. Select a tooth and touch it to the square. Slowly pull the carriage towards you. Observe the tooth and square; if the blade begins to move, *stop* the blade. If you don't, the tooth could climb the square and break. This movement is an indication of arm misalignment. Another indication is space between the tooth and square at the end of the stroke.

Begin the crosscut by placing the work against the fence. The work should also rest firmly on the table. Support long pieces with a dead man. Line the cut up with the blade (Illus. 233). Your layout line should line up

Illus. 231. The blade must be perpendicular to the table to assure a square cut..

Illus. 232. Make sure the arm tracks squarely. Use a framing square for this job. Make any needed adjustments before you begin cutting.

Illus. 233. Stock should be held securely against the fence. The blade should be on the waste side of the layout line. Use a tooth that points towards the work to make this setup.

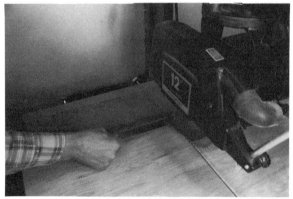

Illus. 230. Check the blade to make sure that it is square with the fence.

with a tooth that points towards the layout line. Note: The saw blade should be on the waste or scrap side of the line.

Turn on the saw and pull the carriage (and blade) into the work. Hold the work securely with your other hand (Illus. 234). Make sure your hand is not in the blade's path. The arm pulling the carriage should be kept slightly stiff. This will keep the blade from climbing the work and jamming or throwing the saw out of alignment. This climbing is sometimes caused by a blade with too much hook. Pull the carriage at uniform speed. If the motor slows down, you are moving the carriage too fast. After the crosscut is complete, return the carriage to the column and shut off the motor. Lock the carriage in position.

When crosscutting, keep scrap off the table. Be sure to shut the saw off before clearing the table. When the cutoff scraps are small, they sometimes become trapped between the blade and the kerf in the fence. To solve the problem, install the desired blade and a new fence with one kerf cut in it. One cut in the fence will keep scrap from getting caught and will minimize tear-out. It will also make it easier to locate the layout line with the blade's path (Illus. 235).

Work wider than the stroke of the radial arm saw can be cut in two operations. First, the stock is positioned and sawn to the end of the stroke (Illus. 236). The piece is then flipped over (Illus. 237) and aligned with the blade's path. This is done with the power off. The cut is then completed with the second stroke of the blade (Illus. 238).

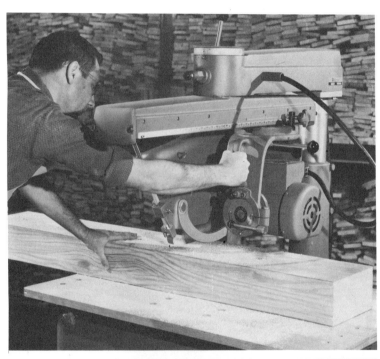

Illus. 234. Pull the carriage (and blade) through the work. The arm pulling the carriage should be slightly stiff. This keeps the blade from climbing the work.

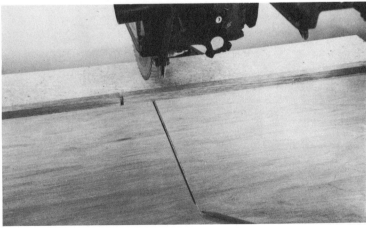

Illus. 235. This fence has been offset slightly so that a new kerf may be cut in it. This new kerf will show you where the layout line should be positioned.

Illus. 236A. Butt the wide stock firmly against the fence. Keep your hands clear of the stroke.

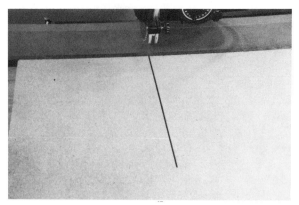

Illus. 236B. Crosscut the piece to the end of the stroke.. Blade diameter and fence position will affect the stroke somewhat.

Illus. 237. Turn the piece over and align the cut with the blade.

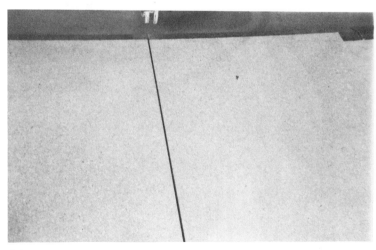

Illus. 238. Complete the cut and return the carriage to the column.

If the arm is not aligned correctly, the 2 cuts will not meet. Try a cut in some scrap stock before attempting a cut in some expensive stock or an important piece for the project you are building.

Sometimes a stop is clamped to the fence or table to help align the two cuts (Illus. 239). This will work only when the end of the piece is square. Most factory edges on plywood are square. Check solid stock with a framing square before using this method.

Pieces that are too thick for the blade should also be handled in 2 cuts. The blade cuts as deep as possible on the first stroke (Illus. 240). The piece is then turned over and the cut is completed (Illus. 241). The blade has to be square with the fence and table or the 2 cuts will be uneven.

Small or short pieces can also be a problem when cross-cutting. These pieces bring your hands too close to the blade. Special clamping mechanisms (Illus. 242–244) can be used to hold the stock in place while the cut is made. A holding device that engages with the fence can also be designed. It does the same job as the clamping mechanisms (Illus. 245).

Sometimes a specialty fence has to be made for this operation. A series of dadoes cut into the fence will do the job (Illus. 246) in most cases. The stick has an offset tongue (Illus. 247) that makes it possible to hold stock of varying thickness. (Plans for this fence appear in Chapter 8.)

The commercial hold-down shown in Illus. 248 hooks into eye-type bolts. The knob on top produces the needed clamping pressure to hold stock in place (Illus. 249). The V in the clamp pad will hold round and irregular pieces in place. The hold-down stays clear of the work during the cut (Illus. 250).

Illus. 240. When stock is too thick to be cut in one stroke, cut as deep as possible on the first stroke.

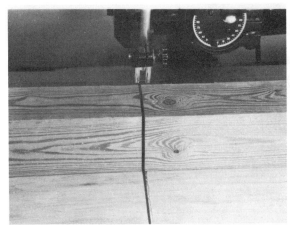

Illus. 241. Complete the cut with the second stroke. Line this cut up carefully.

Illus. 239. A plywood stop can be clamped to the table to locate a wide piece. Be sure the end of the stop is square.

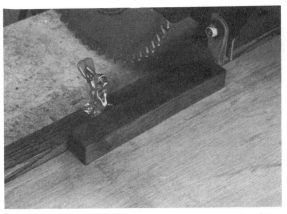

Illus. 242. This snap-type clamp is attached to the fence with sheet-metal screws. It holds stock securely to the fence.

Illus. 243. The snap-type clamp has been engaged. This small piece will not move while the cut is made.

Illus. 244. This small piece is cut safely and accurately with the snap-type clamp. This allows the operator to keep his hands clear of the blade.

Illus. 245. The stick engages the dadoes in the fence to act as a hold-down. This keeps your hand clear of the blade when cross-cutting small parts.

Illus. 246. The series of dadoes in this fence makes it possible to hold stock of almost any thickness.

Illus. 247. The tongue on this stick is offset. You can flip it over for stock of a different thickness.

Illus. 248. The commercial hold-down hooks into an eye-type bolt. The eye-type bolts replace the conventional table bolts.

Illus. 249. Turning the knob on this hold-down produces the clamping pressure. The hold-down has a quick release for faster adjustment.

Illus. 250. The hold-down stays clear of the blade and keeps your hand clear of the blade during operation.

Round stock must be held securely when it is crosscut (Illus. 251). This is because it has a gear-like effect when it is cut; that is, it tends to roll towards the blade and jam into the teeth. In addition to being dangerous, it can throw the radial arm saw out of adjustment or damage the blade. A clamp should be used to hold the round stock to the fence while crosscutting.

Illus. 251. Clamp round stock to the table or fence before crosscutting it. The round stock has a tendency to roll into and jam the blade. The clamp keeps it from moving.

It is frequently necessary to crosscut several pieces to the same length. To eliminate layout of individual pieces, clamp a stop block to the fence or table (Illus. 252). Set the stop block by measuring the distance from the blade. Select a tooth that points towards the stop block and secure it to the fence or table. Make a test cut into a piece of scrap. The scrap does not have to be cut in half. Measure the scrap to make sure the length is correct. Make any needed adjustments and proceed with the operation.

Illus. 252. A stop block is frequently used to control part of the stock length. This block is clamped to the table. It is the square corner from a sheet of plywood.

There are some commercial stop devices that can be secured to the fence (Illus. 253). These devices allow minor adjustment without their removal. Home-made devices (Illus. 254–256) can be made with less expense. A flip-over stop can also be made. This device flips out of the way when the end of the piece must be squared (Illus. 257). It can then be flipped into position as a stop block (Illus. 258). An offset hinge (Illus. 259) will also work as a flip-over stop. It must be screwed to the fence. The offset in the hinge provides a natural stop (Illus. 260).

Illus. 253. This commercial stop attaches to the fence. This stop allows minor adjustment without removal.

Illus. 254. This home-made stop is similar to the commercial stop shown in Illus. 253. A clamp secures it to the fence.

Illus. 255. This stop has a flathead machine screw for minor adjustments in part of the stock length.

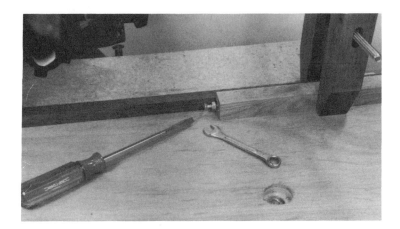

Illus. 256. The nut is loosened with the wrench and the machine screw is adjusted. The number of threads per inch helps you judge how many turns of the screw are needed to make a minor adjustment.

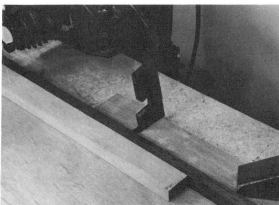

Illus. 257. This simple flip stop clamps to the rear table. It lifts easily to square an end.

Illus. 258. The stop is turned in the dado to locate the square end and control stock length.

Illus. 259. This offset hinge is screwed to the fence. It acts as a flip stop. The stop is up to allow squaring of an end.

Illus. 260. The hinge drops into position to act as a stop. These types of stops are used in cabinet shops where large numbers of uniform length parts are needed.

Whenever you use a stop block, make sure that sawdust does not accumulate between the stop device and the work. A rabbet cut on the end of the stop block (Illus. 261) can eliminate the problem in most cases.

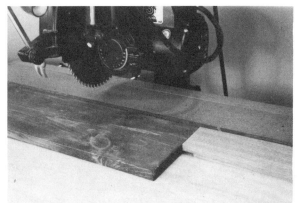

Illus. 261. A rabbet cut on the end of a stop block can eliminate the sawdust problem.

When using a stop that is clamped to the fence or table, handle your stock carefully. Banging the work against the stop can cause it to move slightly. After several pieces have been cut, the length of your pieces may have changed considerably. This could spoil the work or waste time or stock. Push the work against the stop carefully and check the length of the parts periodically.

Sometimes irregular pieces have to be crosscut. A specialty jig can be made for this purpose (Illus. 262). The jig clamps between the table boards and locates the stock for trimming. The stock shown in Illus. 263 are decorative trim I made for an apartment house (Illus. 264).

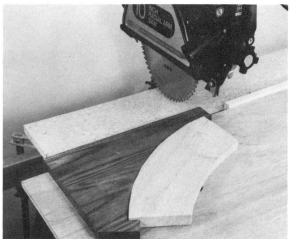

Illus. 262. This jig was designed to trim the ends of some irregular pieces. Part of the jig clamps between the table boards.

Illus. 263. A small amount was trimmed away from the ends to make them fit some decorative millwork.

Illus. 264. The round decorative moulding is made up of the parts trimmed in Illus. 263. They are on several apartment houses in northern Illinois.

Sawdust can also accumulate between the fence and work when crosscutting. This can affect the accuracy of the cut. Some woodworkers cut a groove in the fence (Illus. 265). This keeps the sawdust from affecting the accuracy of the cut (Illus. 266).

There are many commercial stop and table systems that can be added to the radial arm saw. The LG 500™ by Mertes is a length gauge (Illus. 267) designed to ride on an extruded aluminum fence. The LG 500™ accommodates work from 3 inches to 10 feet. Once length is set, lock the cam (Illus. 268) and begin sawing the pieces to length (Illus. 269). The material stop can be lifted so that one end can be squared (Illus. 270).

Illus. 265. The sawdust on this table is not a problem because of the kerf in the fence.

Illus. 266. The sawdust was swept into the kerf by the work. The kerf has to be cleaned occasionally.

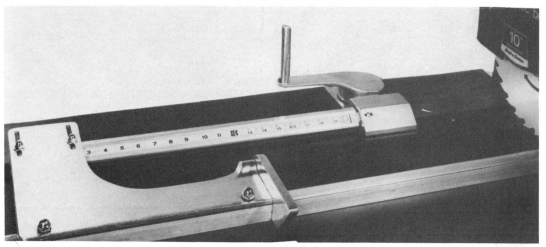

Illus. 267. The Mertes length gauge rides on an extruded aluminum fence. It accommodates work from 3" to 10'.

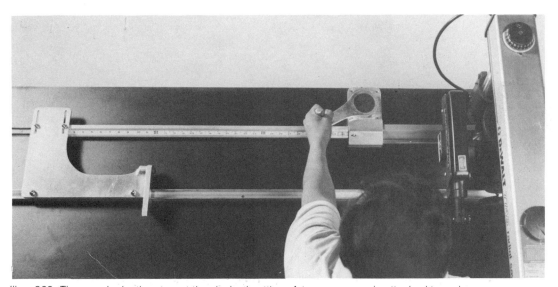

Illus. 268. The cam locks the stop at the desired setting. A tape measure is attached to make setup easier.

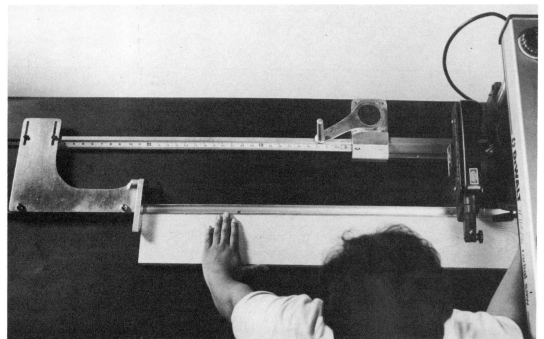

Illus. 269. Stock is butted against the stop and cut to exact length.

Illus. 270. The stop can be lifted for squaring the end. The piece can then be turned over and cut to length.

The Saw Helper™ (Illus. 271) is a combination saw table and length gauge. This device folds up for storage and has a quick coupler system (Illus. 272). This coupler system can be adjusted to about 1/100th of an inch.

The Jigfence™ is an extruded aluminum fence that can be bolted to the front table (Illus. 273). The extrusion accepts ¼″ hex bolts along the entire length (Illus. 274), which enable it to be bolted to table extensions. It, too, has a length gauge, called the Flipstop™ (Illus. 275). This gauge can be lifted up to allow longer pieces to be squared prior to cutting the work length (Illus. 276).

When making repetitive crosscuts, place a stop on the arm of the saw (Illus. 277). This keeps you from pulling the carriage (and blade) further than necessary. It also makes the operation safer. The Occupational Safety and Health Administration (OSHA) requires this in industrial operations. One of the requirements is that:"An adjustable stop shall be provided to prevent the forward travel of the blade beyond the position necessary to complete the cut in repetitive operations."

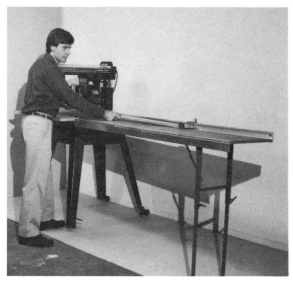

Illus. 271. The Saw Helper is a portable combination saw table and length gauge.

Illus. 272. The Saw Helper is also a folding table that attaches to either side of your saw. It has a quick-coupling system for easy removal.

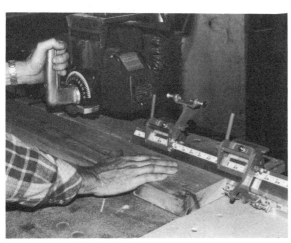

Illus. 273. The Jigfence is an aluminum fence that is bolted to the front table of the radial arm saw.

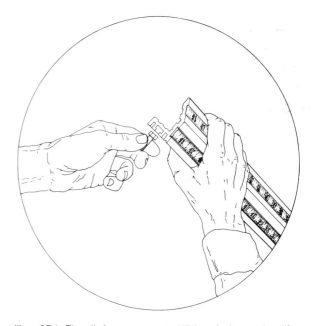

Illus. 274. The Jigfence accepts ¼" hex bolts to simplify mounting. The Jigfence can be mounted on other power tools.

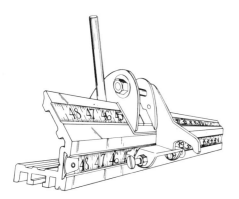

Illus. 275 (left). The length gauge on the Jigfence is called the Flipstop. It flips out of the way for squaring ends.

Illus. 276. More than one Flipstop can be attached to the Jigfence. This allows parts of different length to be cut without changing the setup.

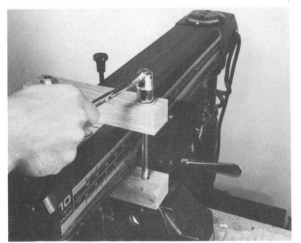

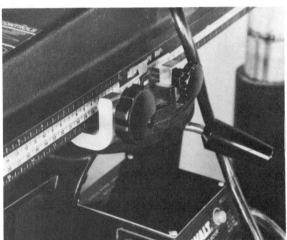

Illus. 277. A stop can be clamped to the arm (left) or track (right) of the saw to control stroke length. This should be attached when making repetitive cuts.

A crosscut crank is sometimes used in industrial applications (Illus. 278). The crosscut crank allows the operator to pull the carriage through the work by turning a crank. This keeps the blade from climbing and reduces the fatigue of the operator. Crosscut cranks are usually a special accessory used by large woodworking industries.

When some materials are crosscut, grain tear-out is a problem. Tear-out usually occurs on the bottom of the piece. This is sometimes caused when the blade is pulled through the work too quickly. A slower feed may reduce or eliminate the tear-out. A table with many kerf cuts will encourage tear-out. This is because the wood fibres are not supported when the blade cuts through. An auxiliary table should improve the cut. Other causes, such as heeling, and cures for grain tear-out are discussed in Chapter 7.

Illus. 278. A crosscut crank is sometimes used in industrial applications. The crank controls carriage feed. Notice that the parts are clamped for greater control.

Cutting Mitres

Mitres are crosscuts made at an angle. Mitres across the face (edge to edge) are usually made by turning the arm to the left or right. Mitres across the end (face to face) are usually made by tilting the motor in its yoke. Mitres along the edge of a piece require that the motor be tilted in the yoke, and the yoke turned 90° into the rip position.

Most mitre cuts are made at a 45° angle, but mitres can be cut at any angle. Determine the correct or desired angle before beginning to make any adjustments.

Face Mitres   Mitres across the face are commonly cut on picture-frame stock and door or window trim. The arm must be turned to the right or left for making the face mitre. Begin by checking the scale on the column. Make sure the indicator is aligned with zero. Then release the arm clamp and pull the locking pin clear of its detent. Now raise the blade out of the table kerf.

For a right-hand mitre (Illus. 279), turn the arm to the right. Keep your eyes on the blade to make sure it does not touch the fence or table boards. If the desired angle is 45°, the arm will lock in position. The pin will drop into a detent. Tap the pin lever with the palm of your hand to make sure it is engaged properly. The arm clamp may now be clamped securely.

The locking pin will not engage at any angle other than 45°. The arm clamp is the only thing holding the setting, so make sure it is clamped securely. The scale on the column can be used to set the mitre angle. For exact angular settings, a sliding T-bevel can be used (Illus. 280). Place the head against the fence; this will bring the blade

Illus. 279. A right-hand mitre is cut when the arm is turned to the right. Position the layout line with reference to the kerf in the fence.

Illus. 280. A sliding T-bevel may be used to set the arm. Keep the tool off the blade's teeth. This could give you an incorrect setting.

into contact with the saw blade. Do not let the saw teeth touch the blade of the sliding T-bevel. This could give you an incorrect adjustment.

A level or straightedge can also be used to copy the angle marked on the work. Place the straightedge on the layout line, and "eyeball" the arm angle (Illus. 281). Pull the carriage towards you and align the carriage with the straightedge. Clamp the arm in position after it is adjusted correctly.

The carriage must now be returned to the column. Lower the blade until it is just above the table. Grab the carriage with one hand and turn on the motor with the other. While holding the carriage, slowly lower the blade into the table. If you have a front table that is higher than the back table, lower it enough to make a kerf in the front

table. The carriage should now be slowly pulled through its entire stroke.

Before beginning to cut the work, take a practice cut in the waste area. This will ensure that the cut is parallel to the layout line (Illus. 282). Use the same practices for making the mitre cut as those made for a crosscut.

To make a left-hand mitre, turn the arm to the left. A left-hand mitre is best made with the table boards shifted and the fence in the rear position. This allows greater mitring capacity. Set the mitre angle and pull the carriage through its stroke. If the blade leaves the table (Illus. 283), set up a stop (Illus. 284). An operating blade should never leave the table! This can lead to a dangerous situation. After cutting a kerf in the table and fence, cut left-hand mitres.

Illus. 282. Take a practice cut in the waste stock near the layout line. The cut should be parallel to the layout line.

Illus. 283. The blade may leave the table on some left-hand mitre cuts. If possible, turn the work over and use the right mitre position, or move the fence back behind the rear table board.

Illus. 281. A straightedge can also be used to figure the desired angle.

92

Illus. 284. A stop or arm clamp may be used to keep the blade from leaving the table when cutting a left mitre.

Illus. 286. End mitres are cut with the arm in the 0° position and the blade tilted to 45° or other desired angle.

Stops can be clamped to the table or fence to control length (Illus. 285). If stock tends to creep during a mitre cut, check the blade for a heeling condition. Your work can be clamped to the fence or table to eliminate any creeping during the mitre cut.

Illus. 285. The stop is clamped to the table. It controls part of the stock length. If stock tends to creep, check your saw for heeling.

Illus. 287. The blade has been raised about 2″ above the table for tilting. The motor clamp may now be released.

End Mitres   End Mitres are commonly used on pieces that edge-band plywood. They can also be found on some picture frames and clock frames (Illus. 286). For end mitres, the arm remains locked in the 90° position and the motor is tilted to the mitre angle. This angle is usually 45°, but other angles may be set according to the job.

To tilt the motor, raise the blade about 2″ above the table. The clamp can now be released (Illus. 287). Lift the locking pin and turn the motor to the desired angle. Use the protractor to determine the angle (Illus. 288). For exact settings, use a sliding T-bevel to set the angle between the table and blade. You may have to lower the blade and carriage to make this adjustment.

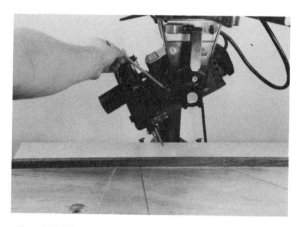

Illus. 288. The protractor scale will tell you the angle setting. A sliding T-bevel can also be used for this purpose.

The carriage must now be returned to the column. Lower the blade until it is just above the table. Grab the carriage with one hand and turn on the motor with the other. While holding the carriage, slowly lower the blade into the table. If the front table is higher, lower it enough to cut a kerf in the front table. Now pull the carriage through its entire stroke (Illus. 289). This will cut a kerf in the fence and table. Cut end mitres using the same practices that are used for crosscutting (Illus. 290).

Illus. 289. Lower the carriage and pull it through its stroke to make a fence and table kerf.

Illus. 290. Make an end mitre in the same way you would make any other crosscut.

Improving Face and End Mitres Even after you have checked all adjustments on the radial arm saw, the mitres may still fit poorly. The following factors can cause poor mitre quality. Eliminating them will improve the quality of the mitre cut.

1. A thin blade that flutters while cutting. This causes dips in the mitre. Use a saw collar(s) to stiffen the blade, and check the arbor washers for distortion.

2. One piece of the frame is too long (or short). Make sure the stop does not move during the operation.

3. The blade may not be perpendicular to the table. Check the motor clamp and lock to make sure they are engaged correctly.

4. The blade is dull and tearing the wood. Replace the blade with a sharp one.

5. The object being framed is not square, thus affecting the fit of the mitre.

6. The framing stock does not have parallel edges.

7. Sawdust is trapped between the fence and the work. Clear the table frequently. Use a fence with a sawdust kerf.

Cutting Edge Mitres An edge mitre is a rip cut made at an angle. To make this cut, the *yoke* must be turned 90° and the blade must be tilted to the desired mitre angle. Before beginning, check the blade for heeling and adjust if necessary. Replace the fence with a true, uncut piece of stock. Raise the blade about 1″ above the front table. Release the yoke clamp and lift the yoke pin. Decide whether you wish to in-rip or out-rip, and turn the yoke 90° (clockwise for in-rip, counterclockwise for out-rip). The yoke pin should drop into position. Give it a tap to make sure it is seated correctly. The yoke clamp should now be locked.

Release the motor clamp and lift the locking pin. Turn the motor to the desired angle. Set the angle with the protractor scale, a triangle, or a sliding T-bevel (Illus. 291). Cut a trough for the blade. Do this by lowering the turning blade until it touches the front table. Pull the blade through its stroke. The trough should be about ¹⁄₁₆″ deep. Shut the saw off after the trough is cut.

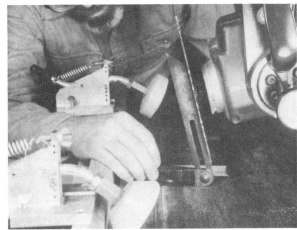

Illus. 291. When cutting an edge mitre, set the saw up for ripping. Set the desired angle with a triangle or other layout tool.

Adjust the distance between the fence and blade to the desired width. Either measure this distance or use a piece of stock. If you measure it, use a tooth that points towards the fence. If you use a piece of stock, move the carriage until the blade is lined up with the layout line (Illus. 292). Since this is done solely by sight, you may wish to make a practice cut in scrap stock.

Before making any cuts, lock the carriage and lower the guard to the work. Next, position the splitter and anti-kickback pawls. A cleat should be clamped to the fence. Also use commercial hold-downs (Illus. 293). They keep stock from lifting during the cut. Select a combination or rip blade with very little hook for this job. The less hook the blade has, the less chance of stock lifting or kickback.

Before doing an edge mitre, review the sections in this chapter on ripping (page 73), ripping narrow pieces (page 77), as well as ripping safety procedures in Chapter 4 (page 64). Follow the same procedures and precautions for edge mitres as those used for ripping.

Stave Work Some stock is edge-mitred on both sides. When several pieces of this stock are joined edge to edge, they form a circle (Illus. 294 and 295). Columns and posts are often made this way. These pieces are known as staves.

The procedure for making staves is the same as that for edge-ripping (Illus. 296 and 297). Another method is to edge-rabbet one edge and leave the other edge square (Illus. 298). This reduces the amount of shifting the pieces do when they are glued up.

To determine the blade angle for stave work, divide the number of sides into 360°. Divide this angle by two; this gives the correct blade setting. The first setting may not produce a perfect fit. Cut only one piece and then cut it into 3″ lengths. These pieces can then be assembled and clamped to determine the fit.

Illus. 292. Move the blade into position with the layout line. Make a trial cut in scrap to be sure it is correct. Note that the splitter, anti-kickback pawls and hold-downs are adjusted correctly.

Illus. 294. When several pieces are edge-mitred, they can be assembled into a circle or column. This is called stave work. The more staves, the more the object appears to be a true circle.

Illus. 293. The commercial hold-downs keep work positioned correctly and guard against kickback while the cut is being made.

Illus. 295. The stave work on the right appears to be more like a circle than the one on the left; yet the left one has one more stave. Shaping the exposed face (right) gives it more of a circular look.

Illus. 296. A stave is made in 2 cuts. One edge is ripped with the first cut.

Illus. 297. The second rip cut turns the work into a stave. Make sure the angle is correct before cutting all the parts.

Illus. 298. This stave procedure leaves one edge square and cuts an angular dado on the other edge. These parts do not shift as much when they are glued together.

Special Mitre Setups For some jobs, a special mitre setup may be needed. A mitring jig (Illus. 299) is commonly used on the radial arm saw for this purpose. Cut the left mitre first (Illus. 300), then move to the other side of the jig. The right mitre may now be cut. A stop can be clamped to the jig (Illus. 301) to control part of its length. When using a jig like this, use a carriage stop. The carriage stop controls the stroke of the carriage. This extra control makes any job (especially repetitive mitres) safer. Repetitive cuts tend to be more dangerous. This is because it is difficult to maintain concentration or attention; the operator tends to daydream or think about the next task.

When using this jig, make the cut the same way a crosscut is made. Pull the carriage towards you at a steady,

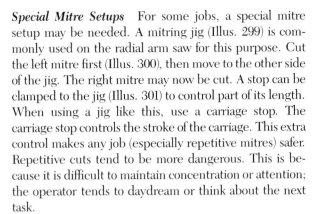

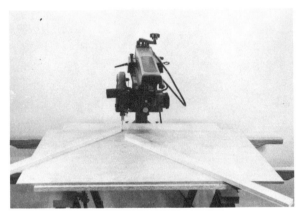

Illus. 299. This mitring jig is clamped between the table boards. The blade should be perpendicular to the table and the arm should be set at "0".

Illus. 300. The left mitre is cut first. Make this cut the same way you would any other crosscut.

Illus. 301. Make the right mitre cut. Use a stop to control stock length.

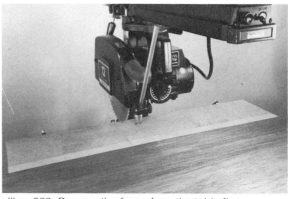

Illus. 302. Remove the fence from the table first.

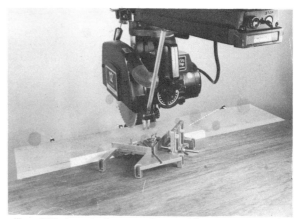

Illus. 303. Locate the manufactured jig on the table. The board to which it is attached is clamped between the table boards. Make sure the blade lines up with the channel in the jig.

Illus. 304. Cut the left mitre after clamping your work to the jig. Make left mitre cuts on all parts before changing the setup. Make sure the blade does not cut into the jig.

even speed. Pulling the carriage too fast can cause tearout or affect cutting accuracy. Complete plans for this jig appear in Chapter 8.

There are also manufactured mitre jigs (Illus. 302–310) that are similar to the shop-made one previously discussed. Both jigs work on the principle of a 90° included angle. While neither angle may be exactly 45°, they are complementary. They add up to 90°. As long as a mitre is cut on each side of the jig, the parts will fit at a perfect right angle.

Manufactured jigs also have a length gauge (Illus. 307) and a clamping device (Illus. 308). The clamping device holds stock securely while the mitre is cut. It also holds stock at any desired angle. This simplifies the cutting of compound mitres.

Another technique for cutting mitres is the special right-hand mitre setup. This technique works well when the accuracy of the radial arm saw is uncertain. Set the arm to the right mitre position and lock it in position (Illus. 311). Get a scrap of plywood ¾″ or greater in thickness. Make sure one corner is a factory corner with a 90° included angle (Illus. 312). Clamp the scrap to the table (Illus. 313). Make sure one edge of the factory corner is against the fence and the other is even with the fresh mitre cut. Move the fence over to keep stock from pinching (Illus. 314).

Stock may now be placed in the corner made by the fence and plywood scrap (Illus. 315). Make the mitre cut the same way you would cut any other mitre (Illus. 316). Move the fence over so a stop can be clamped to it (Illus. 317). The left mitre is now cut (Illus. 318). The mitres may not both be 45°, but they are complementary; that is, they add up to 90° (Illus. 319). This setup compensates for a radial arm saw that may not be in perfect alignment.

Illus. 305. A sharp fine-tooth blade produces a cut as smooth as glass.

Illus. 306. Remember to consider rabbet length when measuring picture-frame stock for mitres.

Illus. 307. Mount the stop rod and move the clamping mechanism to the opposite side of the jig.

Illus. 308. Adjust the stop rod. Note the pencil line, which extends from the rabbet. Adjust the clamping mechanism to hold the stock securely.

Illus. 309. Make the cut as you would any crosscut. Do not pull the blade too quickly. This could increase the tear-out.

Illus. 310. The 2 different lengths are assembled into a frame. The mitres fit perfectly.

Illus. 311. First, turn the arm to the right mitre and kerf the table. Replace the fence with a true piece.

Illus. 312. Get a scrap of plywood with a factory corner (90°). Position it so that the corner lines up with the table kerf.

Illus. 313. Use 2 pieces of frame stock to position the plywood and clamp it to the table.

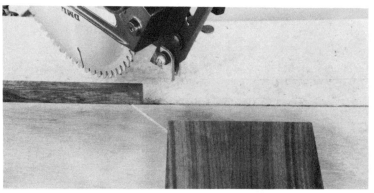

Illus. 314. Move the fence into position for cutting the mitres.

Illus. 315. Locate your stock with the rabbet towards the plywood and make the cut. Cut all parts with this setup.

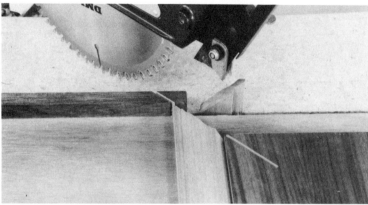

Illus. 316. The short fence is used so that cutoffs are not pinched between the fence and the plywood piece.

Illus. 317. The fence is moved into position to cut the other mitre. A mitre cutoff is clamped to the fence to act as a stop. Keep sawdust clear of the stop for best results.

Illus. 318. Cut all mating mitres with this setup.

Illus. 319. This frame fit perfectly with the first attempt.

Cutting Chamfers and Bevels

Chamfers are inclined surfaces that go from a face to an edge or end. Bevels are inclined surfaces that go from face to face. Edge bevels are rip cuts; in fact, the cutting technique for an edge bevel, chamfer, or mitre is the same. Follow the procedures discussed in the section Cutting Edge Mitres (page 94).

End chamfers and bevels are cut the same way as an end mitre. The angles may vary, but the technique is the same. Follow the procedures discussed in the section Cutting End Mitres.

Special Chamfer Setup Chamfers are sometimes used to decorate the balusters used on porches or decks (Illus. 320). I have made these balusters as a custom job for various apartment complexes. Both ends of the baluster are chamfered. For production work, it is desirable to do the job with a single setup.

The setup shown in Illus. 321 allows both ends to be cut. The pieces are cut to length first. Either end may be chamfered first (Illus. 322). Make the cut as you would make any crosscut (Illus. 323). Hold the work firmly while making the cut. For safety purposes, a crosscut clamp or stop should be used. Turn the work over and cut the other end (Illus. 324).

This chamfer setup is actually a heavy rip-type cut. Select a blade that will do the job without burning or binding.

Illus. 321. A heavy piece of stock is butted to the fence and set at the desired angle. The opposite end is clamped in position.

Illus. 320. Chamfers are sometimes cut on dimensional stock to make porch balusters.

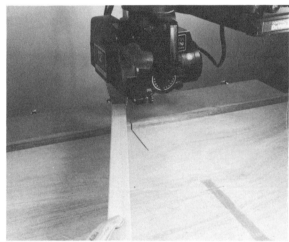

Illus. 322. Pieces are precut to desired length. The end is butted against the fence and the face is butted against the auxiliary fence.

Illus. 323. The cut is made the same way as any other crosscut.

Illus. 324. The piece is flipped end for end and the second cut is made.

Cutting Compound Mitres

Compound mitres are cut when the mitred stock is angled or inclined from the true plane. These cuts are usually made with the arm turned and the blade tilted. Compound mitres are sometimes called bevel mitres or hopper cuts. They are called hopper cuts because frames or objects assembled with compound mitres usually have a hopper or funnel shape.

Compound mitre angles for blade tilt and arm swing are furnished in Fig. 4. Use these settings for making a compound mitre.

Deep picture frames, wastebaskets, and planters are all assembled with compound mitres. Compound mitres require careful setup because the blade is tilted and the arm is turned. Careful adjustment is required. Practice the cuts on scrap until you master them and are certain of their accuracy. Some readjustment is usually required to get a perfect mitre. Do not rush the setup; if you do, the work will be spoiled.

Four-Side Compound Mitre

Angle of Work	Blade Tilt	Arm Turn
5	3½	45
10	7	44½
15	10½	44
20	14	43¼
25	17½	42¼
30	21	41
35	24	39½
40	27	37½
45	30	35¼
50	32¾	32¾
55	35½	29¾
60	37¾	26½

Fig. 4. Use these angles to set up your saw for compound mitres.

Turn the arm to the desired angle, and then tilt the blade. The work should remain flat while the cut is made (Illus. 325). To ensure that all parts are of uniform length, clamp a stop (Illus. 326) to the fence after the mitres have all been cut on one end.

Illus. 325. The work remains flat when a compound mitre is being made. Check your setup to make sure it is accurate before cutting finished parts.

Illus. 326. A stop block can be used to control length when cutting the mating mitre.

Organizing compound mitre cuts is difficult. For picture frames, set the blade for a right mitre slot using the appropriate settings. Proceed as follows:

Right Mitre. Use fence to right of blade. Rabbet faces away from fence, exposed face-down.

Left Mitre. Use fence to left of blade. Rabbet faces away from fence, exposed face-up. Always work on scrap to improve your setup. Compound mitre cuts can waste a lot of good material if the setup is incorrect.

For ceiling cove moulding, there may be both inside and outside mitres. As you look up at the ceiling, the piece on the right is a right mitre and the piece on the left is a left mitre. For inside mitres on cove moulding, adjust the saw for a right mitre, and proceed as follows:

Left Mitre	*Right Mitre*
Exposed face-down	Exposed face-up
Lower edge touches fence	Lower edge away from fence
Stock to right of blade	Stock to left of blade

For outside ceiling cove mitres, adjust the saw for a right mitre and proceed as follows:

Left Mitre	*Right Mitre*
Exposed face-up	Exposed face-down
Lower edge away from fence	Lower edge against fence
Stock to right of blade	Stock to left of blade

Compound mitres can be tricky. Practice first because the corners might not be square. This will require some modification in your blade and arm settings.

A mitring jig (Illus. 327–329) can also be used to cut compound mitres. These jigs hold the stock at their desired angle. This allows the blade to remain perpendicular to the table. A cleat can also be tacked to the table to help hold the stock at the desired angle. Commercial jigs may also be used (Illus. 330–334). The right-hand mitre system discussed in the section Mitres (page 91) may also be adapted to compound mitres.

On wide stock, there may not be enough blade to go through the work when it is tilted to the desired angle. In this case, the stock must be sawn in the flat position. If you are cutting picture-frame stock, remember to lay it out along the rabbet. If the rabbet is not measured, the glass may be too large for the frame.

 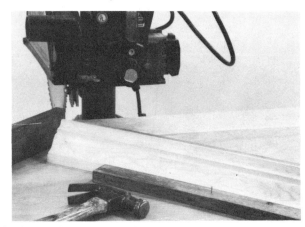

Illus. 327. This mitring jig has high fences for compound mitres. It is clamped between the table boards. At right, a cleat has been nailed to the jig to hold the stock at the desired angle.

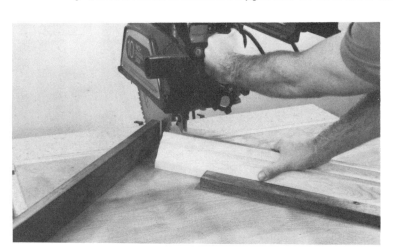

Illus. 328A. The blade is set at 90°.

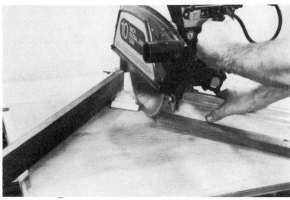

Illus. 328B. The scrap drops free as the blade completes the cut. At right, the right mitre is set up and cut after all left mitres are cut. A stop block can be used to control length.

Illus. 329 (left). Scrap drops clear when the cut is made. The fence is set so that long pieces will extend in front of the column. Illus. 329 (right). When cut correctly, the 2 parts fit together in the jig.

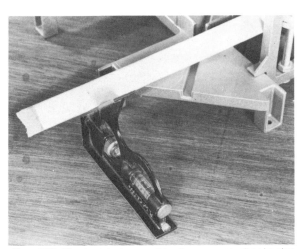

Illus. 330. This commercial jig will cut compound mitres as well as simple mitres. Note how the clamping mechanism is holding the part at the correct angle.

Illus. 331. The head of a combination square checks the angle of the part in the jig.

Illus. 332. The jig allows you to make a compound mitre cut in the same way as a cross-cut. Do not allow the blade to contact the jig.

Illus. 333. The complementary mitre is cut on the other side of the jig. A stop rod is used to control part of the stock length. Remember to consider rabbet length when setting the position of the stop rod.

Illus. 334. The completed cut is smooth as glass with no tear-out. A sharp, correctly aligned blade is essential for this type of quality.

Cutting Dadoes

A dado head is usually installed to cut dadoes. Disconnect the power and remove the blade using the procedures discussed in Changing the Blade (see page 70 and Illus. 335–339). Adjust wobble heads to the desired width (Illus. 340–342) and secure them to the arbor. When tightening the arbor nut, be careful not to change the setting on the wobble head. With blade and chipper dado heads, the correct combination of blades and chippers must be selected. One or 2 cutters (blades) are always used. Chippers make up the rest of the combination. They are sandwiched between the cutters. A ½″ dado uses two ⅛″ chippers.

Minor adjustments in blade and chipper dado size can be made with spacers, Paper or plastic laminate spacers can be placed between the cutters or chippers to increase dado width. Minor adjustments in wobble heads are made by dialing (turning) the washers to increase or decrease dado width.

Mount the dado head carefully. The teeth closest to the table should point towards the fence. The chippers between the cutters should be staggered so the head is balanced (Illus. 343). The chippers closest to the cutters should rest or nestle in the gullets of the cutters. This keeps them from rocking. On some carbide-tipped dado heads, the cutters have 2 teeth missing. This allows for placement of the chippers. Placing the chippers in any other position could smash the carbide tips when the arbor nut is tightened.

After the guard is replaced, turn the dado over by hand to make sure it does not hit the guard (Illus. 339). All setup and preliminary checks should be made with the power disconnected.

Illus. 335. A cutter is installed first. A chipper is installed next. Note that the power has been disconnected.

Illus. 336. Additional chippers are added to achieve the desired dado width.

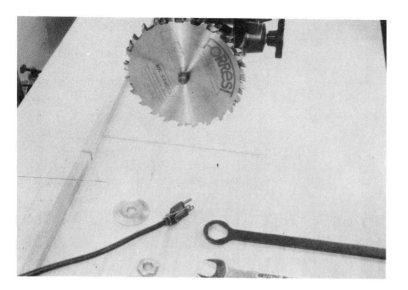

Illus. 337. The other cutter is mounted on the arbor. Check to be sure the chippers are staggered between the cutters for balance.

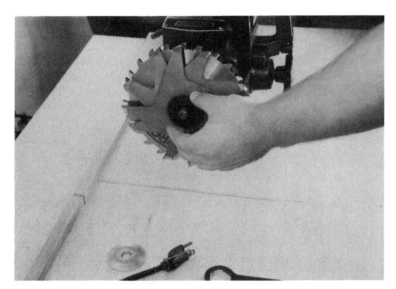

Illus. 338. Replace the arbor washer if possible. If the dado is quite wide, the washer may have to be left off.

Illus. 339. After the arbor nut is tightened and the guard is replaced, the dado should be turned over by hand. This assures the dado has been mounted correctly and will not contact the guard.

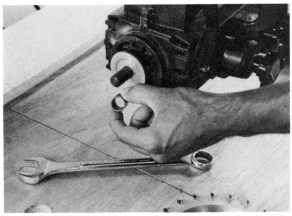

Illus. 340. This wobble dado has a bushing which fits on the arbor before the wobble dado is mounted.

Illus. 341. Adjust the wobble dado to the desired width and mount it over the bushing.

Illus. 342. The arbor nut is attached without the arbor washer. This is because the wobble dado takes up most of the arbor.

Illus. 343. Note how the chippers are staggered between the cutters. This gives the head balance.

A ⅜″ dado depth is suggested for each cut. If a ¾″ dado depth is required, make one cut ⅜″ deep and one cut ¾″ deep. The species of wood, horsepower of the saw, and dado type will determine appropriate dado depth. Generally, harder woods like oak and beech require lighter cuts than softer woods like pine or basswood. As you become familiar with dado operations, you will know the limits of your radial arm saw and dado head.

Set the dado height to take a light cut in a scrap (Illus. 344). Make a cut and check the dado width. Though the dado can be measured, the best check is with the mating part (Illus. 345). The fit should be snug but not tight. Remember, when the glue is added, the fit will be a little tighter. Adjust the dado width if necessary and set the dado depth.

The most accurate depth setting is made when the last movement of the blade is upwards. This ensures that there is no lash or slack between the gears in the elevating mechanism. Any slack in the gears will allow the blade height (and dado depth) to change.

Some dadoes can be cut with the grain or across the grain. Complete setup procedures for each type of cut are discussed in Chapter 6. Not all dadoes are cut perpendicular to the stock. The dado head is sometimes tilted and the arm is sometimes turned to make an angular dado (Illus. 346 and 347). When setting up an angular cut, make sure the dado head does not contact any metal object such as the column or table fasteners.

Illus. 344. Set the dado height and take a cut in scrap stock. Inspect the piece for tear-out or irregularities.

Illus. 345. Check the dado width to the mating part. Be sure to allow a little clearance for glue. Wood swells a little bit when glue is applied.

Illus. 346. The dado head has been tilted to make this angular dado. Make the cut as you would any other dado.

Illus. 347. The arm has been turned to make an angular dado in this setup. Make sure the dado head does not contact any metal on the table or column when making the setup.

Tear-out around the dado is sometimes caused by a lack of set or clearance on the outside cutters. This pinches the dado, causing it to lift the wood fibres near the dado. A dull dado head will also tear the face of the work.

Pulling the carriage across the work too fast can also cause tear-out. Vary your speed and compare the results. Cutting a deep dado can also cause tear-out. Raise the dado head and take a lighter cut. This will usually reduce tear-out.

A new fence can eliminate end or edge tear-out. The fence backs the work and keeps the end or edge from tearing or splintering as the dado head begins its cut. It is worth the time to change or move the fence when using a dado head. It is also possible to cut dadoes in oversize stock. Trim away the tear-out while cutting the piece to finished size.

Some cutter- and chipper-type dado heads make the dado slightly deeper under the cutters (Illus. 348). The cutters scribe the 2 sides of the dado, and the chippers remove the stock in between. The extra depth at the cutters allows the stock cut by the chippers to break off evenly. Other cutter- and chipper-type dado heads cut a dado of uniform depth. Cost and quality vary with the type of dado head selected.

Wobble or Excalibur™ dado heads cut a dado that sometimes has a concave or convex bottom (Illus. 349). This is a result of wobble in the blade. On wider dadoes, the dado head cuts deeper in the middle of the dado than on the edges. The larger the wobble dado diameter, the more pronounced the effect.

A sharp chisel or router plane (Illus. 350) can be used to true-up the dado. If the dado is not visible, the slight irregularity will not affect gluing. Work carefully when trimming a dado. Take light cuts. Heavy cuts can leave the bottom of the dado more irregular than it was.

Keep the dado head sharp and free of pitch. A dull dado head produces poor results. Extra force is needed to cut with a dull dado head. This makes the dadoing operation unsafe. Make sure that all sheet stock is dadoed with a carbide dado head. Steel dado heads become dull rapidly in all materials except solid wood. Also, the glue and other additives in sheet stock are very hard. They take the edge off steel tools quickly.

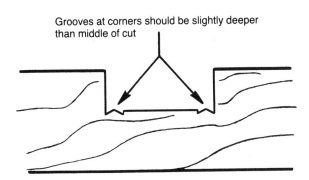

Grooves at corners should be slightly deeper than middle of cut

Illus. 348. Cutter- and chipper-type dadoes are slightly deeper under the cutters. This allows the chippers to break out of the middle of the dado evenly. Chippers with more than 2 cutting faces need less depth under the cutters. Dado heads with an advanced tooth geometry on the chippers may not need any extra depth under the cutters.

TYPICAL PATTERN OF CUT WITH ADJUSTABLE DADOES AT DIFFERENT WIDTHS

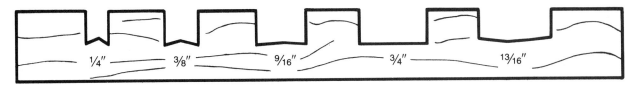

¼"   ⅜"   9/16"   ¾"   13/16"

Illus. 349 (above). Dadoes cut with a wobble head may have a concave or convex bottom. Illus. 349 (below). Excalibur or twin-blade adjustable dadoes leave a slightly different shape.

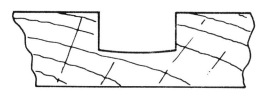

Arbor at the **6 O'CLOCK** position.

Arbor at the **12 O'CLOCK** position.

Illus. 350. A router plane can be used to true up a dado. This is not usually necessary unless the dado is visible.

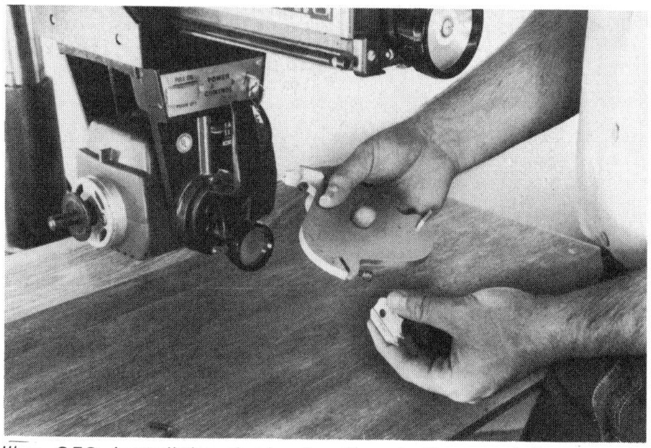

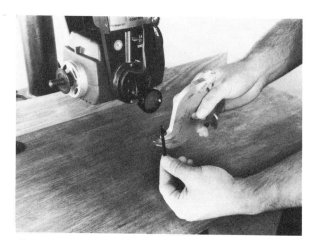

Illus. 352. Install the desired cutters in the moulding head. Be sure the cutters are mounted correctly.

Cutting Moulding or Shaping

Moulding cut on the radial arm saw requires careful attention to detail (Illus. 352–370). The moulding head or cutter is attached to the arbor and may be used in a vertical, tilted, or horizontal position. The stock is always fed against cutter or moulding head rotation. The cutterhead is never pulled across the work; the carriage remains stationary when moulding is being cut.

When cutting moulding or shaping on the radial arm saw, take light cuts. All adjustments and setups must be carefully checked before you begin. Install the desired cutters in the moulding head (Illus. 352) or select the desired cutterhead. Follow the manufacturer's instructions for installing the cutters. Make sure the cutters are locked securely and that they are all pointing in the same direction (Illus. 353).

Illus. 353. Tighten the cutters securely. Check them periodically while shaping to be sure they haven't loosened. Make sure they are all pointing in the same direction.

Disconnect the power to the saw and remove the guard. Mount the cutterhead (Illus. 354); the flat side of the cutters face the direction of rotation. Replace the guard and turn the cutter over by hand. Make sure the cutters do not touch the guard. Note: For some shaping operations, a specialty guard is used. Follow the saw manufacturer's recommendations concerning guard selection.

Position the cutterhead for shaping, and install the appropriate fence. For edge shaping, the fence has to be cut out to accommodate the cutterhead. When face-shaping, use a true, uncut fence. This will allow the work to ride along the fence without interference.

Adjust the cutter height and carriage position. Cuts of $\frac{1}{8}$ to $\frac{1}{4}''$, depending on species hardness, are best. Deeper cuts require 2 or more passes. Make the final cut only $\frac{1}{16}''$. Use featherboards, commercial hold-downs, or

Illus. 351. Check the saw for heeling before you do any shaping. Make any needed adjustments before you continue.

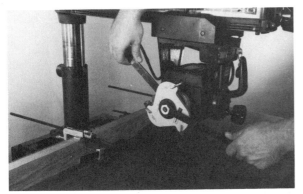

Illus. 354. Mount the cutterhead on the arbor and tighten it securely.

hold-down rollers to control the stock while cutting. Use a push stick or other device to feed the stock. This will keep your hands clear of the cutterhead.

When the face of a piece is being shaped, it is trapped between the table and cutter. A warped or twisted piece is likely to kick back under these circumstances, so work with true stock. Edge shaping is done along the fence. If the entire edge is cut away, the fence on the outfeed side of the cutters must meet the cut edge for support. This means that the outfeed fence will be offset from the infeed fence. The amount of offset equals the amount removed from the shaped edge.

Work carefully when shaping. Keep your hands clear of the cutterhead and kickback zone. Stand to the side of the stock as you feed it into the cutter. Take light cuts for smoother shaping and less chance of kickback. Feed stock slowly when shaping. This improves surface smoothness and minimizes surface tear-out. If the motor slows down, take a lighter cut.

Make sure the stock being shaped is true and free of knots or other defects. Shaping operations can destroy pieces containing loose knots and other defects. When in doubt, do not shape the piece.

In some operations, the piece used to feed the work can be used to control tear-out. Sometimes oversized pieces are shaped and the tear-out is then sawed off. Shape end grain first when doing all 4 sides of a piece. Any tear-out at the ends will be removed when the edges are shaped.

Fancy pieces of moulding can be made by shaping stock with 2 or more cutters. Remember to retain 2 true surfaces to control the stock. One true surface should rest on the table, and the other should ride along the fence.

When the motor is tilted, additional profiles can be cut using the same cutters. After tilting the arbor, make sure it does not contact the table, fence, or column. Turn the cutterhead over by hand. Change the setup if the cutterhead contacts anything. Note: When turning the cutterhead over by hand, make sure the power is disconnected.

Small pieces of moulding are safer and easier to cut when they are part of a larger piece. Wider, heavier pieces do not vibrate or chatter as much as a thin strip. A thin strip is likely to shatter and kick back during the shaping process. It is much safer to shape both edges of a wider piece. The moulding can then be ripped from both edges of the wider piece. Use a fine-cutting blade to rip the moulding from the wider piece. This will keep the edge smooth and eliminate the need for planing.

Illus. 355. Turn the yoke to the desired position for in-shaping or out-shaping. Lock it securely in position.

Illus. 356. Feed stock into cutter rotation. Take light cuts.

Illus. 357. Commercial hold-downs control stock. A second piece is fed right behind the first. The last piece is followed by a push stick.

Illus. 358. The motor is tilted for angular shaping. Cutters can make different shapes when the motor is turned. The saw is set up for out-shaping.

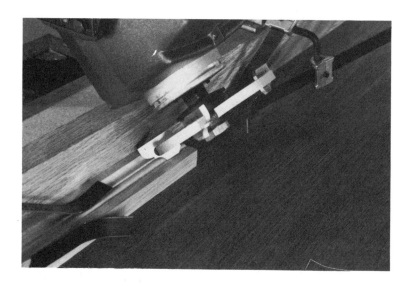

Illus. 359. Hold-downs are adjusted and the shaper head is positioned on the work. Lock and clamp all adjusting mechanisms after the setup is complete.

Illus. 360. Pieces can be fed one after the other into the cutter. The last piece must be followed by a push stick.

Illus. 361. This setup is using commercial hold-downs for in-shaping. Note that the stock is clear and free of defects.

Illus. 362. The stave is shaped again for a balanced look.

Illus. 363. This angular setup is using a horizontal guard. The tilt is so slight that this guard gives enough protection.

Illus. 364. The commercial hold-down has wheels that turn the opposite way for out-shaping operations like this. A planer knife is cutting a chamfer on this stock.

Illus. 365. A fence with a cutout is being used for horizontal shaping. The front table is about 1" higher than the rear table. This gives the arbor clearance.

Illus. 366. The commercial hold-downs are adjusted for the work.

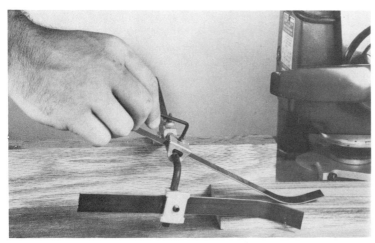

Illus. 367. The hold-downs are tightened securely after adjustment.

Illus. 368. The horizontal guard is then mounted and adjusted to clear the workpiece.

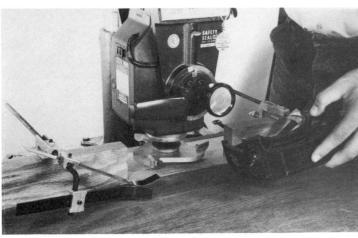

Illus. 369. Stock is fed into or against cutter rotation. The hold-downs resist vibration and make the job safer.

Illus. 370. One piece can follow another when hold-downs are used. A push stick should follow the last piece.

117

Sanding Operations

The radial arm saw is quite versatile as a sanding machine. It is capable of disc-sanding, spindle-sanding, and stroke-sanding. Each of these operations requires a different setup. The specifics of each are discussed on the following pages.

Whenever you use the radial arm saw for sanding operations, wear a dust mask. The dust of some woods is capable of causing bronchial problems and cancer. Using dust masks and other dust collection systems can make the sanding operation much safer.

Regardless of what type of sanding operation is being set up, make sure the attachments are secured properly and that all adjustments are locked securely before you begin sanding. Make all adjustments and setups with the power disconnected.

Disc-Sanding The sanding disc is mounted on the arbor in the same way as a blade (Illus. 371 and 372). The yoke is then turned so the disc faces forwards. A special sanding table (Illus. 373) is used to support the work while it is being sanded. The sanding table is clamped to the table of the radial arm saw. It should be adjusted so that it is about ⅛″ from the disc. Make sure the arm and carriage are locked securely before you begin sanding.

All sanding is done against disc rotation. For an outside curve, turn on the power and feed the work into the disc (Illus. 375). Take a light cut and keep the work moving. This will keep the abrasive from burning the wood. Always work on the half of the disc that is moving downwards towards the table (Illus. 376). If you work on the half of the disc moving upwards, the disc will lift the work.

If the edge of the curve is chamfered or bevelled, the arbor can be tilted to the desired angle. For chamfered ends, a mitre gauge may be used with the sanding table (Illus. 378).

A special circle-sanding jig can also be used with the disc-sanding attachment (Illus. 379). The jig is clamped to the radial-arm-saw table. Circular blanks are set over the pin. The tongue is moved towards the jig until contact is made. The work is then sanded as it is turned. When the stop on the tongue hits the jig (Illus. 380), the circle has been sanded to the correct diameter.

Illus. 371. The sanding disc replaces the saw blade when disc-sanding. Disconnect the power before you begin.

Illus. 372. This disc has abrasives on both sides. Select the side which has the correct abrasive grit. Tighten the arbor nut securely before you begin.

Illus. 373. This special sanding table is clamped to the saw table. It should be mounted about 1/8" from the disc. Be sure it is clamped securely in position.

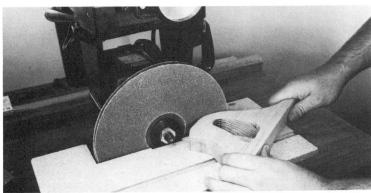

Illus. 374. All sanding is done on the side of the disc that pushes the work down on the table.

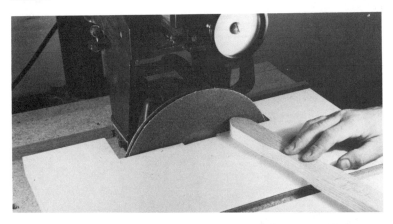

Illus. 375. The disc is turned on and allowed to come to full speed. Stock is sanded against disc rotation.

Illus. 376. Keep the work moving. Do not force the work into the disc. This letter is part of a sign made in my shop.

Illus. 377. Recognize the letter? This business belongs to a different Roger.

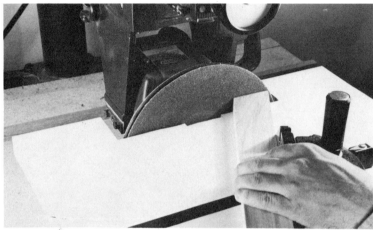

Illus. 378. A mitre gauge can also be used with the sanding table.

Illus. 379. This circle-sanding jig is clamped to the radial-arm-saw table. Stock is placed over the pin on the tongue.

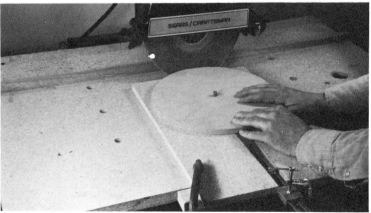

Illus. 380. Stock is fed into the turning disc. When the stop on the tongue hits the jig, the circle is the correct diameter.

In some cases, pattern-sanding can be useful. The pattern is made slightly smaller than the work. The work is then placed over the pattern. The pattern rubs on a pin located on the sanding table and controls sanding (Illus. 381–384). The pin and pattern control the pattern and the amount of stock removed. Pins of different sizes will produce different results.

When sanding a straight edge, pinch the stock between the face of the disc and the fence. Take a light cut when edge-sanding. A heavy cut can burn the wood and cause a kickback. Some discs require a slight offset (2°) for edge-sanding with the fence. This reduces the stress on the disc and makes sanding marks run parallel to the edge.

The most common error made when disc-sanding is to load or burn the disc with wood particles. A stick-type abrasive cleaner such as the Pro Stik™ (Illus. 385) will keep the disc from loading. A loaded disc gets hot and will become burned quickly. A burned disc will not cut.

Though burning is most often caused by a loaded disc, it can also be caused in part by using too fine of an abrasive for the job or not moving the part as it is sanded. Keeping the part stationary while sanding causes heat to build up on both the disc and the wood. Move the wood and use the entire downwards moving half of the disc. This spreads the heat over the wood and disc. Remember, heat will build up faster at the outer edge of the disc. This is because the disc turns faster at the outer edge.

Because a sanding disc does not have teeth, some people feel that it is not as dangerous as a saw blade. A sanding disc is full of abrasive particles, which are small teeth. These teeth make smaller bites, but cut just the same. Keep your hands clear of the disc and table. If your finger becomes pinched between the disc and sanding table, a serious injury can occur.

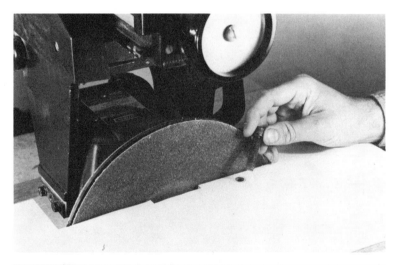

Illus. 381. A pin is screwed into the disc-sanding table for pattern sanding.

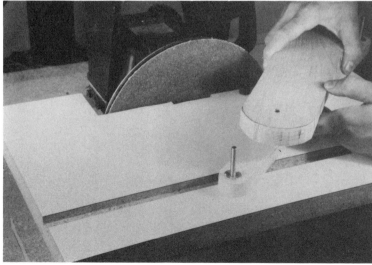

Illus. 382. The work has been rough-cut and is set over the pattern. The bolts coming through the pattern locate the work.

121

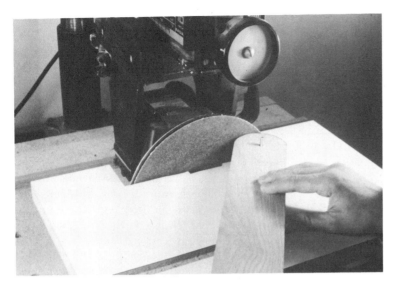

Illus. 383. The work is placed against the disc and sanded in the normal way.

Illus. 384. When the pattern touches the pin, the sanding will cease and the work will be the correct size and shape.

Illus. 385. An abrasive cleaner can be used to keep the abrasive working better and longer.

Spindle-Sanding When internal curves or irregular edges must be sanded, spindle-sanding works better than disc-sanding. Spindles come in diameters from about ½ to 3″. Their length varies from 1″ to 3″. Sanding spindles can be mounted on the blade arbor, an auxiliary arbor, or in a chuck attached to the blade or auxiliary arbor (Illus. 386–390). Where the sanding spindle mounts depends on the type of radial arm saw and the type of sanding spindle.

Spindle-sanding is much like disc-sanding. After the spindle is mounted, an auxiliary table is clamped to the saw table (Illus. 391 and 392). Work is fed against spindle rotation (Illus. 393). Use very light pressure and keep the work moving. Heavy pressure may cause burning. This ruins the abrasive.

Illus. 386. On some saws, an auxiliary arbor is used for spindle sanding. The blade, arbor washers, and guard must be removed from the other arbor when spindle-sanding.

Illus. 387. The spindle is turned onto the auxiliary arbor. A wrench can be used on the other end of the arbor to hold it stationary.

Illus. 388. On some machines, the spindle is mounted on the saw arbor. The arbor washers and nut are left in place when the spindle is mounted.

Illus. 389. Sometimes a chuck is mounted on the auxiliary arbor.

Illus. 390. This chuck accommodates smaller spindles with a shank.

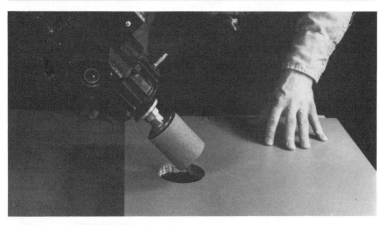

Illus. 391. The spindle is dropped into the spindle-sanding table. Be sure to lock the bevel clamp after it is in position.

Illus. 392. The spindle and table are located. Clamp the table to the saw and lock the carriage.

Illus. 393. Work is fed against spindle rotation. Keep the work moving so that you do not burn the abrasives or the work.

To sand bevels or chamfers, tilt the spindle (Illus. 394). Make sure all locks are secure after adjusting the spindle. Use relatively coarse abrasives (40- to 80-grit) when spindle-sanding and use an abrasive cleaner to keep the abrasives from loading and burning.

The spindle sander may also be adapted to pattern-sanding. A pin is added to the table so that the pattern may follow it. Use the table shown in Illus. 381 as a model if you wish to make such a table.

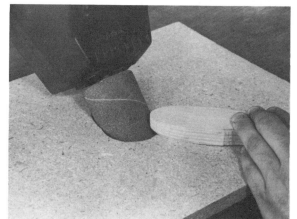

Illus. 395. For some jobs, it is easier to put the spindle in the horizontal position. Keep your fingers clear of the abrasives.

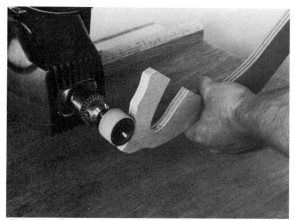

Illus. 394. The spindle may be tilted for sanding chamfers and bevels. Lock the bevel clamp after tilting the spindle.

The spindle may be used in any position depending on the work. In some cases, it is easier to put the spindle in the horizontal position (Illus. 395) and sand the work freehand. Exercise caution when freehand sanding. Keep your fingers clear of the abrasives at all times. Abrasives can tear the skin very quickly.

Abrasive sleeves must be changed when they are torn, dull, or burned. Before changing, be sure to use the entire abrasive. Keep the abrasives clean to prolong their lives (Illus. 396). When the column is raised or lowered, new abrasive grits are positioned next to the table. Some sleeves are held in position by internal pressure (Illus. 397). A screw in the middle of the spindle exerts pressure on the sleeve to hold it in position. This must be loosened to remove the sleeve. Tighten the screw securely after replacing the sleeve (Illus. 398). Always disconnect the power before changing the abrasive sleeve.

There are other sleeves that are held with a cam-type clamp (Illus. 399–402). These sleeves use portions of a sandpaper sheet instead of a sleeve. The paper is cut to exact size and fit into a slot in the spindle. An eccentric spindle is then inserted and turned with a wrench. When using this type of spindle, use sandpaper with a "C" or "D" weight backing. Lighter-weight paper will tear easily.

Illus. 396. Use a stick-type abrasive cleaner to prolong abrasive life and increase abrasive efficiency.

Illus. 397. Some abrasive sleeves are held on by compression. The screw in the middle of the spindle is loosened and the sleeve is removed.

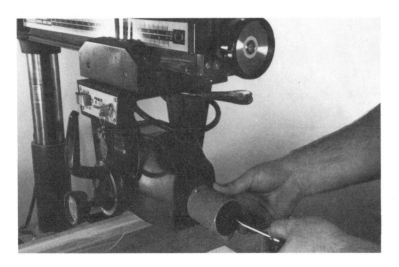

Illus. 398. Install a fresh sleeve and compress the rubber spindle to hold it in position.

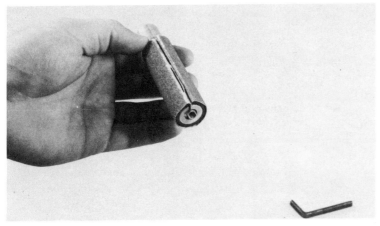

Illus. 399. This sleeve uses paper-backed abrasives. They wear a little quicker, but they are less expensive.

Illus. 400. Release the eccentric tube with a wrench and remove the abrasive.

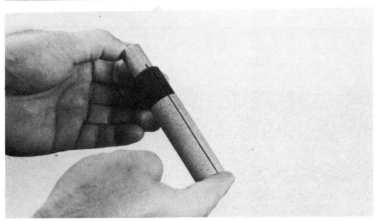

Illus. 401. Roll the abrasive paper into a sleeve with tightly folded edges. The folds go in the slot cut in the spindle.

Illus. 402. Push the eccentric tube in the hole and turn it to secure the abrasive paper.

Stroke-Sanding Stroke-sanding is similar to belt-sanding. It is well-suited to wide, flat panels. The stroke sander is attached to the radial-arm-saw motor (Illus. 403–411). A pulley is attached to the saw arbor. This pulley drives a V belt, which drives another pulley attached to the rear drum of the sander. This drum drives the belt. Sanding pressure comes from a handheld pad (Illus. 412). This pad is pushed against the belt while it is moving (Illus. 413). The pad is moved back and forth on the inside of the belt while the carriage is moved in and out with the other hand (Illus. 414).

There are a specific set of instructions for mounting the stroke sander. Refer to the product's manual for safety instructions and assembly sequences and procedures. The stroke sander is not designed for continuous use. It should be run only for periods of one hour or less.

When stroke-sanding small pieces, clamp a cleat to the table. This holds the work stationary while it is being sanded. Larger pieces should be moved according to the sequence in the manufacturer's manual.

When using the stroke sander, look through the tracking window occasionally to make sure that the belt is tracking properly. Readjust it with the tracking or clamping knob. Prior to operating the stroke sander, review the owner's manual for proper setup and safety procedures.

Illus. 403. The stroke sander is mounted in the same groove as the blade guard. It is levelled and screwed down securely.

Illus. 404. A pulley is mounted on the stroke sander after the back of the guard is installed.

Illus. 405. A pulley is secured to the saw arbor. The saw motor will drive the stroke sander.

Illus. 406. The V belt is mounted over the pulleys, and the guard is screwed in position.

Illus. 407. The tracking adjustment is centered in its adjustment prior to running. Minor adjustments can be made while the abrasive belt is running. Notice that the stroke sander has been rotated 180° by turning the yoke.

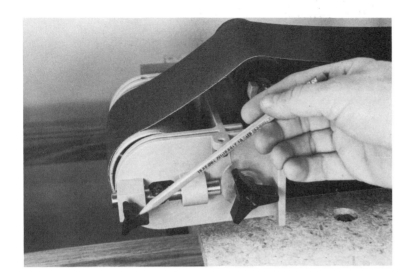

Illus. 408. The lock-knob holds the tracking adjustment. This knob must be released before making any tracking adjustment.

Illus. 409. The front abrasive guard is now mounted. This helps prevent contact with the abrasive belt and makes dust collection more efficient.

Illus. 410. There is a window in the front guard. This window allows you to see how the abrasive belt is tracking on the drum.

Illus. 411. The rear abrasive guard is now attached. It has an outlet on the back for dust collection. It accommodates a standard vacuum hose.

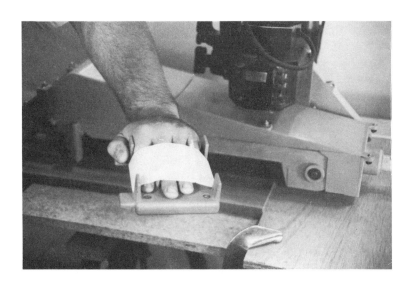

Illus. 412. This handheld pad exerts pressure on the moving belt to make it sand the work beneath the belt.

Illus. 413. One hand holds the pad and does the sanding while the other moves the carriage in and out. Note the stop clamped to the table to hold the work in position. Dust collection is important. This sander has been hooked up to a collector.

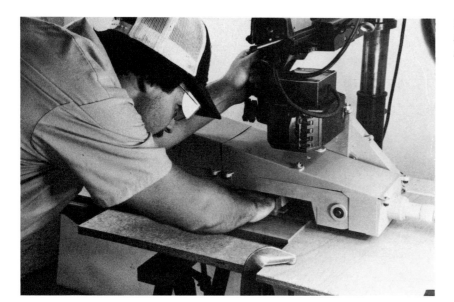

Scrolling Attachment

A scrolling attachment is available for certain radial arm saws (Illus. 415–417). This device works like a sabre saw in cutting irregular curves. The attachment is bolted over the arbor and clamped to the motor housing. The blade has teeth that point downwards towards the table. It is held in the chuck with 2 set screws.

Before the scrolling attachment is attached to the motor, a ⅜″ hole must be drilled in the front table. This is to accommodate the blade when it reciprocates. It is also possible to make an auxiliary table that can be clamped to the front table. The one shown in Illus. 417 has a plastic laminate surface. It was made from a countertop sink cutout.

The hold-down must be in contact with the workpiece before sawing. This is controlled with the elevating crank. Light pressure is all that is needed (Illus. 418). Heavy pressure makes it difficult to feed the work.

Use conventional scroll saw practices when using the attachment. Avoid sharp turns and feeding too fast (Illus. 419). Do not let your thumb or fingers line up with the blade. If you slipped, they would be pushed directly into the blade. It is good practice to leave the layout line when scroll-sawing. This leaves some extra stock for disc- or spindle-sanding to finished size. A slow, steady feed usually produces the best results.

The scroll attachment can be turned by pivoting the yoke; it can be moved in and out by moving the carriage on its arm. For angular cuts, release the bevel latch and turn the motor to the desired angle (Illus. 420). The downward cutting stroke of the blade tends to push the work away from the layout line when an angular cut is made. A fence could be used to help position the work in some cases. (For more information about sabre-sawing and jig-sawing, refer to *Woodworking Principles and Practices* [American Technical Publishing Co., 1981].)

A mount can be made on the front table for a sabre saw (Illus. 421). This mount does the same things a scrolling attachment does, and is portable. Vertical (Illus. 422) and angular cuts can also be made with this mount. For best results, select a saber saw with a stroke of ⅝″ or greater (Illus. 423).

Illus. 415. This scrolling attachment is used on DeWalt (Black & Decker) radial arm saws. The blade and the arbor washers must be removed to mount this attachment.

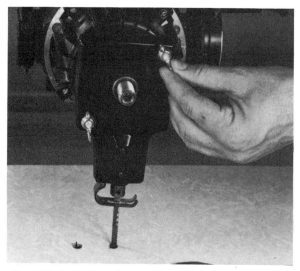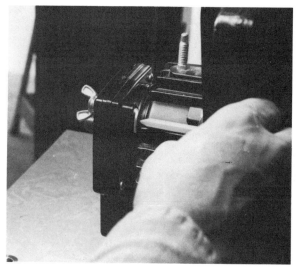

Illus. 416 (left). The wing nuts have a hook device on the opposite side. (Right). The hooks clamp on the ring designed for the saw guard.

Illus. 417. The arbor nut is tightened against the scrolling attachment. The auxiliary table has a hole into which the blade drops. The auxiliary table is adjusted and clamped in position.

Illus. 418. The hold-down keeps the work on the auxiliary table. The blade-elevating crank is used to control hold-down pressure.

Illus. 419. Feed only as fast as the blade will cut. Leave the layout line for disc sanding. Note how the operator's hand does not line up with the blade.

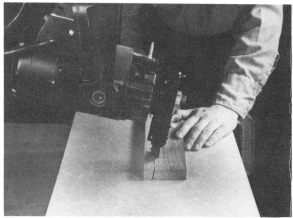

Illus. 420. The motor may be turned for bevel cuts. Remember, this scroller cuts on the downstroke. It may push the work away from the layout line.

Illus. 421. A conventional sabre saw can be mounted to the underside of your radial-arm-saw table. Drill a hole to accommodate the blade.

Illus. 422. The sabre saw is used to make this irregular cut. Angular cuts may also be made this way.

Illus. 423. The sabre saw is cutting a tight turn in red oak. Speed of feed is dependent upon stroke length, blade coarseness, and wood hardness.

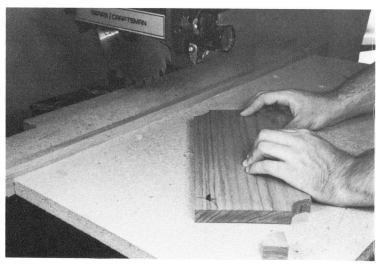

Buffing

Buffing wheels can be mounted on the radial arm saw for polishing metal and honing cutting edges. The buffing wheel (Illus. 424) is mounted the same way as a saw blade. Be sure to disconnect the power before changing from blade to buffing wheel. Replace the guard to control the dust (Illus. 425).

An abrasive material is used to achieve the polishing action. The abrasives are called buffing compounds. These come in several different abrasive grades. Be sure to select the correct one for the job being done.

The buffing wheel is "charged" or loaded with compound by rubbing the stick against the wheel while it is turning. The work is then pushed against the wheel until the desired result is achieved (Illus. 426).

The buffing wheel must be unloaded or discharged to change compounds. Do this by holding a putty knife (Illus. 427) or similar object against the wheel while it is turning. After the compound is removed, the wheel may be recharged.

Some cutting tools, such as chisels, can be honed with a buffing wheel (Illus. 428). If the tool is not nicked, the cutting edge may be touched against the wheel to form the secondary cutting angle. Work slowly and check the edge frequently. Rust can also be removed from tools with the buffing wheel (Illus. 429).

Illus. 424. The buffing wheel is bolted to the arbor in the same way as a saw blade.

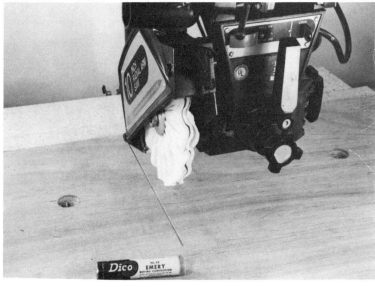

Illus. 425. The guard is used when buffing to control dust.

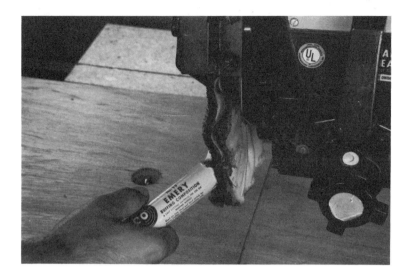

Illus. 426. The buffing wheel is loaded or "charged" with buffing compound. Be sure to use the correct buffing compound for the job you are doing.

Illus. 427. When changing buffing compounds, use a putty knife to unload the buffing wheel.

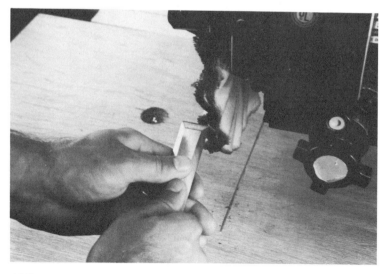

Illus. 428. The buffing wheel is being used to hone this chisel. The buffing compound provides the abrasive action.

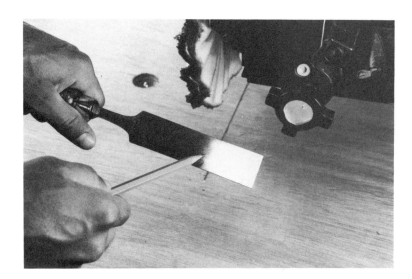

A buffing wheel throws off many small particles while it is in operation. Use the guard to control the debris, and wear a dust mask to protect your lungs. Hold the work firmly so that the wheel does not pull it out of your hands.

Observe the following precautions when buffing on the radial arm saw.

1. Do not force the work against the wheel. Let the buffing wheel and compound do the work.
2. Keep your work slightly below the center line of the wheel. This will minimize the chance of the wheel grabbing the work. It also keeps the work from raking the buffing compound off the wheel.
3. Hold the work firmly. Work with sharp corners or projections can be grabbed by the wheel and thrown with great force.
4. Wear a dust mask while buffing to protect your lungs.
5. Wear protective glasses when buffing, and keep your eyes on the work. Avoid distractions of any kind.

Here is a list of available buffing compounds and their uses.

Buffing Compounds

NAME	USE
Emery	Removes rust and corrosion from iron, steel, and other hard metals. Cuts very fast.
Tripoli	For aluminum and pewter. Also used on plated objects. Mild-cutting action.
Stainless	For stainless steel and other hard alloys containing chromium and nickel. Moderate-cutting action.
Rouge	For precious metals such as silver and gold. Also used as a final buffing compound on other materials.
Jeweler's Rouge	For use on jewelry as a final buff or for touch-up work. Very slow cutting—more of a polishing agent.

6

Intermediate and Advanced Operations

As you become experienced with your radial arm saw, you will want to try some of the intermediate and advanced operations presented in this chapter.

Remember, new experiences can present new hazards! Review Chapter 4 before attempting any new operation. The information presented there will help you identify a potentially dangerous situation and suggest ways of avoiding it.

Cutting Rabbets and Dadoes

Rabbets are L-shaped channels along an edge or end. Dadoes are U-shaped channels through a piece of stock. Rabbets and dadoes can be cut with a dado head or a single blade. For 1 or 2 rabbets or dadoes, it is probably faster to use a single blade because it takes longer to set up a dado head than it takes to make the cut with a single blade. For cutting multiple parts, the dado head is much faster. The cut is made in one pass.

Single-Blade Rabbets and Dadoes   A single-blade end or edge rabbet consists of 2 cuts. For an edge rabbet, the

yoke is pivoted to the rip position. The first cut is in the face of the work. The depth of cut is controlled by the blade elevation. Set the blade to rabbet depth or slightly less (Illus. 430). The distance from the fence to the far side of the blade determines rabbet width on an edge rabbet. Lock the carriage after making this adjustment. For some rabbets, this cut can be made at an angle (Illus. 431).

For an end rabbet, the depth of cut is set the same way as an edge rabbet. The width of the rabbet is set from the blade to a stop (Illus. 432) clamped to the fence. The end-rabbet face cut is made by pulling the carriage through the work (Illus. 433). The edge-rabbet face cut is made the same way a rip cut is made (Illus. 434). Observe the same precautions and safety procedures.

To make the second cut in the rabbet, turn the blade down into the horizontal position (Illus. 435). An auxiliary table has to be placed on the front table for this cut, and a low fence must be used (Illus. 436). The safest way to make this cut is with an 8″ blade or smaller. This allows you to use the shaper guard for this cut. Make sure the blade does not touch the column (Illus. 437).

Illus. 430. The face cut for an edge rabbet is cut to full depth or slightly less.

Illus. 431. The face cut on some edge rabbets can be made at an angle.

Illus. 432. The rabbet width is set with a stop. Use a tooth that points away from the stop.

Illus. 433. Pull the carriage through the face of the work for an end rabbet.

Illus. 434. The face cut in an edge rabbet is made the same way as any rip cut. Observe the same safety precautions you would observe for ripping.

Illus. 435. The second cut or edge cut in a rabbet is done with the blade in the horizontal position. Be sure the blade does not contact the column.

Illus. 436. A low fence and auxiliary front table are used for this cut. A mitre gauge can be used for this operation. Push blocks may also be used.

Illus. 437. A blade smaller than usual makes horizontal sawing safer. This increases the space between the blade and column.

The blade is lined up with the other cut and locked in position. Use a tooth that points towards the table for this setup. Install the shaper guard (Illus. 438) and make the cut. On an edge rabbet, the edge rides along the fence as the cut is made. This is very similar to a rip cut. Use a push stick or hold-down to increase your control. End rabbets should be fed with a wide pusher or mitre gauge (Illus. 439). This keeps them from turning as the cut is made. Some woodworkers cut a dado in the auxiliary table so a mitre gauge can be used to feed the piece (Illus. 440). This can be a commercial mitre gauge (from a table saw or shaper) or shop-made.

The end rabbet can also be made with a series of crosscuts. After the first cut is made at the stop (Illus. 441), the work is moved one saw blade away from the stop for another cut (Illus. 442). This is repeated until the rabbet is completed (Illus. 443). Trim the rabbet with a chisel if necessary (Illus. 444).

Illus. 438. The shaper guard is used for horizontal sawing. This makes contact with the blade difficult. Note the commercial hold-downs used to increase control over the work.

Illus. 439. A wide pusher or mitre gauge should be used to control end rabbet cuts.

Illus. 440. The dado in the auxiliary table allows a mitre gauge to be used. This provides positive control over the workpiece.

Illus. 441. The face cut of this end rabbet was made while the work was butted to the stop.

Illus. 442. Additional face cuts have been made instead of turning the blade to the horizontal position.

Illus. 443. The rabbet is completed with a few additional face cuts. For cutting a few rabbets, this method is the most efficient.

Illus. 444. Use a chisel to trim up the single-blade rabbet if necessary. In most applications, it will be smooth enough.

To cut a dado across the face of your work, make a series of cuts. Line up your layout line with the blade and clamp a stop in position (Illus. 445). Use a tooth that points towards the layout line. Make this cut in all pieces (Illus. 446). Now move to the other layout line and position the blade. Use a tooth that points towards the layout line. Clamp a stop in position and make the cut (Illus. 447). The piece is then moved one saw blade distance away from the stop and another cut is made (Illus. 448). This is repeated (Illus. 449) until you reach the first kerf (Illus. 450). Cut all pieces before removing the stop. Avoid banging into the stop, as this may change your setup. Clean the dado up with chisel or router plane.

To cut a groove or dado along the face of the work, position the yoke for ripping. Set the blade height to dado depth first, then position the blade to the layout line closest to the fence (Illus. 451). Use a tooth that points towards the fence. Lock the carriage to the arm after setting the blade distance from the fence. Adjust the anti-kickback pawls and attach any available hold-downs or a cleat to the fence. This will provide greater control as you make the cut. Use a push stick to keep your hands clear of the blade. Observe all other safety procedures described in the sections on ripping in Chapters 4 and 5. Make this cut in all pieces.

Release the carriage and adjust the blade with the other edge of the dado. Use a tooth that points away from the fence. Lock the carriage to the arm and make the cut in all parts (Illus. 452). The carriage is then moved one saw kerf closer to the fence, and a cut is made (Illus. 453). Another cut (Illus. 454) is then made in all parts. This is repeated until the dado has been completed (Illus. 455).

The procedures for cutting single-blade rabbets and dadoes in sheet stock are similar to those used for solid stock. The difference is that grain direction in sheet stock is not as important as the dimensions of the part. An end rabbet on a small piece of sheet stock would be done in the same way as an end rabbet on solid stock, but an end rabbet on a large awkward part of sheet stock would be treated as an edge rabbet in solid stock.

Single-blade rabbets and dadoes are sometimes called lazy dadoes. This implies that the operator is too lazy to set up a dado head. For a few rabbets or dadoes, the single blade may be the best. When several dadoes or rabbets must be cut, the dado head should be set up. This reduces handling, labor, and setup time.

Illus. 445. For a cross dado, line up the right layout line with the blade. Use a tooth that points towards the line. Clamp a stop to the fence or table to position it. Make sure blade height is set for dado depth.

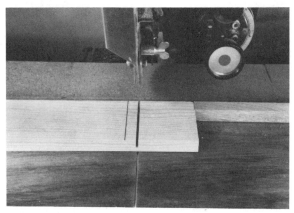

Illus. 446. Make this cut in the face of all pieces.

143

Illus. 447. Adjust the left layout line with a tooth that points towards it. Clamp a stop to the fence or table to position the work.

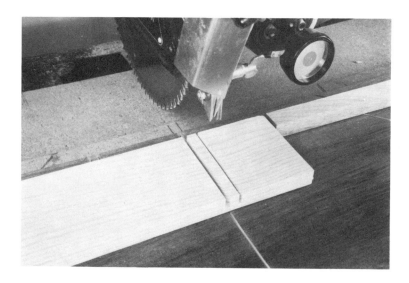

Illus. 448. The piece is moved one saw blade's distance from the stop for another cut.

Illus. 449. The piece is moved repeatedly to the left of the stop for additional cuts.

Illus. 450. When you reach the first kerf, the dado is complete.

Illus. 451. To cut a single-blade dado in the rip position, line up the blade with the layout line closest to the fence. The blade height should be adjusted to the dado depth.

Illus. 452. After the first cut is made in all parts, the carriage is moved. The blade is lined up with the layout line furthest from the fence.

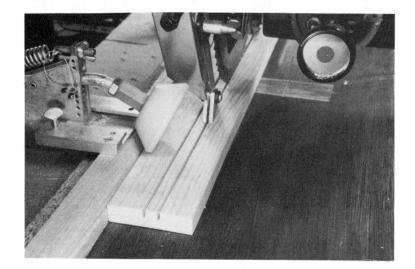

Illus. 453. The second cut is made in all parts. Hold-downs provide greater control over the work.

Illus. 454. The carriage is moved one saw blade's width closer to the fence and another cut is made. Note that the anti-kickback pawls are engaged with the work.

Illus. 455. After a series of cuts, the dado is completed.

Cutting Rabbets with the Dado Head End rabbets are cut much like single-blade rabbets. The saw arm is pulled across the work. Edge rabbets require a special fence used with the dado head in the rip position. To cut an end rabbet, mount the dado head on the radial arm saw. The dado should be as wide or slightly wider than the rabbet. Make this setup with the power disconnected.

Replace the guard and set rabbet depth on a scrap. Mount a stop on the fence. Position it so that it locates the rabbet correctly on the work. The work should be squarely against the fence and touching the stop. Turn on the saw and pull the carriage through the work (Illus. 456). Inspect the rabbet for accuracy and smoothness. An angular end rabbet can be made in the same way (Illus. 457). The only difference is that the motor is turned. When many of these rabbets must be cut, it is a good idea to secure a carriage stop. This limits the travel of the arm and minimizes the chance of error during repetitive cuts.

Edge rabbets are set up differently. First the dado head is mounted on the arbor. The dado head is about ¼″ wider than the desired rabbet. The yoke is turned to the in-rip position, and a new fence is installed. The fence is then marked for rabbet height above the table. The dado head is elevated above the fence and positioned so that about one-third of the dado head is over the fence. The carriage is locked securely and the guard is positioned horizontally. The saw is turned on and the moving dado head is slowly lowered into the fence.

Keep an eye on the mark scribed on the fence. When the dado head cuts the mark (Illus. 458), begin elevating the head. Elevate it just enough to take any lash or slack out of the threads. Turn off the saw and allow the head to come to a complete stop. Set the distance from the head to the fence to the desired rabbet size (Illus. 459). Use a tooth on the outside cutter that points away from the fence. Position the hold-downs and kickback devices and make a trial cut in a scrap. Make any needed adjustments and begin rabbeting (Illus. 460).

Illus. 456. The stop locates this rabbet cut which is made with the dado head. Note the fresh cut in the fence to control tear-out.

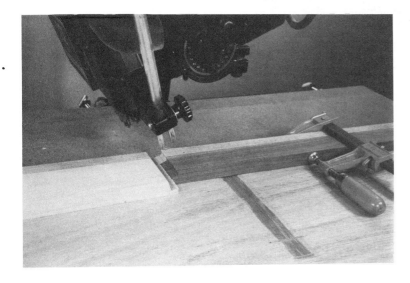

Illus. 457. When the motor is tilted, an angular end rabbet can be cut.

147

Illus. 458. A special fence is used for rabbeting with the dado head. Part of the dado head cuts into the fence.

Illus. 459. The distance from the outer edge of the dado head to the fence determines the size of the rabbet.

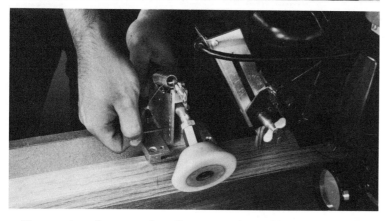

Illus. 460. All hold-downs and anti-kickback pawls should be adjusted before the cut is made.

Use a push stick to control smaller pieces when rabbeting (Illus. 461). Remember that hold-downs can make the operation much safer and the stock easier to control (Illus. 462). If the saw slows down during the rabbeting operation, take a lighter cut. With practice, you will learn the correct depth of cut and feed speed for your radial arm saw.

A shaper head equipped with jointer knives can also be used to cut rabbets in solid stock. The shaper head can be used just like the dado head in the vertical position. In fact, the same fence can be used in many cases.

When the shaper head is used in the horizontal position (Illus. 463), a special fence is used. The shaper guard also replaces the regular guard for this operation. Shaping

of rabbets should be done while observing all safety precautions discussed in Chapter 4 and in the section Shaping in Chapter 5. Take light cuts and avoid sheet stock. The steel knives dull very quickly in sheet stock.

With large pieces of sheet stock, the edge-rabbeting method with a dado head is preferred (Illus. 464). Smaller pieces are usually rabbeted with the end-rabbet technique. This is also best done with a dado head.

Hardwood plywood may require a slower feed speed than other materials. This is because the face veneers are so thin. These veneers tend to tear or break when cut at a high-feed rate. Remember, carbide is best for sheet stock because the glue will dull tool steel very quickly.

Illus. 461. A push stick or push block should be used to control smaller pieces when rabbeting.

Illus. 462. Hold-downs make the job safer and the stock easier to control.

Illus. 463. The shaper head can be used in the horizontal position for cutting rabbets.

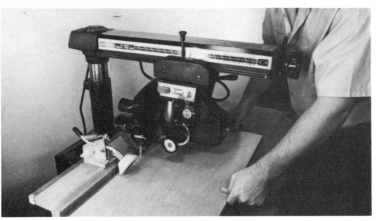

Illus. 464. When working with large pieces of sheet stock, use the edge-rabbeting dado technique.

Cutting Blind Dadoes Blind dadoes are dadoes that do not go completely from end to end or edge to edge. They stop somewhere in the part. They are sometimes called stopped dadoes. Blind or stopped dadoes are often used in cabinetwork. They look like butt joints from the front.

A blind dado shows no tear-out, and a loose fit is not visible from the front. It is cut the same way as a regular dado except it is not fed completely through.

A cross-grain blind dado is cut with the help of a pencil line or a carriage clamp. After the dado head is set up correctly, the stock is marked. The mark indicates where the dado is to stop. The carriage is pulled back to the pencil line and then returned to the column for a single blind dado. When several are to be cut, the carriage clamp or other device (Illus. 465) should be secured to the arm. This will stop the carriage and dado head at that point. For repetitive blind dadoes, a stop or clamp is the best practice. It is safer and there is less chance of error.

A blind dado that goes with the grain can also be marked with a pencil line (Illus. 466), but a stop clamped to the table or fence works best. The stop locates the end of the dado (Illus. 467). It offers greater control over the stock when the cut is completed. A long fence may be used to control blind dadoes in longer pieces of work; simply replace the short fence with a longer one. It is also possible to clamp a cleat to the underside of your work. This cleat will hit the table and stop the work at the desired location.

Cut a blind dado as you would a regular dado. In the rip position, feed the stock normally. When the stop is hit or the mark lines up with the dado head, shut off the saw (Illus. 468). Let the dado head come to a complete stop before releasing the work. Release the hold-downs if used, and lift the anti-kickback pawls. The piece may now be removed.

In the crosscut position, locate the work and pull the carriage out until the carriage clamp is hit or the mark lines up with the dado head. Return the carriage to the column and shut off the saw. Lock the carriage in position. Inspect the work to be sure the setup is correct. You can either square out the end of the dado with hand tools or cut an arc on the mating part with a scroll saw.

Illus. 465. A carriage clamp controlled dado length in this side. The dadoes are uniform in length.

Illus. 466. A pencil line has been used to mark the end of this blind dado. The guard has been removed for illustration purposes.

Illus. 467. A stop can be clamped to the fence or table to locate the end of a blind dado.

Illus. 468. When you reach the end of a blind dado, shut off the saw. Allow it to come to a complete stop before you release the work. The guard has been removed here for illustration purposes.

Cutting Lap Joints Lap joints are corner or cross joints where one piece laps over the other. They are used for cabinet faceplates and for cross braces. The lap joint is usually cut with the dado head. Adjust the dado head depth to one-half stock thickness (Illus. 469). For end laps, use stock width to locate a stop (Illus. 470). Use a tooth that points away from the stop. Clamp the stop securely to the fence or table. The distance from the stop to the fence should equal stock width or slightly more. By making a slight allowance, the overlapping ends can be sanded slightly after assembly for a nice-looking corner.

Mark the pieces. One half will be cut on the good or exposed face (Illus. 471). The other half will be cut on the back. Butt the stock to the fence and stop just as if you were cutting an end rabbet (Illus. 472). The stop locates the end of the cut. Pull the carriage through the work and return to the column. Now move the stock just enough to make another cut (Illus. 473). Continue this practice until the cut is completed (Illus. 474). Note: If the pieces tear out at the back when they are cut, back them up with a new fence. The new fence will control tear-out. Careful layout and setup will yield a good-fitting lap joint (Illus. 475).

When cutting a cross-lap joint, 2 stops must be used.

This is because they are not on the end of the piece. Set the first stop to the end closest to the stop or on the right-hand side of the layout (Illus. 476). Remember, this will be lined up with the right side of the dado head (the side closest to the stop). Butt the work against the fence and stop. Make the first cut (Illus. 477) and check the setup. Make this cut in all parts and remove the stop.

Locate the second stop to the left layout line. Use the left side of the dado head (Illus. 478). Position the work and make the cut (Illus. 479). Both ends of the cross-lap joint are now cut. If more stock remains, continue cutting until it is gone (Illus. 480). Several identical cross-lap joints can be produced accurately with this method (Illus. 481).

When making cross-lap joints, make sure stock is of uniform thickness and width. Wide pieces will need trimming, and narrow pieces will fit poorly. Uniform stock thickness is also important to any lap joint. Thick or thin stock will produce a shoulder at the joint. This spoils the appearance of the work and wastes material.

Remember to use an arm stop or clamp if multiple parts are being cut. This reduces the chance of error and accident. It also saves time since the pull stroke is only as long as necessary.

Illus. 469. When cutting lap joints, adjust the cut to one-half stock thickness. Make sure your last adjustment is an elevation of the blade. This will eliminate problems due to lash in the elevating mechanism.

Illus. 470. Use stock width to locate the stop when cutting end laps.

Illus. 471. Mark the pieces so that you know which side to cut. Remember to cut the good face of one part and the bad face of its mate.

Illus. 472. Cut a lap joint the same way you would cut an end rabbet.

Illus. 473. Move the stock over to make another cut in the face of the work.

Illus. 474. Continue cutting with the dado head until the lap joint is complete.

Illus. 475. Careful setup and layout will yield a good-fitting lap joint.

Illus. 476. For cross-lap joints, the first stop is set on the right-hand side of the layout.

Illus. 477. The first cut is made in all the parts. The stop controls their location.

Illus. 478. The second stop is located to the left of the layout line. Use a tooth that points towards the line for setup.

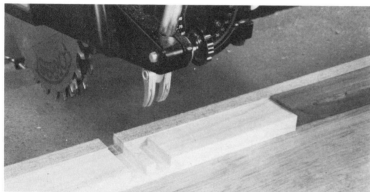

Illus. 479. The first cut is made using the left stop.

Illus. 480. Continue cutting until the lap joint is complete.

Illus. 481. The two-stop method produces accurate, good-fitting lap joints.

Cutting a Series of Dadoes Often, a series of equally spaced dadoes is needed for a shelving system or for some other purpose. A special fence can be used to control this spacing. One type of fence simply has a stop clamped to it to locate each dado. This method is slow because all parts must be handled for each dado. Another fence uses a self-closing hinge with a piece of stock screwed to it (Illus. 482). The stock fits in the rabbet or dado (Illus. 483) and controls the distance to the dado head. As each dado is cut, the hinge is lifted and the work is moved. The hinge is then turned down into the dado, and another cut is made. This is done until all dadoes are cut.

When cutting a series of dadoes, do not let sawdust get between the work and fence. This could throw the dado out of square. If blind dadoes are needed, a carriage clamp can be used.

Dadoes that go with the grain cannot use the stop method. The carriage has to be moved for each successive cut. Instead, lay out one piece of stock with all the cuts to be made marked on it (Illus. 484). Use this piece to set up each cut.

It is a good idea to make a few extra parts for setup purposes. Measure carefully when making the setup and remember which edge of the part goes against the fence (Illus. 485). On wide parts, you may have to switch from the in-rip to the out-rip position in the middle of the job.

Illus. 482. The piece of stock on this self-closing hinge helps locate equally spaced dadoes.

Illus. 483. The stock attached to this hinge fits in the dado. It controls spacing between the dadoes.

Illus. 484. For dadoes cut with the grain, the setup piece should be marked with all the dadoes.

Illus. 485. When cutting successive dadoes with the grain, remember which edge of your work goes against the fence.

Cutting Mortises and Tenons

A mortise and tenon is a two-part joint. The mortise is a slot or hole cut in one part. The tenon is a mating tongue that fits into the mortise. The 3 most common mortise-and-tenon joints are the blind, haunched, and open (Illus. 486). Both parts of the open mortise and tenon can be cut with a saw blade or dado head. The blind and haunched tenons can also be cut with a saw blade or dado head. The mating mortises cannot be cut with a saw blade. The mortises must be cut with a router bit or drill bit. Both of these bits can be attached to the radial arm saw and are discussed later in this chapter.

Saw-Blade Tenons   The way a saw-blade tenon is cut is very similar to the way a rabbet is cut. First, the shoulders are cut using a stop (Illus. 487). The stop locates the end of the tenon. This is called the shoulder cut. Shoulders may be cut on just the faces or on the faces and edges (Illus. 488). The cheek cuts are then made. The cheek cut joins the shoulder cut, and the tenon is formed.

To make the cheek cut, mount a 7½ or 8″ blade on the arbor and turn the arbor so that it is in the vertical position. The blade is now in the horizontal position (Illus. 489). An auxiliary table and cutout fence must be used for this operation. The blade is adjusted for the correct cut (Illus. 490) and is locked in position. The cut should be in the waste portion of the cheek. Check all clamps, locks, and adjustments to make sure they are secure. Install a shaper guard and adjust it to accommodate the wood you are working with (Illus. 491).

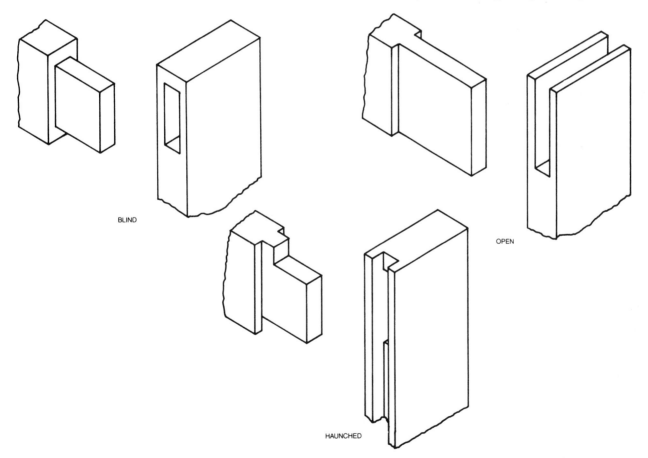

BLIND

OPEN

HAUNCHED

Illus. 486. Three types of mortise-and-tenon joints. The haunched tenon has a step (haunch) cut into it. This allows it to fit in the groove and mating mortise.

157

Illus. 487. When making a saw-blade tenon, cut the shoulders first. A stop is used to locate them.

Illus. 488. Shoulders are cut on both faces here. They can also be cut on the edges for some tenons.

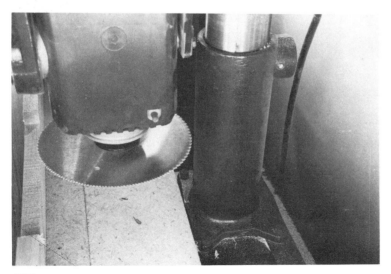

Illus. 489. For cheek cuts, the blade is turned to the horizontal position. Use a smaller blade (8") and make sure it does not come into contact with the column.

Illus. 490. The blade is adjusted for the correct cut.

Illus. 491. A shaper guard is used to make the job safer. Stock is controlled by a mitre gauge that moves in a slot on the auxiliary table.

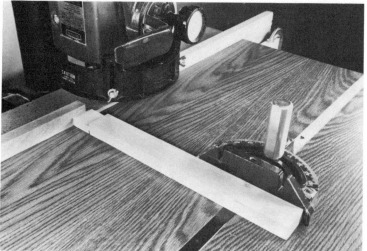

Use a mitre gauge to control the work. A mitre slot must be dadoed into the auxiliary table. Turn on the saw and feed the stock into the blade. Make sure it is being fed against blade rotation. Hold the stick firmly against the table and mitre gauge. Turn the piece over and make the cheek cut on the opposite face (Illus. 492). If the edges also require cheek cuts, readjust blade height. This process can also be used for lap joints.

The shoulder cut for a lap joint is made in the same way as a shoulder cut for a tenon. Shoulder-cut depth for a lap joint equals ½ stock thickness (Illus. 493). The stop is set to the width of work or slightly greater (Illus. 494). Use a tooth that points away from the stop to set the width. Mark all pieces so you know which face must be cut away (Illus. 495). This will eliminate confusion as you work at the saw. Remember, when making a lap frame cut away the good face of one part and the poor face or back of the mating part. If parts are not marked, you may have the back of some parts facing out. Test the fit on a trial setup to make sure it is correct (Illus. 496).

Illus. 492. The stock is now turned over and the cheek cut is made on the opposite side.

159

Illus. 493. Shoulder depth for this cut should equal one-half stock thickness or slightly less.

Illus. 494. The stop is set to the width of the stock or slightly greater when making lap joints.

Illus. 495. Mark the faces so that you know which one is to be cut away.

Illus. 496. Make a trial cut in scrap stock to be sure of the fit.

Saw-Blade Mortises The open or through mortise can also be cut with the blade in the horizontal position. Use the tenon to lay out the mortise (Illus. 497). Readjust blade height and shaper guard position. It will usually take 2 cuts to complete the mortise (Illus. 498). Feed only as fast as the saw can cut. Forcing the wood into the blade encourages a kickback or binding. It can also throw the machine out of alignment (Illus. 499).

A chisel may be needed to true-up the bottom of the mortise or improve the fit between the mortise and tenon. Work carefully and take light cuts. Removing too much stock will ruin the fit. Check the fit frequently to make sure too much stock has not been removed (Illus. 500).

A haunched tenon is cut to fit the groove made on the vertical parts (Illus. 501). The haunch is usually as long as the depth of the groove and ½″ deep. The haunch can be cut with a saw blade or dado head (Illus. 502).

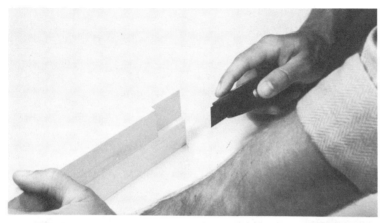

Illus. 497. Use the tenon cut to lay out the mortise. Mark the line with a utility knife and shade the area to be removed with a pencil.

Illus. 498. The first cut has been made to form the mortise. The piece must be turned over for the second cut.

Illus. 499. Feed the stock only as fast as the machine can take it. After the second cut has been made, any remaining stock can be sawed or chiselled away.

161

Illus. 500. Check the fit in scrap stock before you begin working. If the stock must be custom-fitted, check your progress frequently.

Illus. 501. A haunch can also be cut with the saw blade in the horizontal position. The haunch fits the groove on the mating part.

Illus. 502. A dado head can also be used to cut the haunch. A wobble-head dado has been used here.

Dado-Head Mortises and Tenons The dado head can be mounted on the radial arm saw to cut tenons. These tenons can be cut with the dado head in the horizontal or vertical position. When the dado head is in the horizontal position, tenons and through mortises are cut using an auxiliary table and mitre gauge or push block.

The process is the same as the one described for single-blade tenons. If you are using a sharp dado head of good quality, there may not be a need to make a shoulder cut on the work. The dado will make the cheek and shoulder cut in one pass. There may be some tear-out on the back edge of the work where the dado head exits. If this occurs, back the workpiece with a scrap of the same thickness. This will control tear-out.

Slot mortises can also be cut with the dado head in the horizontal position. The amount of dado head extending beyond the fence determines the depth of the mortise.

The bottom of the mortise will be curved instead of square. It will be the same as the arc of the dado head. The mating tenon can be trimmed to fit the arc.

Lay out the mortise on the work and set the dado height. Locate the mortise in relation to the dado and clamp a stop to the fence or table on the thrust side of the blade (Illus. 503). Make sure all locks and clamps are secure and that the guard is positioned correctly.

Turn the saw on and butt the work to the stop (Illus. 504). Push the work into the dado head and cut the mortise (Illus. 505). Push the work forward until it touches the other stop (Illus. 506). Pull the work off the dado head slowly and carefully. Twisting the work could enlarge the mortise or cause a kickback. The curve at the end of the mortise is caused by the shape of the dado head (Illus. 507).

Illus. 503. A stop for cutting a slot mortise is clamped to the table on the thrust side of the dado head.

Illus. 504. The stock is butted to the stop but clear of the dado head. The motor is then turned on.

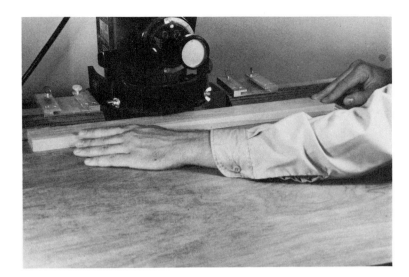

Illus. 505. Stock is pushed into the turning dado head and the mortise is cut.

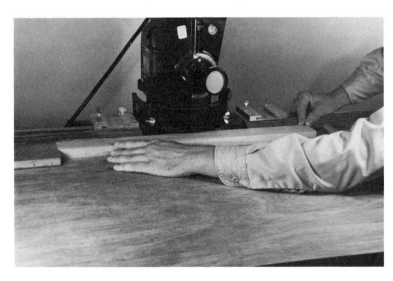

Illus. 506. The dado is pushed forward to another stop which locates the opposite end of the slot mortise. Pull the work away from the cutter.

Illus. 507. The curve at the end of the mortise is caused by the arc of the dado head.

Tenons can also be cut when the dado head is in the vertical position. Usually the dado is at maximum width (approximately ¾″ or slightly more). The arm is usually set at 0 degrees and the blade is set perpendicular to the table. A stop (Illus. 508) locates the shoulder of the tenon. Dado height determines the size of the tenon.

Butt the work against the fence and the stop. Turn the saw on and pull the dado across the work. Move the work away from the stop so that another cut can be made (Illus. 509). Turn the piece over so that the tenon can be completed (Illus. 510 and 511).

Haunched tenons may also use the dado head setup (Illus. 512). Some dado heads can cause tear-out on the work. Slower feed may reduce it. A new fence may also be helpful. The fence will have only one dado cutout. All cuts will be backed by the fence. This backing usually controls all tear-out problems. Note: A deep cut is more likely to cause tear-out. Deep cuts may require 2 consecutive cuts to control tear-out.

Blind mortises can be drilled-out and squared-up with a chisel. These may be cut on the radial arm saw. The saw must be set up for drilling. This technique is discussed later in this chapter (page 230).

Mortises can also be cut with a mortising machine. Mortising machines cut mortises of a nominal size, such as ¼″, ⅜″, ½″, ⅝″, and ¾″. Keep this in mind when you first lay out the tenons. Odd-size tenons can make the mortises more difficult to cut.

Illus. 508. The dado stop locates the shoulder of the tenon when using a dado head.

Illus. 509. Work is butted to the stop and the dado head is pulled across the work. One-half of the tenon is formed. The piece is turned over and again butted to the stop.

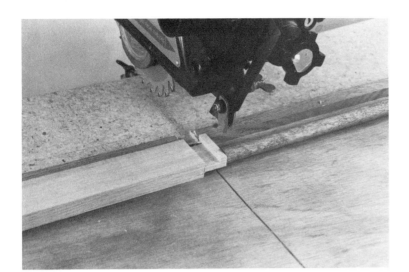

Illus. 510. A cut is made with the work butted to the stop. This locates the other shoulder.

Illus. 511. To make the final cut and form the tenon, move the work away from the stop.

Illus. 512. The same dado setup can be used for haunched tenons.

Cutting Keys and Splines

Keys and splines are reinforcing members added to mitre joints. Most mitre joints are end-grain joints. An end-grain joint is the weakest type of wood joint. (Face-grain-to-face-grain gluing is the strongest bond in wood joinery.) When a key or spline is added to the mitre joint, it becomes stronger. This is because the key or spline is glued face to face in the 2 parts of the mitre joint.

To install a key, cut a keyway into the mitre joint after it has been assembled and the glue has cured. The keyway jig (Illus. 513) has a V-shaped cradle mounted on a true base of plywood. The cradle locates the mitre joint while the keyway is cut. The strong back holds the frame to the plywood base while cutting takes place. Plans for this jig can be found in Chapter 8.

Determine the key size before beginning. For a thin key, use an 8″ blade or smaller. For thicker keys, use a dado head. Turn the blade to the horizontal position, adjust the depth of cut in relation to the mitre joint, and lock the carriage. Adjust the blade height to the correct position and lock the horizontal blade guard in position. Make sure the frame is clamped securely to the jig with the strong back.

Turn on the saw and grasp the jig by both handles. Feed the jig along the fence to cut the keyway (Illus. 514). A special cutout fence may be needed depending on what type of saw is being used. Repeat this process for each corner. Make sure the frame is clamped securely with each repetition.

Rip some stock to fit the keyways. The stock is going to be glued in place, so make some allowances for glue. A key that is too thick for the keyway could break the joint during installation. Make a trial fit of the keys (Illus. 515). Mark them and cut them slightly long. Apply glue to the key and keyway. Insert the key and allow the glue to cure. It is difficult to clamp keys, but masking tape will hold them securely until the glue cures. Sand the key flush with the stock after the glue cures.

Splines are similar to keys except they run the entire length of the mitre. Splines are cut into both parts of the mitre joint before assembly. They are positioned and glued when the frame or mitre joint is assembled.

A spline jig (Illus. 516) is used when cutting splines. It is similar to a keyway jig. The spline jig positions stock at a 45° angle. A clamping device holds the stock against the plywood base. The stock is fed along the fence with the blade in the horizontal position.

Use the same setup procedure as that used with the keyway jig (Illus. 517–519). Keep the exposed faces of the frame all facing up (or down) when making the cut. This will ensure proper fit when assembling the frame. Plans for the spline jig appear in Chapter 8.

Illus. 513. This keyway jig can be used to kerf stock for keys. The wooden support clamps the stock for kerfing.

Illus. 514. After all adjustments are made, the jig can be pushed along the fence to cut the keyway. Four cuts are needed on a picture frame.

167

Illus. 515. The keys should fit snugly, but there must be room for glue. Trim the keys after the glue cures.

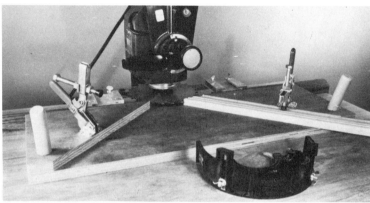

Illus. 516. The spline jig is used to cut grooves in unassembled frame parts. The industrial clamp holds the part for machining.

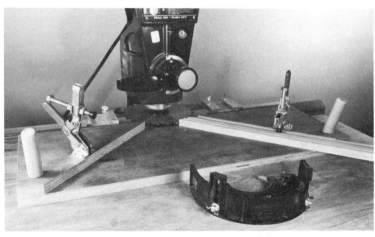

Illus. 517. The piece is located in the jig and the blade is adjusted with reference to the frame part.

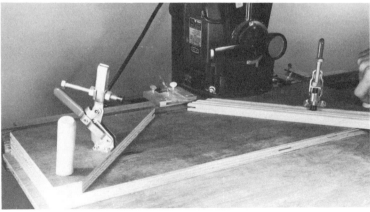

Illus. 518. The right mitre is splined in this operation. Handles on the jig provide greater control.

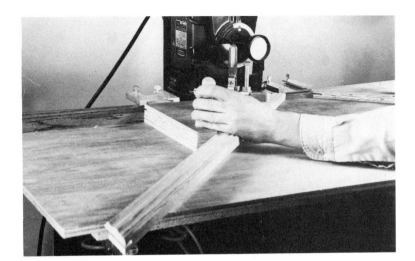

Illus. 519. The left mitre is splined in this operation. The shaper guard prevents contact with the blade.

Resawing

Resawing is the process of ripping a thick piece of stock into 2 thinner pieces. Resawn pieces are often glued together to make wider panels for cabinet sides or doors. The grain of the 2 thinner pieces is often matched at the glue line to give it a book effect. This is commonly known as a bookmatch. Sometimes resawn pieces are used side by side or consecutively to make matching drawer fronts.

Stock to be resawn should be true. Edges and faces should be parallel. There should be no knots or other defects. Choose a fine-cutting rip or combination blade. The teeth should have moderate set. The set will minimize pitch accumulation and the chance of kickback. Make sure the blade being used has a very low hook angle. This will also minimize the chance of lifting or kickback.

Select a piece of stock that is thick enough to yield pieces of the desired thickness. For example, a ¾" piece cannot be resawn into 2 pieces ⅜" thick. This is because the blade will turn ⅛" or more of thickness into saw kerf. A ¾" piece will produce 2 pieces of ¼" stock with no trouble. This allows ¼" for a saw kerf and sanding or planing of the sawn surfaces.

Resawing follows the same general procedures for ripping except no rip trough is needed. An uncut fence works best. It may be a little higher than typically used when ripping. This gives the work more surface control and reduces the chance of deflection. Check out the saw before you begin. Make sure the blade is not heeling. If the blade is heeling, resawing will be difficult, if not impossible.

Set the distance from the fence to the blade at the desired stock thickness. Allow a little extra thickness for sanding or planing away saw marks. Set the blade at a point slightly less than half the stock width or no more than 1". Lower the nose of the guard so that it just clears the work, and position the splitter and anti-kickback pawls.

With the face against the fence and the edge on the table, make a rip cut through the piece (Illus. 520). Featherboards or commercial hold-downs can be used here to hold the stock in position while the cut is made (Illus. 521). Turn the piece over so the other edge is on the table. Keep the same face against the fence. Make another rip cut (Illus. 522). On narrow stock, there will be a thin strip separating the 2 pieces. In most cases the pieces will split apart easily. They can then be sanded, planed, or glued together. Note how the splitter and guard are positioned for this cut (Illus. 523).

On wider stock (Illus. 524), the blade will have to be lowered another inch or slightly less than half the stock width. When the blade is lowered, the guard and anti-kickback pawls must be readjusted. Do this carefully with the power off. Make another rip cut from each edge. Keep the same face against the fence (Illus. 525). Use a push block to feed stock. Feed only as fast as the blade will cut. Keep the feed pressure close to the center line of the work. Feed pressure from a push block below center can sometimes cause stock-lifting as the cut is completed. Limit resaw operations to pieces no less than 24" long. Separate the resawn pieces when a thin strip remains.

Set the blade for a 1" cut to reduce stress on the blade and minimize the chance of a kickback. The stock hardness and the horsepower of the radial arm saw may allow a slightly higher or lower setting. Experience will tell you the correct setting for your saw. While you are gaining that experience, remember that light cuts work best.

When resawing some pieces, you may wish to make some cuts with both faces touching the fence (Illus. 526). This will make the saw kerf wider and ensure that the resawn pieces are the same thickness. It will be easier to glue up panels when the resawn pieces are the same thickness.

Illus. 520. The first resawing rip is made about halfway through the work.

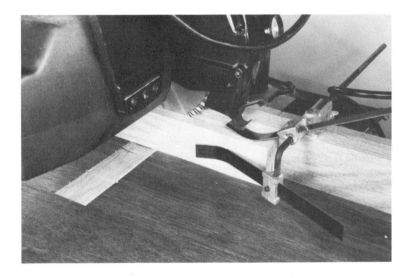

Illus. 521. Hold-downs can position the work while the cut is made.

Illus. 522. The second resawing rip is made with the same face against the fence. These pieces will split apart easily when removed from the saw.

Illus. 523. When resawing, it is important to have the splitter and anti-kickback pawls positioned correctly.

Illus. 524. On wider pieces like this one, the blade will have to be lowered for another cut. This will require readjustment of the guard and anti-kickback pawls.

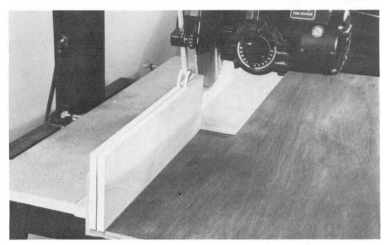

Illus. 525. In this operation, it is important to keep the same face against the fence. This keeps the kerfs in the same plane.

Illus. 526. In some resawing operations, cuts are made with both faces against the fence. This ensures that the pieces are the same thickness.

Kerfing Stock for Bending

Cutting kerfs in the back of a piece of solid stock allows it to be bent easily. The apron for a round table is one application of kerf bending. The depth of the kerfs is about ¾ to ⅞ of stock thickness. Kerf-bending works best in stock ¾" thick or greater. Shallow kerfs make the curve or arc appear to have flats opposite the kerfs. Kerfs ³⁄₃₂ to ⅛" wide usually work best.

Kerf-spacing is important. The kerfs must be uniformly spaced to produce a smooth arc. To determine spacing, use a scrap about 5" longer than the radius of the bend. Cut a kerf about 3" from the end of the piece. This kerf should be at the desired depth. Mark a line parallel to the kerf. The distance from the line to the kerf should equal the radius of the bend. Clamp the layout board with the kerf up to a true surface. Clamp it on the short side of the kerf. Raise the long side of the board until the kerf closes. Measure the distance from the surface to the bottom of the board at the radius line. This distance equals the kerf spacing (Illus. 527).

These kerf cuts can be laid out on the stock, or a spacing device can be attached to the fence. More uniform spacing is achieved when a device is attached to the fence. A metal pin is usually used for spacing. The pin may be a machine screw and bolt or a finishing nail. The machine screw and bolt require predrilling, but will remain rigid (Illus. 528). The nail may bend or split the wooden fence. A pencil line on the fence may also be used, but it does not yield the same uniformity.

Determine where the kerfs are to start and begin making the cuts (Illus. 529). Move the stock carefully and continue making the kerfs (Illus. 530 and 531). Do not test the bending ability of the piece until all kerfs are cut. Otherwise, the work will have a bend to it that may affect the kerfing operation.

There are many species that lend themselves to bending. These species produce the best results. Generally, those woods which steam-bend easily also kerf-bend easily. Regardless of species, best results will be obtained with clear, straight-grained stock (Illus. 532). Better bending will also occur if you expose the kerfed side to heat or sunlight before attempting the bend.

Illus. 527. When kerf-bending, the distance from the table to the work at the radius line determines spacing of the kerfs.

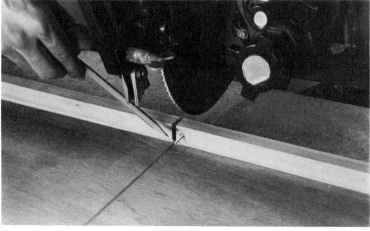

Illus. 528. The machine screw will remain rigid and keep kerf spacing uniform.

Illus. 529. Begin making kerf cuts at the starting point. Hold the stock firmly on the table.

Illus. 530. Continue making kerf cuts along the rear face of the work.

Illus. 531. Avoid trial-bending the work until all kerfs are cut because the work could curl and make the bending more difficult.

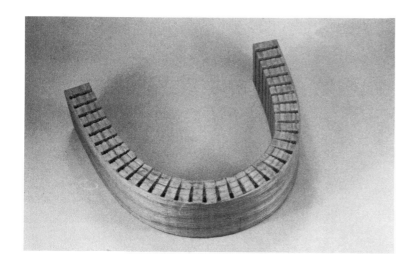

Illus. 532. Clear, straight-grained stock kerf bends the best.

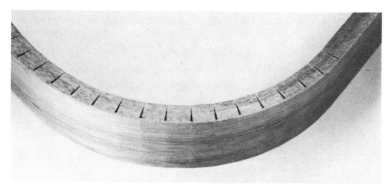

Illus. 533. The kerf bend in this piece caused "flats" to appear on the exposed face of the work.

Cutting Plastic Laminates

In small shops, plastic laminate sheets are sometimes cut on the radial arm saw (Illus. 534). For best results, a carbide-tipped blade with fine teeth and very little hook should be used. Laminates are quite thin and tend to lift when cut. Use commercial hold-downs or a cleat clamped to the fence to control this problem.

Because of the blade's thrust, there may be some tear-out when cutting laminates. This is due to their brittle nature. Some woodworkers prefer to cut the laminate stock with the good side down. Any tear-out then occurs on the back side. This is usually of no consequence since laminates are cut oversize and trimmed after they have been glued in position.

When long sheets of plastic laminate are being cut, the counter blank can be used to support the laminate while it is cut. Lay the counter blank on two sawhorses on the infeed side of the saw. The laminate can rest on the counter blank while the cut is made. This process eliminates unrolling the laminate as it is fed into the saw. This approach also minimizes any chance of breakage.

Sometimes laminated counters are cut on the saw (Illus. 535). Again, a fine-cutting carbide blade works best. It is best to cut the work with the laminate down on the table to guard against tear-out (Illus. 536). Be sure the table is smooth and free of nails. Nails or a rough surface could scratch or damage the laminated surface.

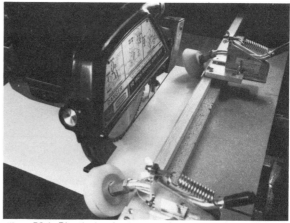

Illus. 534. Plastic laminates can be cut on the radial arm saw. Commercial hold-downs reduce the chance of lifting. A cleat clamped to the fence also increases control.

Illus. 535. When counter stock is being cut, fine carbide-tipped blades work best.

Illus. 536. Cutting laminated counter with the good face down can control tear-out, but the counter may get scratched.

Making Decorative Diamonds

Decorative diamonds (Illus. 537 and 538) are used to accent doors and panels. They are also used as clock faces. Begin with some strips of stock about 2″ wide and 2 to 4 feet long. These strips should be bevelled on each side. Refer to the sections on bevels, edge mitres, and staves in Chapter 5 (pages 103, 94, and 95) to prepare these pieces.

Mount a fine-cutting blade on the saw, and tilt the blade (Illus. 539) to the same angle as the bevel on the strips being used. The bottom of the blade should move to the right as you face the saw. Clamp the blade securely. A fine-cutting blade is used because end grain is being cut. These cuts should be as smooth as possible.

Determine how many diamonds you want in the circle. Divide this number into 360°. (For example: If you want 6 diamonds, divide 6 into 360°. The answer is 60°.) Next, subtract the answer (60°) from 90°. The remainder is 30°. This is the arm setting for a 6-diamond circle. Turn the arm to the right and clamp it at 30° (Illus. 540).

Install a new fence or move the fence over and make a new cut. Place the stock on the left side of the blade (Illus. 541), and cut both ends of all pieces. The edges will tilt towards the work (Illus. 542).

Now place the stock on the right side of the blade. The cut should be parallel to the first cut (Illus. 543). Through trial and error, determine the correct length of the diamonds (Illus. 544). Mark the table and fence with a pencil (Illus. 545). A stop is not practical because it will be in the way for the first cut and could pinch the work.

After the diamonds have been cut, move back to the left side of the blade and repeat the process (Illus. 546). Trim at least ½″ off the end. Smaller pieces tend to pinch and be thrown from the saw.

When gluing the diamonds to a board, find the centers horizontally and vertically; locate the first diamond at the intersection. One point touches the intersection and the other point touches the vertical line. It is best to line up the first diamond with the vertical line. That way, if there are an odd number of diamonds, the top one points straight up.

Illus. 537. This 8-point star is made up of decorative diamonds. The diamonds are red oak on a walnut board.

Illus. 538. This star has 9 points. Determining the cutting angles is discussed on page 175. These decorative diamonds are yellow poplar on a walnut board.

Illus. 539. Tilt the blade to match the angle on the strips you are working with. Lock the setting securely.

Illus. 540. Turn the arm to the right and clamp it at the calculated angle. This securely locks the arm in position.

Illus. 541. A new fence is used and the stock is placed to the left of the blade.

Illus. 542. After the ends are cut, the edges tilt towards the middle of the work.

Illus. 543. Place the stock on the right side of the blade so that the cut you make is parallel to your first cut.

Illus. 544. Trial-and-error cutting determines the diamond length.

Illus. 545. Mark the table and/or fence for correct diamond length, and cut all parts.

Illus. 546. After all pieces have been cut, move to the left side of the blade and repeat the process. Trim off at least ½". Smaller pieces tend to be thrown from the saw.

Cutting Scallops

Scallops are decorative cuts that appear as arches on the edge of your work (Illus. 547). The arch matches the cutter's periphery (Illus. 548). Scallops are usually cut with a dado or shaper head. Lay out scallops on your work carefully. Find the centers of the scallops and mark them (Illus. 549).

If you are using the shaper head, you may wish to shape the bottom edge of the work before cutting scallops. This will give the entire edge a uniform shape. This may also be done with the dado head. All cuts should be made with the shaper or dado head in the horizontal position. The amount of shaper or dado head extending beyond the fence determines the shape of the scallop.

Adjust the work so that the layout line of the scallop is centered on the arbor. Clamp a stop block on the fence or table to hold the work while the scallop is cut (Illus. 550). The stop must be on the thrust side of the moulding or shaper head. Adjust the height of the dado or shaper head with reference to the work and secure the shaper guard in position.

Turn on the saw and butt the work to the stop block with the exposed side up. Slowly push the work into the shaper or dado head. Turn off the saw and let the cutter come to a complete stop. Retract the work and adjust the stop block for the next scallop cut. Make the cut using the same procedure. Continue until all scallops are cut.

If you are using the dado head, you may wish to raise the dado head and readjust the carriage towards you. When you make this second cut, the scallop will have a 2-step look. If you are planning to do this, mark the position of the stop block for each scallop when making the first cut. This will allow you to reposition the work correctly.

If the workpiece is quite long, you will have to use a long fence or an extension table for a clamping base. A stop block *must* be used when making scallop cuts. If it is not used, a kickback is sure to result. Exercise caution when making a scallop cut. If the stock has a warp in it, it could spring up into the cutter. This could cause it to grab and kick back, or it could cut the work deeper at this scallop and ruin the overall appearance.

Illus. 547. Scallops are decorative cuts that appear as arches on the edge of your work. The decorative moulding on this chest has been scalloped.

Illus. 548. The scallops have an arch that matches the cutter's periphery. Plans for this chest appear in Chapter 8 (page 330).

Illus. 549. The centers of the scallops should be located and marked.

Illus. 550. A stop must be clamped to the table or fence when scalloping. The stop must be located on the thrust side of the cutter or blade.

Illus. 551. Note the two level scallops on the right half of the work. The cutter was raised and the carriage was moved towards the work for the second cut.

Jig- and Pattern-Cutting

Jig- and pattern-cutting are commonly employed when cutting wedges, tapers, and polygons. The jigs and patterns are designed for special purposes. Each of the jigs and patterns is discussed separately.

Pattern-Cutting For some shapes—such as diamonds, hexagons, and heptagons—pattern-cutting works well. For best results, the pattern should be smaller than the desired part. The pattern is attached to the back of the workpiece with screws or nails (Illus. 552). The blade is turned to the rip position (Illus. 553), and an auxiliary fence is clamped to the fence (Illus. 554). The auxiliary fence now controls the pattern and acts as a blade guard. The work rides on the table and slides under the fence.

The distance from the face of the guide to the blade

must be subtracted from each side of the pattern. The blade can be moved to make minor adjustments in the relationship between the pattern and the part. The pattern should be made accurately. Lay out the pattern carefully and cut it precisely. Use a dense hardwood, particle board, or plywood for pattern stock. The pattern must hold up well and resist wear as it rides along the fence.

Anchor the pattern securely to the workpiece. Nails or screws work best. On thin stock, double-faced tape can be used. Usually, the pattern is attached to the back of the workpiece so that the nail or screw holes are not visible. When attaching the pattern to the work, pay attention to the grain direction of the work. If the pattern is attached incorrectly, the grain direction of the part will be incorrect.

Illus. 552. Screws or nails in the pattern are used to attach it to the work.

Illus. 553. The blade is moved to the out-rip position for pattern cutting.

Illus. 554. An auxiliary pattern fence houses the blade. It is clamped to the saw's fence.

Feed the stock slowly into the blade, with one side of the pattern in full contact with the fence (Illus. 555). Avoid twisting the pattern; this could cause a kickback. Make sure that pieces trimmed away from the workpiece do not get caught between the fence and blade. This could also cause a kickback. Make the workpiece as close as possible to the desired size, as this minimizes the amount of cutting needed and the amount of scrap or waste. Remove scraps from the table frequently. Do this with the power off. Do not attempt to remove scrap while the blade is turning. Avoid pattern-cutting stock greater than ¾" thick.

Some patterns are nothing more than a straightedge. In the case of rough-cut hardwood, it is difficult to square-up the stock. This is because there is no true edge on the stock. A straightedge clamped to the work (Illus. 556) becomes the pattern used to cut a true edge. The straightedge rides along the front edge of the front table. The blade is set in the out-rip position and adjusted for the desired amount of stock removal. The guard and anti-kickback pawls are then adjusted to the workpiece.

Turn on the saw and begin the cut. Keep the straightedge against the front table (Illus. 557). This cut is the same as a rip cut except the straight edge clamped to the work becomes the fence. Do not turn or twist the work, as this may cause a kickback. If the front edge of the table is not parallel to the fence, the blade can heel. Measure the distance between the front edge and the fence in 2 or 3 places. If the dimensions are not the same, trim the front edge of the table before making the cut.

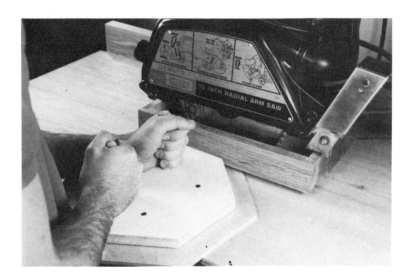

Illus. 555. All cuts are made with the pattern in full contact with the fence. Avoid twisting the work while cutting. This could cause a kickback.

Illus. 556. The pattern in this operation is a simple straightedge.

Illus. 557. The straightedge becomes the fence in this pattern rip. This approach can also be used for tapers. Note that the guard and anti-kickback pawls have been positioned correctly for greater safety.

Cutting Wedges Wedges are cut for many purposes. They sometimes hold pieces in a fixture for gluing. They can also be used to hold a door in the jamb when marking where hinges will be positioned. Wedge-cutting is done with a jig. The jig is made for the specific wedge size. This jig clamps between the table boards and replaces the fence (Illus. 558). Wedge jigs can be made of solid stock or sheet stock. A wedge-shaped notch is cut out along the blade side of the jig. The wide end of the wedge is cut first.

When clamping the jig between the table boards, make sure a spacer of equal size is placed between the table boards at the opposite end. Make sure the jig is clamped securely before you proceed. Place the stock on

Illus. 559. Stock is positioned in the jig's cutout. Grain should run parallel to the blade's path. The workpiece is flipped over for the next cut.

the table and position it in the cutout (Illus. 559). The grain should run parallel to the blade's path. The carriage is then pulled towards the work. Hold the stock securely as the blade makes it cut. After the first wedge has been cut, turn the workpiece over. The wide side of the workpiece will now face the wide end of the cutout. Turning the work over between cuts allows more wedges to be cut from the workpiece. It also keeps the grain running straight in all of the wedges.

As the workpiece becomes smaller, a hold-down or table clamp (Illus. 560) can be used to hold the workpiece. This keeps your hands well away from the blade. Work carefully and all wedges will be uniform in size and shape (Illus. 561).

Illus. 558. This wedge jig clamps between the table boards and replaces the fence.

183

Illus. 560. A hold-down or table clamp can be useful when the workpiece gets too small to hold safely.

Illus. 561. When set up correctly, all wedges are uniform in size and shape.

Cutting Tapers Tapers are inclined surfaces along the edge of a board. They can be cut on the radial arm saw in both rip and crosscut setups. Both setups require a jig to cut the tapers. Some taper jigs are single-purpose, and others are adjustable. Adjustable jigs are usually used in a rip setup. Fixed jigs are used in both rip and crosscut setups. A taper is measured or laid out by the amount of incline per foot. A taper of ⅜″ per foot would equal a ¾″ incline on a board 2 feet long.

Crosscut taper jigs are held between the table boards at one end and clamped to the table at the other end (Illus. 562). The cutout is made with reference to the edge of the jig. The jig lines up with the blade's path. Be sure the jig is clamped securely and that a spacer is clamped between the table boards at the end opposite the jig. Clamp the front of the jig securely to the table after it is adjusted.

Position the stock in the jig and secure it with the quick-acting clamp (Illus. 563). Turn on the saw and pull it through the work. Use the same procedures you would for a typical crosscut (Illus. 564). Return the carriage to the column and turn off the saw. Release the clamp and remove the tapered piece.

Tapers in the rip setup follow a different procedure. A commercial adjustable jig can be used (Illus. 565). Make a rip cut, with one leg of the jig against the fence and the other leg offsetting the work in order to cut a taper.

The uplifting thrust of the blade makes control of the work difficult when these jigs are used because there is no cleat or hold-down to resist the thrust. For this reason, these jigs are better suited for the table saw. The fixed tapering jig shown in Illus. 566 has a cap over the work. This cap resists the blade's upward thrust. The notch (Illus. 567) offsets the work to make the taper.

Tapering jigs with a base seem to be a better design. This base rides on the saw table and provides a rigid surface for clamping (Illus. 568). The piece is locked securely to the base (Illus. 569), so it will not lift as the cut is made (Illus. 570).

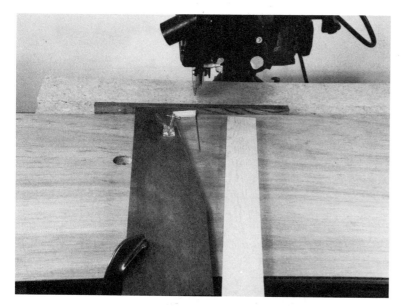

Illus. 562. The crosscut taper jig is positioned between the table boards at one end and clamped to the table at the other end.

Illus. 563. Stock is positioned in the jig and secured with the quick-acting clamp.

Illus. 564. The cap on this taper jig helps resist uplift blade thrust.

Illus. 565. Commercial taper jigs can be used on the radial arm saw, but they do not control uplift thrust of the blade.

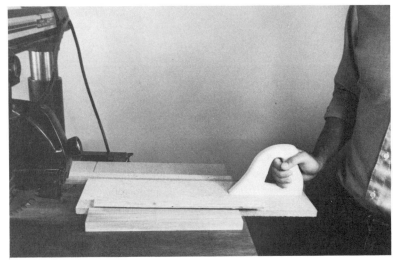

Illus. 566. The cap on this taper jig helps resist uplift blade thrust.

Illus. 567. The notch on this jig offsets the work to cut a taper.

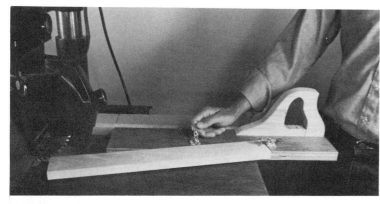

Illus. 568. This taper jig has a base which allows for solid clamping of the work.

Illus. 569. The work is locked securely to the jig. It is able to resist uplifting blade thrust.

Illus. 570. No lifting occurred during the cut. Note that the operator's hand was clear of the blade. A handle makes any jig safer.

To cut a single-step taper, position the stock in the jig and clamp it securely (Illus. 568). Set the blade to the correct position with reference to the jig and adjust the guard and anti-kickback pawls (Illus. 571). The stock is fed into the blade at a uniform speed and the taper is cut (Illus. 570). Two identical pieces can be cut from one piece if the jig is adjusted correctly.

A 2-step taper jig cuts equal tapers on both sides of the work. This requires 2 cuts. The inner step (Illus. 572) is used for the first cut. The cut follows the same procedure as a single-step taper (Illus. 573). Observe the same precautions. After the wedge is cut away (Illus. 574), the piece is turned over and positioned in the outer step (Illus. 575). The cut is then repeated (Illus. 576). The cut produces a piece with equal tapers on both sides of the work (Illus. 577).

A single-purpose jig can be made from sheet stock (plywood or particle board). Select a piece 4 to 8″ longer than the stock that will be tapered. Square-up the workpiece and lay out the step or steps on the edge of the piece. One step is equal to the desired taper. On a 2-step jig, one step equals the desired taper per foot, and the other step equals twice the desired taper.

On a tapered piece 18″ long with a taper of ½″ per foot, the first step would be ¾″. If you are making a 2-step jig, the second step would be 1½″. To cut the steps, use the rip fence to cut the long layout lines. Stop the cut at the layout line. Finish up the cuts with a scroll attachment or a hand saw. Mount the handle and attach a base. Install some quick-acting clamps. Be sure to keep them clear of the blade's path. The jig is now ready to cut tapers.

187

Illus. 571. When a taper jig is being used, the guard and anti-kickback pawls should be adjusted the same way they would be for ripping.

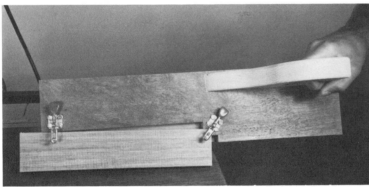

Illus. 572. The inner step is used for the first cut.

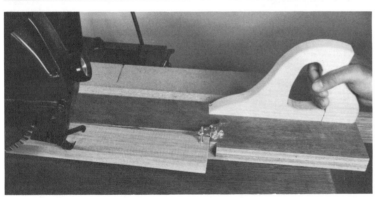

Illus. 573. This cut removed a wedge from the outer edge.

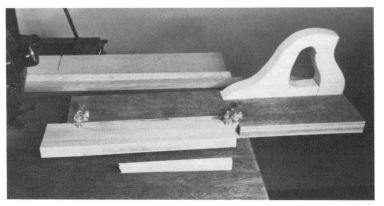

Illus. 574. Allow the wedge to fall clear, and shut the saw off.

Illus. 575. Place the cut edge of the work in the outer step of the jig.

Illus. 576. The cut is repeated on the opposite edge of the work.

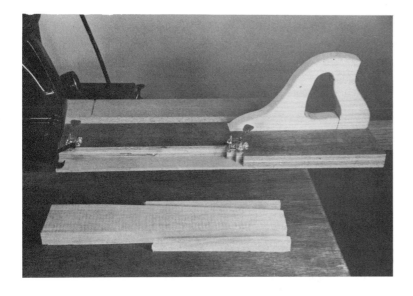

Illus. 577. The result is a piece with equal tapers on both sides.

Cutting Coves

A cove is a curved recess cut into a piece of stock. Most simple coves are cut with a shaper head and cove cutters. Many coves do not follow the arc of a machined cutter. These coves can be cut on the radial arm saw with a saw blade or dado head.

Many objects require this method of cutting coves. In restoration work, cove cuts are often required to reproduce some type of moulding. The brush shelf shown in Illus. 578 has a coved base. This keeps hairpins, combs, and brushes from being easily knocked off the shelf. Many picture frames with graceful coves are also cut with a saw blade.

Begin by laying out the cove. Determine the arc of the cove and its relative position in the piece of stock. The layout can be done on paper and photocopied, then glued to the ends of the work to help keep parts oriented correctly. Patterns can also be made to trace the profile on your work.

Remove most of the waste stock in the cove with a blade or dado head (Illus. 579). This will reduce the number of cuts required to complete the cove. It will also put less stress on the blade.

Select the appropriate blade for cove-cutting and install it (do this with the power off). For shallow, wide coves, a 10″ blade works well. For coves with a semicircular shape, an 8″ blade works well. The blade selected should have fine teeth. This will reduce the amount of sanding required. Tilt the blade about 15° to the right (bottom of blade moves to the right) and lock it in position.

Place a parallel guide over the work and adjust it to the cove width (Illus. 580). Adjust the blade so the lowest tooth is even with the bottom of the desired cove (Illus. 581). Now raise the blade 4 to 6 turns. Record the number of turns that you have raised the blade.

Illus. 578. This brush shelf provides an opportunity to make a cove cut.

Illus. 579. Most stock should be removed from the cove with a dado head or single blade. This makes the coving job more efficient.

Illus. 581. Blade height is adjusted even with the bottom of the cove.

Loosen the yoke and turn it almost to the in-rip position. Position the parallel guide under the blade with the long legs parallel to the fence. Lower the blade the exact number of turns that it was raised earlier. Now turn the yoke so that one tooth of the saw blade touches each side of the parallel guide (Illus. 582). Lock the yoke in this position. The blade angle is now set for cove-cutting. Note: To be absolutely accurate, make sure the parallel guide is the same thickness as the stock you intend to cove. Any deviation will affect the setup.

Move the carriage so that the blade lines up with the cove. Lock it in position. Raise the blade so that it just touches the work. Adjust the hold-downs so that the stock is controlled. Featherboards can also be used. Plug in the saw and turn it on. Make your first cut in the work (Illus. 583). Mark the fence edge on the top face of each piece. This will help you keep the correct edge against the fence, which is very important if the cove is not centered.

Lower the blade about ⅛″ and make a second cut (Illus. 584). Light cuts produce the best results. If you encounter any resistance, take a lighter cut. Remember, as the blade is lowered more teeth come in contact with the work. This means the blade has to work harder and is more likely to kick back.

As you near the desired shape, continue taking light cuts (Illus. 584). This will reduce the amount of sanding needed. Feed slowly on the final pass to make it smoother. Sometimes 2 passes at the final setting makes the cove smoother. The cove must be sanded after machining. Begin with 60- or 80-grit abrasives and work up. A dowel or piece of stock cut to the shape of your cove can be used as a sanding block (Illus. 585).

Cove-cutting can also be done with a dado head. The head is tilted about 15° in the same way as a saw blade. Layout of the cove and setup of the saw remains the same. Feeding procedures remain the same. A straightedge clamp can also be used for control.

The chief difference between a single blade and a dado head is that each of the cutters and chippers takes a small bite when the dado head is tilted (Illus. 586). This allows you to take a little heavier cut and usually produces a smoother cove. Follow the same procedures with a single blade or a dado head. Keep hands clear of the cutter and use hold-downs. If you do not use hold-downs, use a push stick to feed stock. This will keep you well away from the cutter.

191

Illus. 582. *The parallel guide is positioned under the blade to set the yoke angle. Lock the yoke securely. One tooth touches each side of the parallel guide.*

Illus. 583. *Make the first cut in the work. Hold-downs or featherboards can make the job safer.*

Illus. 584. *As you near the layout line, take light cuts. This will reduce the amount of sanding needed.*

Illus. 585. A piece of stock the same shape as your cove can be used as a sanding block.

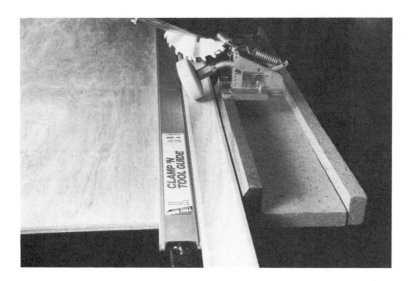

Illus. 586. When the dado head is tilted, each of the cutters and chippers takes a small bite. This is a heavier cut than a single blade. Use the same procedure you would use when cutting a cove with a single blade. Note the straightedge clamp used for increased control.

A partial cove is sometimes cut to make moulding or a raised panel. If part of the blade is moved behind the fence, a partial cove is cut (Illus. 587–590). A push block is used to feed the stock (Illus. 587). The fence is cut away to accommodate the dado head. Notice that part of the fence remains. This acts as a control surface when the stock passes under the dado head. Without a partial fence the work would slip under the dado head and jam. This could possibly cause injury.

The coving operation is not easily done with most lower guards in position. For that reason, the lower guard is removed. As a result, there is a large amount of dado blade exposed and you are feeding directly into it. Keep firm footing and balance, take light cuts, and use a push block when making a cove cut.

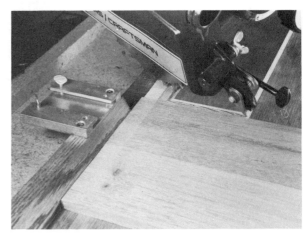

Illus. 587. This partial dado cove is made with the help of a push block. Light cuts produce the best results.

193

Illus. 588. The lower guard cannot be used with this operation, so work carefully. Make this cut on true, clean stock only.

Illus. 589. Use light cuts. Make 2 passes under the dado head at its final setting.

Illus. 590. This raised panel was produced using the partial cove cut. Very little sanding will be needed on this piece.

Cutting Edge Joints

Edge joints are often glued together without any joinery. For certain applications, a spline or tongue-and-groove reinforcement would increase the strength. Splines are commonly used when banding the edges of plywood with solid stock. Tongue-and-groove joints are used to line up pieces that are not perfectly true. Gluing and clamping pieces with a tongue-and-groove joint usually makes the panel much truer.

Tongue-and-Groove Joint   Tongue-and-groove joints are best cut with the moulding or shaper head. A twist cutter can also be used. Install the groove cutters in the shaper head and mount it on the radial arm saw. Set the head in the horizontal position. Adjust cutter height so that the center of the groove cutter is aligned with the center of the work (Illus. 591). In most woods, the groove can be made in one cut (Illus. 592). Very hard wood may require 2 cuts to shape the groove.

Set up featherboards or hold-downs to control the work. Install a shaper guard and adjust it. Make a trial cut and any minor adjustments before beginning. Cut a groove on one edge of all pieces. Note: If you are making a panel, the first piece should not have a groove, and the last piece should not have a tongue.

After all grooves have been cut, remove the shaper head. Remove the groove cutters and replace them with the tongue cutters. Mount the shaper head, and adjust the head relative to the fence and the work (Illus. 593). Tongues may require 2 successive cuts. This is because twice as much stock is removed. Make a trial cut to determine the correct depth of cut (Illus. 594). Make sure the tongue lines up with the groove before cutting any parts.

Work slowly and carefully when shaping tongue-and-groove joints. Guide the stock with commercial hold-downs or featherboards and push sticks. Avoid defective pieces or pieces with loose knots. Straight-grained pieces shape easily; pieces with slanted grain may kick back. Lighter cuts minimize the chance of a kickback.

A tongue-and-groove joint can also be cut with a dado head. The groove is cut first. Then, 2 rabbets are cut to form a tongue. More cuts may be needed when using the dado head, and the surfaces of the tongues and grooves may not be as smooth.

Illus. 591. The middle of the groove cutter is aligned with the middle of the work.

Illus. 592. A groove can usually be made in one cut. Hold-downs and featherboards make the cut safer. The guard has been removed for illustration purposes.

Illus. 594. The second cut forms the tongue. Make sure the tongue matches the groove. The guard has been removed for illustration purposes.

Glue Joint   A glue joint is a form of edge joint similar to a tongue-and-groove joint. It is cut with a shaper head or twist cutter. The middle of the cutter is lined up with the middle of the work (Illus. 595). All parts are cut with this setup. This is because the cutter is a mirror image of itself from the center line.

Feed stock slowly across the cutterhead (Illus. 596). Use a featherboard or commercial hold-downs to hold the stock against the fence and table. Check your setup in scrap stock before cutting the work (Illus. 597). Mating pieces are fed across the cutter—one with the good face up, the other with the good face down. Mark your pieces accordingly.

Spline Joint   Spline joints use a thin piece of stock as a tongue. It fits into a groove cut on both pieces. Splines line up the 2 parts and provide an increased gluing surface. Splines can be cut with a dado head or a single blade. The groove should be centered in the piece and should be no wider than ⅓ of the stock thickness. The groove must be slightly larger than the stock. This is to allow for glue.

Cut a spline joint the same way you would cut grooves (Illus. 598 and 599). The spline should be slightly deeper than it is wide. Keep all exposed faces pointing towards (or away from) the table when cutting the grooves. This will make it difficult to align the pieces when fitting them together (Illus. 600).

Illus. 595. The middle of the cutter is lined up with the middle of the work. The guard has been removed for illustration purposes.

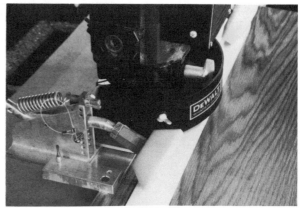

Illus. 596. Feed the stock slowly across the cutterhead. Be sure to use hold-downs or featherboards to control the work.

Illus. 597. Check your setup in scrap stock before cutting your actual work. The guard has been removed for illustration purposes.

Illus. 598. The spline groove is cut in the plywood. The good face is up.

Illus. 599. The spline groove is cut in the solid stock with the same setup. The good face is up.

Illus. 600. The notch (rabbet) formed by the plywood and solid stock is caused by a difference in thickness. The good face matches. The bottom or unexposed face has the irregularity.

Making Cabinet Doors

Most cabinet doors consist of a frame around some type of panel. The panel may be glass, cane, solid stock, or plywood. The joinery and panel differ from one door style to another.

Frame and panel doors can be flush, ⅜″ offset (rabbet), or overlay (Illus. 601). Flush doors sit in the door frame. Offset or rabbeted doors have a ⅜″ rabbet on all edges. The rabbeted part of the door sits in the door frame. The perimeter of the door is actually larger than the opening. Overlay doors are also larger than the door frame. They simply cover the opening.

Flush doors are the most difficult to fit because the door frame and the door must both be square for a nice fit. When the door and/or the door frame is out of square, hand fitting and planing are required.

Rabbeted doors are easier to fit. The door is cut ½″ longer and wider than the opening. A ⅜″ rabbet is cut on all edges. The dimensions of the door (rabbet to rabbet) are ¼″ smaller than the opening. This allowance makes adjusting the door to the opening easier and makes room for the offset hinge.

Overlay doors are the easiest to fit. They are cut ¾ to 1″ wider and longer than the opening. They are located over the opening and hinged. Handwork is rarely required on overlay doors.

Cope Joints   Cope joints are two-part joints (Illus. 602). They are cut with the moulding or shaper head. The panel edge of the vertical pieces (stiles) and horizontal pieces (rails) is shaped with a panel-door cutter (Illus. 603). This cutter grooves the edge of the stock and leaves a decorative radius in front of the groove (Illus. 604). This shaping operation is performed the same way as the other shaping operations depicted in Chapters 5 and 6.

The groove accommodates the panel. The radius gives the exposed side of the door a decorative shape. The door rails have to be shaped again with the rail end cutter. The end grain is being shaped in this operation. The stock is best controlled with a mitre gauge (Illus. 605). A backing block can also be attached to the mitre gauge to eliminate tear-out. Once the cutter height is adjusted for the panel door cutter, the rail end cutter will also be adjusted. The cutters can be changed while the shaper head is on the saw. Be sure to disconnect the power before changing cutters.

The rail end cutter cuts the complementary shape of the edge on the rail ends (Illus. 606). The panel is then fitted to the frame, and the door is assembled. Be sure to allow some space for panel expansion. Some cabinetmakers drive metal pins through the mating parts for greater strength. These pins are a little shorter than the thickness of the stock. They are driven from the back side and are not visible on the front of the door.

FLUSH

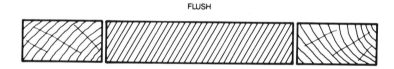

Illus. 601. These are the common types of doors used on cabinets.

LIP

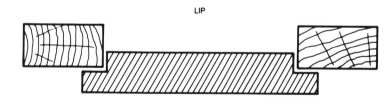

OVERLAY

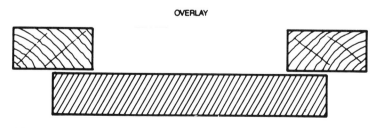

Illus. 602. A cope joint is a two-part door joint. The rails have a coped end that fits the cope made on the inside edge of the stiles.

Illus. 603. All inside edges (rails and stiles) are shaped with the panel-door cutter. The setup is made so the panel is centered. The guard has been removed for illustration purposes.

Illus. 604. The guard protects the operator while the panel-door cutter shapes an edge. Note the commercial hold-downs. They make the job safer.

Illus. 605. The ends of the rails are shaped with a rail-end cutter. A mitre gauge is used with an auxiliary table to control the cut.

Illus. 606. The rail-end cutter cuts a shape that is complementary to the panel-door cutter. This makes a good-fitting glue joint.

Illus. 607. A rabbet is routed on the back of the lap-joint frame. A wood or glass panel can be held in the rabbet with moulding. Square the corners with a chisel.

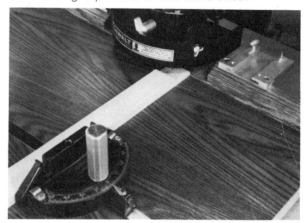

Illus. 608. A lap joint can be cut with a dado head in the horizontal position. A mitre gauge is used to control the stock.

When shaping door edges, make sure the pieces are marked so the best sides become the door front. Set up the shaper in the manner discussed in Chapter 5. When edge-shaping, keep your hands clear of the cutters. Use commercial hold-downs, or featherboards and push sticks. Use a mitre gauge and auxiliary table when shaping rail ends. This will control the stock and minimize tear-out.

Cope joints can also be made with router bits. These bits have a ½″ shank and must be used in a powerful router. With practice, this setup will produce excellent results. Read the section on Routing (page 213), and set up the router accordingly. Follow the same safety practices you would for shaping or other routing operations. Read the instructions that accompany the bit for specific operating information.

Lap Joints Lap joints work well for doors. The stiles are completely exposed. The rails go behind the stiles and are not visible at the joint. They are only visible on the back of the door. Lap joints appear as blind mortise-and-tenon joints when the door edge is rabbeted. This is because the rabbet hides the lap joint. The easiest way to make a lap-joint door is to glue up the frame and then rout a rabbet for the door panel. The rabbet is routed from the back of the door (Illus. 607). The panel is then slipped in from the back. Moulding can be made to hold the panel in place.

This door works quite well for glass panels. The glass can be held securely with the moulding. The moulding also allows the glass panel to be changed easily in the event of breakage.

Lap joints can be cut with the dado head in either the horizontal (Illus. 608) or vertical position. Use a stop to control the length of the lap when the dado head is in the

vertical position. When the dado head is in the horizontal position, control the stock with a mitre gauge and auxiliary table.

Lap joints can also be cut with a single blade. Two cuts are required for this operation, which has already been discussed (page 151). Open mortise-and-tenon joints are also discussed (page 157). These doors may also be glued-up and then routed for a panel.

When using any of the joints discussed in this section, remember the stile is completely visible. Lap joints are cut on the back of the stile and the front of the rail. Mark your stock before going to the saw. This will eliminate the chance of cutting a lap joint on the wrong side of the work.

Mitre Joints Doors using mitre joints give the door panel a wrapped look. The frame wraps around the panel (Illus. 609). All frame parts are grooved and shaped before the mitre joints are cut. The arm can be turned to cut the mitres, or a mitring jig can be used. It is a good idea to key the mitres after the door has been assembled. This increases the strength of the door.

Mitred trim doors look like mitred frame doors, but require less work to make. The trim is purchased in

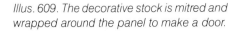

Illus. 610. This trim is mitred to fit the door panel. A piece of stock lifts the stock so that a true mitre can be cut.

Illus. 611. The offset on the back of the door provides the correct fit for this offset hinge.

random lengths. It is mitred (Illus. 610) and glued or nailed around a ¾″ panel. The rabbet on the trim butts against the panel and leaves a ⅜″ offset. This offset is the ⅜″ lip that is common on rabbeted or lipped doors. After the trim is installed, the door is ready for hinges (Illus. 611). Similar trim can be made using the shaper head on the radial arm saw.

Raised Panels Many doors use plain hardwood or plywood panels. These panels are usually ¼″ thick. Raised panels are ½ to ¾″ thick. They have edges that taper to ¼″ and appear to be raised in the middle.

Raised panels are more decorative than plain panels (Illus. 612). The raised panel is first cut to the desired width and length. A typical panel is ½″ thick. This thickness makes the panel even with the front of a ¾″ door frame when assembled.

Begin by sanding and kerfing the face of the panel. Set the distance from the fence at about 1½″. (Illus. 613). Adjust the blade height so that it cuts a kerf about ⅛″ deep in the work (Illus. 614). Make a kerf along both ends and edges. There will be 4 kerfs that intersect near the corners (Illus. 615). Note how the panel profile has been drawn in for layout purposes.

Illus. 612. Raised panels look more decorative than plain panels. Would this chest be as dramatic with plain panels?

Illus. 613. The blade is positioned for kerfing the panel edges. Sand the face of the panel before you begin. End grain is kerfed first.

Illus. 614. The kerf cut is shallow. A push block is used to control the panel.

Set the blade in the horizontal plane. Use a blade 8″ or less in diameter. Adjust the blade so that it cuts up to the kerf and tilt it so that it leaves the stock ¼″ thick at the edge (Illus. 616). Lock the blade in position. Now raise the blade with ½ revolution of the hand crank. Install the guard and cut the end grain using a push block (Illus. 617). Control the stock on the edge grain with a push stick (Illus. 618 and 619).

After all 4 cuts have been made on all the panels, lower the blade ½ revolution and make a second cut. The second cut has much less resistance and makes the panel smoother. This means there will be less sanding (Illus. 620).

Raised panels can be made in other ways. See the sections on cove-cutting with the dado head and the planer head on pages 191 and 227.

Raised panels can be used in almost any type of door frame. Coped joints and haunched mortise-and-tenon joints are the highest quality frames for raised panels. Lap joints, open mortise-and-tenon joints, and mitre joints also make a nice frame for raised panels.

When using solid panels in a door frame, allow for expansion and contraction. Make the grooves in the rails and stiles about ⅛″ deeper than the panel width and length. This allows for panel movement in the frame.

Raised panels are sometimes used as lids. The decorative shape of the panel makes it appealing as a box top. Cut the panel slightly larger than the box. Trim it after it is glued to the box. Box tops may be thicker or thinner than the raised panel used in a door. Adjust your cutting plan accordingly.

Illus. 616. The blade is tilted and aligned with the layout line. Note how the fence controls the stock through the entire cut.

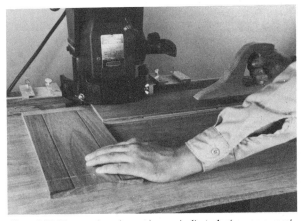

Illus. 617. The end-grain cut is made first. A shaper guard conceals the blade and a push block guides the work.

Illus. 618. Edge grain is cut after end grain. Push sticks may be more convenient for edge cuts.

Illus. 619. The opposite edge is cut. Hold stock securely and guide it carefully. Feed only as fast as the blade will cut.

Illus. 620 (right). Make a second cut on the ends and edges after lowering the blade half a revolution. This light cut will reduce the amount of sanding.

Shaping Door Edges   Most lip doors have a rabbet cut on all 4 edges. This rabbet is usually ⅜″ × ⅜″. The rabbet can be cut with a single blade, a dado head, or a moulding head. The straight or jointing shaper cutters are used in the moulding head. Use the accepted dadoing, rabbeting, or shaping practices when working door edges. Take light cuts. A heavy cut could damage the door or cause a kickback.

Some door frames have a decorative shape cut on the exposed edge. These shapes can be made with various shaper cutters. Roundover cutters and cabinet-door lip cutters can be mounted in the moulding head for shaping the edges.

The cabinet-door lip cutter cuts a rabbet on the back of the door and a radius on the front of the door edge in one cut (Illus. 621). Review shaping procedures before making this cut. Remember, harder woods will require 2 or more light cuts to shape the door edge; there is a great deal of material being removed.

Illus. 621. The cabinet-door lip cutter cuts a rabbet on the back of the door and a radius on the front. This is done in one cut. Harder woods might require 2 light cuts.

Cutting Drawer Parts and Joints

Cutting drawer joints and drawer parts on the radial arm saw are common operations. Drawers, like cabinet doors, can be flush, lip, or overlay. The joinery differs with the type of drawer, but the drawer sides and back are all made about the same way.

Making Drawer Parts Most drawer parts are made from ½″ stock. Drawer parts usually have a groove cut near the lower edge to hold the drawer bottom in position. The drawer bottom is usually ¼″ thick, but may vary according to drawer size and purpose.

The groove is at least ¼″ from the edge (Illus. 622). This

Illus. 622. Drawer stock is grooved to accommodate the drawer bottom. Keep this groove at least ¼″ away from lower edge.

minimizes the chance of splitting or breaking. With some types of drawer guides, the drawer bottom must be higher to accommodate the drawer guide. Select the drawer guides before cutting drawer parts.

Grooves can be cut with a saw blade or dado head. The dado head allows easy adjustment to slightly more than ¼″. The increased size makes it easy to drop the bottom in position. It is best to cut lengths of drawer stock 16″ long or longer. It is safer to dado longer pieces. The pieces can be cut to size after the dado is cut. Always check the groove size with a piece of stock used for drawer bottoms. Too large a groove causes excess drawer rattle when opened or closed.

After the groove has been cut, the top edge may be "radiused" or "nosed." This makes the drawer side less likely to catch on clothing or other articles. Some pieces are radiused from end to end. Others are radiused to within 1″ of the front or front-and-back ends (Illus. 623). This is common with flush drawers. The square end helps guide the drawer into position and makes the joint between the front and side look neater.

Illus. 623. The drawer side has been "radiused" to reduce friction and enhance its appearance.

To radius drawer sides, set up a router in the table and install a roundover bit (Illus. 624). The bit should have a pilot tip to control the cut. Mark the starting and ending points on the work. Install a fence that lines up with the pilot tip (Illus. 625). Clamp a stop to the fence to locate the starting point. Start the router and butt the work to the stop (Illus. 626). Push the work into the cutter and make the cut. Turn the work 90° and repeat the process (Illus. 627 and 628). The edge will now have a smooth radius.

205

Illus. 624. A roundover bit is first installed in the router and mounted in the front table.

Illus. 625. A fence is aligned with the pilot tip to control the door side. Clamp the fence securely.

Illus. 626. A stop is used to control the work. The router is turned on, and the work is pushed into the bit. The edge is fed across the bit while in contact with the fence.

Illus. 627. The piece is turned 90° and moved into the cutter.

Illus. 628. The work is fed across the bit while in contact with the fence. Do all drawer sides before changing the setup.

Overlay Drawers Overlay drawers usually have 2 drawer fronts. The decorative front is larger than the opening. It is screwed to the false front. The false front is part of the drawer assembly (Illus. 629).

The joints on an overlay drawer can be as simple as butt joints. Butt joints are glued and nailed together. A rabbet dado joint on the drawer front and a dado joint on the back make the drawer stronger (Illus. 630). Drawers made with these joints are easier to glue and assemble.

The dadoes at the back of the drawer are wide enough to accommodate the drawer back (Illus. 631). The dado depth is ½ the thickness of the side. A stop locates the dado relative to the end. Make sure you mark the sides right and left. The sides are not the same. They are mirror images of each other.

The dadoes at the front of the drawer are narrow (Illus. 632). They should be about ⅓ of the drawer-side thickness. A saw kerf is often good enough. The depth of these dadoes is equal to those of the back of the drawer. When cutting these dadoes, make sure the distance from the stop to the far side of the blade equals the thickness of the drawer stop.

Drawer backs need no dado work. They are ready to install. The false front must have a tongue cut on each end. This tongue fits the dado on the drawer side. A stop is clamped to the fence to locate the tongue (Illus. 633).

Mark the pieces before cutting the tongue. The groove for the drawer bottom should be down when the tongues are cut. Test the fit and make any needed adjustments. After the drawer has been assembled, the exposed front can be attached. Screws are usually driven through the false front into the exposed front.

Illus. 629. Overlay drawers usually have 2 fronts—a decorative front and a false front. The decorative front is usually screwed to the false front.

Illus. 630. A rabbet dado corner joint is much stronger than a butt joint. The joint makes the drawer easier to glue and assemble.

Illus. 631. The dado at the back of the drawer side is wide enough to accommodate the drawer back. Its depth equals one half drawer-side thickness.

Illus. 632. The dado width at the front of the drawer is about one third the drawer-side thickness. The dado at the front is the same depth as the one at the back.

Illus. 633. The tongue on the false front is cut with the help of a stop. The groove for the drawer bottom should face down when the false front is cut.

Lip Drawers   Lip drawers often have a rabbet joint at the front and a dado joint at the back. The drawer front is usually ¾″ thick. The rabbet is ⅜″ × ⅜″ on the top and bottom. The sides have a wider rabbet. It is ⅜″ plus the drawer-side thickness.

The rabbets can be cut in many different ways. The sides are glued and nailed to the rabbet joint. The drawer front must also have a groove for the drawer bottom. Use a drawer side to locate the groove on the drawer front.

Flush Drawers   Flush drawers can be joined with many different types of drawer joints. The rabbet joint is probably the simplest (Illus. 634). Rabbets are cut on both ends of the drawer front. These rabbets are slightly wider than the drawer sides to allow some clearance for fitting. The depth of the rabbets should be at least ½ the thickness of the drawer front. The sides are dadoed so that the back can be joined to them.

Illus. 634. The rabbet joint is one of the simplest joints used on a flush drawer.

A drawer corner is similar to a rabbet joint except the drawer front has a tongue that goes into the side for added strength (Illus. 635). A dado is cut on both ends of the drawer front (Illus. 636). The dado is about ¼″ wide (on a ¾″ drawer front). The depth is slightly greater than the thickness of the drawer side. The dado may be centered in the stock, or off-centered so that the tongue on the drawer back is slightly smaller than the one on the front.

Illus. 635. A drawer corner joint is similar to a rabbet, but it has a tongue that increases its strength and glue surface.

Illus. 636. A dado is cut on both ends of the drawer front. The guard has been removed for illustration purposes.

A mating ¼" dado is then cut in the drawer sides (Illus. 637). This dado should be about ¼" from the end. Remember the right and left sides are not the same. Mark the pieces carefully before making any cuts. The side should now fit the tongue on the drawer front (Illus. 638). The tongue will have to be trimmed so that the side can be butted against the drawer front (Illus. 639 and 640).

A lock corner is another variation of the drawer corner. The lock corner has a tongue on the drawer front and a tongue on the drawer side (Illus. 641). This joint must be slid together. The back slides into the dadoes in the sides and is not grooved. It rests on the drawer bottom. The sides and front are grooved to support the drawer bottom.

With the exception of one dado, drawer fronts with a drawer corner joint or a lock joint look alike. They are cut in the same way. The first dado cut on the ends of the drawer front is closer to the back (Illus. 642). The second dado cut trims the tongue and puts a dado in the front (Illus. 643).

The drawer side is then cut to fit the front. A tongue is cut on the front of the side (Illus. 644), then a dado is cut on the inner side (Illus. 645). The pieces should slide together without force. If the pieces must be forced together, the glue will make it impossible to put the parts together. This is because the glue causes both parts to swell slightly.

Flush drawers using metal side guides can be joined with through dovetails. The drawer front is dadoed to accommodate the sides. Determine where the drawer sides should be placed. Mark the center line and cut a ¼" dado ½" deep (Illus. 646). Lay out the dovetail over the dado. Use a saw blade to cut the dovetailed sides (Illus. 647 and 648). The blade must be tilted for this operation. The bottom of the dovetail dado should be ½" wide.

Cut a kerf ¹⁄₁₆" deep on each face of the ½"-thick drawer side (Illus. 649). The distance from the stop to the far side of the blade should be ½". The blade is now set slightly off the horizontal plane to cut the angular edges (Illus. 650 and 651). Use a mitre gauge or push block to control the work while the angular faces of the dovetail are cut. Check the fit of the mating parts. They should slide together easily (Illus. 652).

The drawer back should be fitted to a dado. The drawer back will rest on the drawer bottom. It could not be installed if it were grooved.

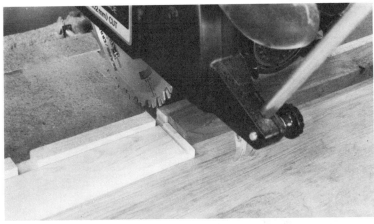

Illus. 637. A dado is cut on the inside of both drawer sides. A stop has been used to locate the dado.

Illus. 638. The dado on the drawer side fits the tongue on the drawer front. The tongue must now be shortened.

Illus. 639. The tongue is shortened with a saw blade. A stop has been used to position the drawer front.

Illus. 640. The drawer corner fits together snugly without force. Glue will make the fit even tighter.

Illus. 641. The drawer corner joint has 2 tongues: one on the inside of the drawer side and one on the front of the drawer side. This joint must be cut carefully.

Illus. 642. The drawer corner joint begins with a dado cut on both ends of the drawer front.

Illus. 643. The crosscut trims the tongue and puts a groove in the drawer front.

Illus. 644. A tongue is cut on the front of the drawer sides. It will mate the groove in the drawer front.

Illus. 645. A groove is cut on the inside edge of the drawer sides. This will mate the tongue on the drawer front. Test the fit with scrap before cutting all parts.

Illus. 646. A through-dovetail drawer joint begins with a dado at both ends of the drawer front. The dado is cut on the inside face.

Illus. 647. The blade is tilted to the layout angle, and a stop is clamped to the table. One cut is made on both ends of all drawer fronts.

Illus. 648. The stop is positioned on the opposite side of the blade for the second cut. The second cut is made on both ends of all drawer fronts.

Illus. 649. A kerf is cut in both faces of the drawer side. These cuts are made on the front of the drawer side.

Illus. 650. The blade is adjusted to slightly off-horizontal to the dovetail layout line. This is about a 6° angle.

Illus. 651. The angular cut is made on both faces of the drawer side. The mitre gauge and auxiliary table are used to control the stock.

Illus. 652. The drawer side slides directly into the front. The fit is snug, but not tight. The drawer guide can now be mounted to the drawer side.

Routing

Routing may be done several ways on the radial arm saw. A chuck or collet can be mounted on the auxiliary arbor. A router bit is then inserted for routing (Illus. 653). Some machines have a special routing attachment (Illus. 654) that is mounted to the saw arbor. This device has a pulley system to boost the cutter speed. Some machine manufacturers sell a bracket or mount for their machine (Illus. 655–660). This bracket attaches to the motor of the radial arm saw. A portable router must be mounted in the bracket after it is attached. The saw motor has no effect on the routing operation. In fact, the manufacturers recommend disconnecting the saw before attaching the bracket.

All 3 systems use the radial-arm-saw table and fence for stock control. The chuck or collet system turns the router bit at 3,450 rpms. This speed is too slow for efficient routing. Router bits are designed to turn at about 20,000 rpms. The 2 other methods turn the bit at the appropriate speed. For most home and small shop radial arm saws, the bracket method of routing is selected. Industrial applications would be more likely to use the special routing attachment.

The routing attachments allow you to use the radial arm saw as a stationary or overarm router. It will perform the operations of a stationary machine without taking up any extra floor space. This is an important advantage for the person with limited shop space.

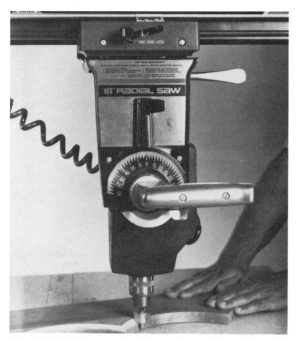

Illus. 653. Routing can be done on the auxiliary arbor of the radial arm saw. This arbor turns at 3,450 rpm, which is very slow for routing.

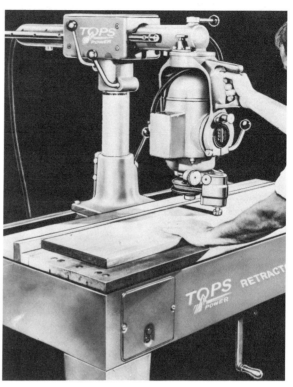

Illus. 654. This special routing attachment has a belt drive, which boosts the spindle speed to make it appropriate for routing.

Illus. 655. The guard is removed and the power is disconnected. The router bracket may now be mounted.

Illus. 656. The bracket bolts to the motor. The groove in which the guard is mounted helps locate the bracket.

Illus. 657. A router base is attached to the bracket. Several routers of the same make can now use this setup.

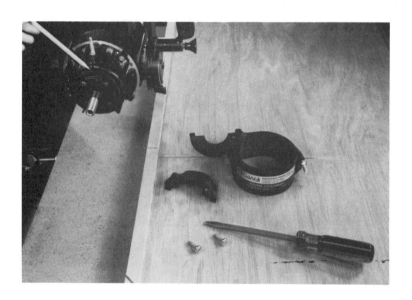

Illus. 658. The guard and all related hardware are removed from the saw, and the saw is disconnected. This bracket also is mounted in the guard groove.

Illus. 659. The bracket is mounted. The screws are tightened securely after the bracket is set parallel to the table.

Illus. 660. The router motor is set in the bracket without a router base. The router cord is threaded through the yoke to keep it out of the way.

Illus. 661. The elevating crank usually sets the depth of cut. Some routers can be raised and lowered in the bracket.

Illus. 662. An uncut fence and a true table make routing much easier and more accurate.

Mounting Follow the manufacturer's instructions for mounting the bracket. Some brackets fit in the groove designed for the guard, and others are held in place by the arbor nut. All blades or accessories should be removed from the radial arm saw before the bracket or router are mounted. Make sure the router is disconnected before it is mounted. Disconnect the saw before beginning. Lock the bracket in position securely. Check the clamping mechanisms periodically while you work.

The router is now fitted to the bracket. The brand of router and bracket will determine the correct mounting procedure. Some clamp the motor of the router into the bracket, others hold the router base to the bracket. Those that clamp the router motor require a router that separates from its base. Thread the router cord through the yoke to keep it out of the way after it is mounted.

Bits can be mounted in the router collet before or after the router is set in the bracket. In most cases, it is easier to install the bits before installing the router in the bracket.

Routing Faces Generally, faces are routed to make joints, but some decorative face cuts are also made. Stock can be moved under the bit, or the stock can remain stationary while the bit is moved across the work.

When moving the work, the bit is positioned relative to the work and the carriage is locked. Use the elevation crank to set the depth of cut. Light cuts are best (Illus. 661). Your fence and table should be true and free of cuts (Illus. 662). This eliminates obstructions that could stop the work or cause it to veer off course.

Turn on the router and let it come up to full speed. Keep the work clear of the bit when you turn on the

router. Feed the work into the bit against cutter rotation. The bit should push the work towards the fence. The router will tell you if the cut is too deep. If it slows down, raise the bit and take a lighter cut. When the bit turns slowly or the work moves slowly, it causes abnormal bit wear. Two light cuts usually work better (and increase bit life) than a single heavy cut.

Keep your hands well away from the router bit at all times. Use a push stick to guide the work and provide a margin of safety. Keep yourself well-balanced so that you do not slip towards the cutter. Router bits are as dangerous as any blade, dado, or shaper head. Extension tables and hold-downs will be helpful on large pieces. Set them up before beginning work.

When moving the carriage and bit, clamp or hold the work securely in position. Hand pressure may be enough in some cases, but with larger bits, the rotating force tends to move the work. Position the work and set bit height. Turn on the router and let it come up to full speed. Grasp the carriage and pull it slowly into the work. Position yourself and use the same grasp as you would for crosscutting. Your arm should be rigid so that the bit cannot climb the work.

For angular cuts, the arm can be turned. Always check the setup carefully before beginning. Make sure all stops and clamps are positioned and locked. The bit can be tilted in cuts where the work moves or remains stationary. If the bit is tilted, more of the bit is in the work. Be sure to check the depth of cut before starting. Tilting a decorative bit can produce a cut that is different from the one made when the bit is in the vertical position.

The hold-downs used for shaping or ripping on the radial arm saw can also be used for routing. These hold-downs can reduce vibration and keep the work from creeping. Use them to make the job safer and more accurate.

Edge-Routing Edge-routing can be done by moving the carriage or the work. In most cases, the work is moved. A fence with a cutout for the bit is used when the work is moved (Illus. 663). This fence replaces the sawing fence. On some router bits, the pilot tip contacts the work and controls the depth of cut (Illus. 664). A fence increases your control over the work and should be used in conjunction with the pilot tips. The work should *never* go between the fence and the bit (Illus. 665). This could cause a kickback.

Begin by adjusting the position of the bit in relation to the edge of the work. Remember that light cuts work best. Bit height is always most accurate when the last adjustment is upward. This takes any lash out of the elevating mechanism. If planning a series of cuts along the edge, make sure you do not rout away the control surfaces that ride on the table and along the fence. If you are tilting the bit, make sure the cut is not too deep. Secure all clamps and locks before you begin cutting. Check them periodically while working.

Turn on the router with the work well away from the bit. Let the router come up to full speed before you begin cutting. Feed the edge along the fence against cutter rotation. The bit should force the work against the fence (Illus. 666). Use a push stick to keep your hands clear of the bit. If you are routing all 4 edges of a panel, begin with the end grain and work your way around the panel. This way any tear-out that occurs on end grain will be removed when the edge grain is routed.

Support long or large pieces with commercial hold-downs and extension tables. If the work is hard to control, get help. A second person should assist you on difficult operations. Continue taking light cuts until you reach your desired shape.

Some edges may require more than one bit or setup to obtain the desired shape. Disconnect the router when changing bits. If removing the entire edge, use shaper fences to control the offset edge of the workpiece. Again, be sure to take light cuts.

Illus. 663. The fence for edge routing has a cutout to accommodate the pilot tip on some router bits.

Illus. 664. The pilot tip can be used to control the cut when edge-routing.

Illus. 665. Never allow the work to go between the fence and router bit when edge-routing. Routing should be done adjacent to the fence.

Illus. 668. The ends of the rails are routed to the mating-cope profile. These ends fit snugly against the inside edges of the door frame.

Illus. 666. The router bit should force the work against the fence. This means you feed into the turning bit. Feed is against the flat face of the router bit.

Routing Panel Doors With the proper router bits, raised panel doors can be made on the radial arm saw with a ½″ router. The router is mounted in a bracket. The first cut is made with a cope bit on the inside of all the frame parts (Illus. 667). The fence and the pilot tip on the bit control the depth of cut. The rails are routed with the mating cope bit (Illus. 668). Usually the cutters in the cope bit are reversed to make this cut. Control the stock with a mitre gauge or a push block. End grain is more difficult to rout than edge grain.

The raised panel is routed with a larger raised-panel bit (Illus. 669). This bit is quite large. Light cuts work best with this bit. Control the stock with a push block or mitre gauge. Cut end grain first (Illus. 670). This will compensate for any tear-out.

The door parts should fit together easily (Illus. 671) if they have been routed correctly. All rails and stiles must be the same thickness for best results and the raised panel must be free of warp.

Illus. 669. This bit is used to make the raised panel. This requires a router of 2 horsepower or more.

Illus. 667. The cope bit routs the inside edge of all door-frame parts. Hold-downs have been used to increase control over the work.

Illus. 670. Be sure to rout the end grain of the panel first. Control stock with a push block and take light cuts.

218

Illus. 671. The door parts fit together easily, and the mating fit is snug.

Pin-Routing Pin-routing is a type of routing that uses a metal, plastic, or wooden dowel (pin) in the table to control the cut. A jig or fixture can be used in conjunction with the pin to control the cut (Illus. 672). In some setups, the edge of the work rubs against the pin to control the cut (Illus. 673). Pin-routing is considered a production setup, but the small shop can adapt the radial arm saw to this operation.

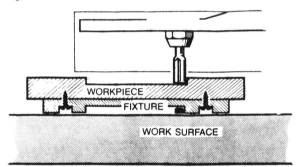

Illus. 672. A jig or fixture can be used with a table pin for routing.

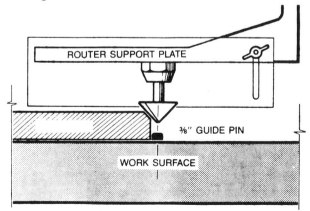

Illus. 673. The pin can act as a pilot tip in some routing operations. Note how the bit is positioned directly over the pin.

The first step in pin-routing is to locate the position of the pin. For large work, it is usually centered in the table. For smaller work, it is centered end to end but moved closer to the operator (away from the column). For large production jobs, a steel pin is used because it resists wear (Illus. 674). For smaller jobs, wood or plastic may be used. Pin diameter is usually the same as the bit diameter. This allows any jig or fixture to be made exact size.

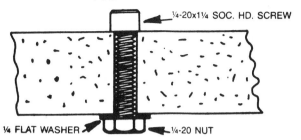

Illus. 674. A steel pin or a round-head screw can be used as a table pin. A threaded pin is better able to resist wear.

Next, remove the fence and clamp the table boards together to make a smooth surface. An auxiliary table may also be desirable since the table should be smooth and true. Next, position the bit directly over the pin (Illus. 675).

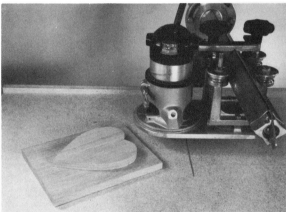

Illus. 675. The bit is positioned directly over the pin for most pin-routing operations.

For external cuts, raise the bit relative to the work. Light cuts work best. After all adjustments have been made, the external edge cut can be made (Illus. 676). Turn on the router and move the jig or edge of the work up against the pin. Feed the work against cutter rotation. Keep hands well away from the cutter. If the bit were to grab the work, it could pull your hand into the rotating bit.

Many different templates may be used for pin-routing (Illus. 677). Remember, the better the template, the better your work will be.

A starting pin can be used to support some edge cuts. This pin supports the work as it is fed into the cutter. The

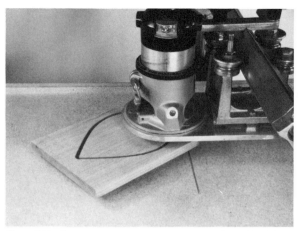

Illus. 676. An external edge cut is made after all adjustments are locked in. Remember, light cuts work best.

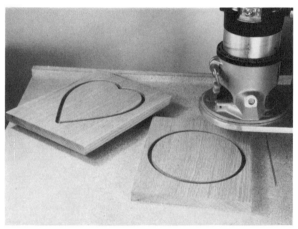

Illus. 677. There are many different templates that can be used for pin-routing. The better the template, the better your work will turn out. It pays to cut your templates carefully.

starting pin helps resist kickback forces. The work is in contact with the starting pin and then it is slowly pushed into the cutter. The pin helps eliminate grabbing as the work contacts the cutter. The pin is usually located on the infeed side of the bit.

For internal cuts, elevate the arm (and bit) so that the bit clears the work. Set the jig or fixture over the pin. The pin now limits the travel of the jig or fixture. Turn the router on and lower the bit slowly into the work. Stop the bit when it is taking a light cut. Hold the jig or fixture while lowering the bit. Now, move the jig or fixture until all the stock is cut away. When the stock is cut away, the bit may be lowered for another cut if needed.

Internal cuts are common for inlays, coasters, and serving trays. Roundnose cutters are used for trays. This gives the cutout areas radiused sides. Templates are easy

to make for these projects. Remember when making the template that it should be larger than the work. If the work is small, make a large template. This will keep your hands clear of the cutter while routing. It is also good practice to put handles on the templates. Handles provide a good grip so your hands do not slip into the rotating bit.

Router Selection When routing on the radial arm saw, select a router of more than 1 horsepower. It is best to use a router with a ½″ collet. The larger shank on these bits minimizes bit deflection. Bit deflection on ¼″ bits can snap the bit when it makes a heavy cut. Make sure the router has been well-maintained. A defective collet can cause the bit to turn an eccentric orbit. This is a contributing cause of bit deflection and breakage. When in doubt, install a new collet in the router. One or 2 broken bits will easily pay for the new collet.

Routing Practices When routing on the radial arm saw, follow the same practices used when sawing, dadoing, or shaping. Only rout true, clear stock that is free of defects. Twisted stock could become trapped between the table and bit and cause bit breakage and/or a kickback. Avoid trapping the work between the bit and fence when edge-routing. This could also cause a kickback. Edge-routing should be done with the router bit next to the fence. Many routing operations will require a takeoff table and can be made safer with the use of hold-downs.

Whenever mounting a router attachment on a radial arm saw, make sure it is mounted securely and all clamps are locked. Check the attachment and clamps periodically while working. The vibration of the router can cause clamps and other fastening devices to loosen. This increases vibration, which could dull or break bits and cause abnormal router wear.

The design of some router attachments makes no provision for a guard. In some routing operations, this could be dangerous. It is good practice to make a guard when you feel the job could be hazardous. When in doubt, make a guard or design a safer setup. Use push sticks whenever they will make the job safer. Push sticks provide a comfortable margin of safety on many router setups.

Router Table For some jobs, it is easier to make a router table out of the front table on the radial arm saw. A router base is mounted under the table (Illus. 678). The router bit protrudes through the table. Bit height is adjusted by raising or lowering the motor in its base (Illus. 679). A straightedge and/or clamp may be used as a fence when cutting dadoes (Illus. 680). Bits with a pilot tip can be used to rout straight or irregular edges. The pilot tip controls the depth of cut (Illus. 681).

The router table approach is not as versatile as the router attachment. It will not allow you to do pin-routing, but it is less expensive. On one of my radial arm saws, I mounted an extra router base permanently to the table. Now I can pull my router out of its other base and slip it into the one under the front table. This makes the routing setup quick and convenient.

If you decide to make your radial arm saw into a router table, follow the routing practices discussed earlier in this section. Always double-check your router to be sure that it is clamped securely in its base. Check the setup periodically while working. Router vibration can sometimes loosen clamps or screws.

Illus. 678. A router base is bolted to the front table. The router can be mounted in the base whenever it is needed.

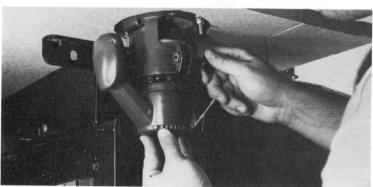

Illus. 679. Bit height is controlled by raising or lowering the router in its base. Lock it securely after it has been adjusted.

Illus. 680. A straightedge clamp has been attached to the router table. This will control the work as it is fed into the bit.

Illus. 681. On irregular shapes, the pilot tip controls the path of the router bit. Handle stock carefully and keep your hand well away from the bit.

Using the Planer Head

The planer head or rotary planer is used for planing or smoothing wood (Illus. 682). It can also be used to cut rabbets and bevels. The guard and saw blade are removed before the planer head is mounted. The arbor nut fits in the underside of the planer head casting. Tighten the planer head securely.

The planer head is used in the horizontal position. Loosen the bevel clamp and turn the motor into position. Install an auxiliary table and fence. The fence must have a cutout that accommodates the planer head. This cutout should still control the stock as it is fed under the rotary planer.

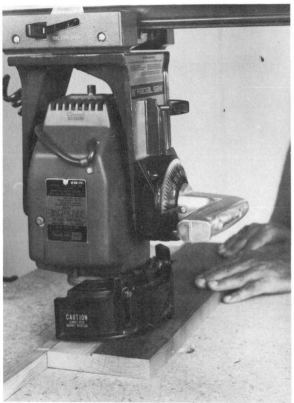

Illus. 682. The planer head can be used for planing or smoothing wood and for many other operations.

Planing Stock   Rough stock can be planed to uniform thickness with the planer head. The truer the stock you begin with, the better the results will be. Twisted, warped stock tends to twist and turn when it is planed. This makes good results more difficult.

Begin by measuring your stock to determine the high point. For safety, stock must be at least ½″ thick. Adjust the planer head height so that it will take a light cut (¹⁄₁₆″)

on the high spot of your work (Illus. 683). Move the carriage so that the planer head is making a cut equal to ½ its diameter or less. Lock the carriage securely, and make sure all locks and clamps are secure. Position the shaper guard so that it will hold down the wood as it is fed into the planer head (Illus. 684).

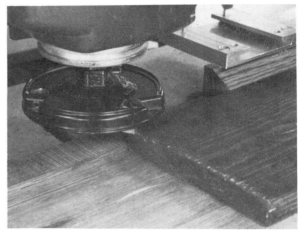

Illus. 683. Adjust the planer head to take a light cut in your work. The width of cut should be less than half the cutter-head diameter. Make sure all adjustments are locked securely.

Illus. 684. The shaper guard is used as a hold-down and to prevent contact with the cutterhead.

Turn on the saw and feed the stock slowly into cutter rotation. On wide pieces, you can feed the stock by hand. Narrow pieces will require a push stick. When using a push stick or push block, retract it slowly after the work has cleared the planer head. Commercial hold-downs can also be used to help guide the work when surface planing.

Readjust the planer head for the next cut. Usually the entire surface is planed to a uniform thickness first. This requires that the carriage be moved away from the fence. Both edges can be placed against the fence for a planer cut before the carriage is moved (Illus. 685). On narrow boards, a second setup may not be needed. When moving the carriage, set the cut for no more than ½ the planer head diameter. After the entire surface has been planed, the planer head can be lowered for a second cut. Keep the cut light (¹⁄₁₆″). You will probably be planing the entire surface with this adjustment. Too deep of a cut will only tax the machine (Illus. 686).

If the stock you are working with is rough on both sides, plane the back side after the front side is flat enough to ride on the table without rocking. Always begin planing with the best face down. This will minimize the chance of rocking when the first side is planed.

Support the entire length of your work. It may be necessary to use an extension table when planing long pieces. If the stock binds between the table and planer head, it may kick back.

Planing Rabbets The planer is capable of making rabbets. Several consecutive cuts will form a rabbet when the planer head remains in the same position. Stock of uniform thickness is usually selected for rabbeting. The planer head is set up the same way it was for planing. Feed edge grain along the fence for control (Illus. 687). Use a mitre gauge to control end grain. Take light cuts. Keep lowering the planer head until the desired rabbet has been cut.

It is possible to cut rabbets by loosening the carriage and pulling the planer head across the work. The work must be butted against the fence for this operation (Illus. 688). This method requires light cuts, and complete guarding is not possible (Illus. 689). It would be much safer to use a dado head on the saw if you plan to pull the carriage across the work to make a rabbet.

Illus. 685. Both edges can be planed from the same setting to reduce the number of setups.

Illus. 687. An edge rabbet is made by feeding the work along the fence. Lowering the cutterhead will increase the depth of the rabbet.

Illus. 686. Light cuts like this are best. Deep cuts will tax your machine and cause excess wear.

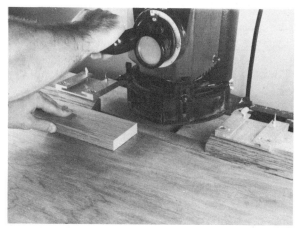

Illus. 688. To make a cross-grain or end rabbet, pull the planer head across the work. The work must be butted against the fence for this operation.

Illus. 689. Light cuts give the best results. Note the well-formed shoulder. Deep cuts would cause tear-out.

Illus. 690. To make a raised panel with the planer head, the yoke and blade must be turned. Make these adjustments with the power disconnected.

Raised Panels The planer head can also be used to make raised panels. The same auxiliary table is used for this operation. Stock is prepared by kerfing it first. A kerf about 1/16″ deep is cut 1½″ from the ends and edges. The edge of the panel is laid out to determine the angle of the planer head. Mark the desired edge thickness on the edge. Allow some extra thickness for sanding. Draw a line from the bottom of the kerf to the edge thickness mark. Measure this angle and set the planer head at the desired angle. On ½″ stock with a ¼″-edge thickness, the angle is about 6°.

Adjust the cutter head with reference to the layout line and lock it in position (Illus. 690–692). Raise the cutter-head so that it is taking a light cut. Begin with the end grain (Illus. 693). Use a mitre gauge or push block. The first cut just knocks off the corner. Lower the cutter and make a second cut (Illus. 694). When you approach the layout line, take light cuts and feed slowly. This will make the surface much smoother and reduce the amount of sanding required (Illus. 695).

Control end grain with the fence and mitre gauge or push block. This may not be necessary if the panel is quite wide. Long panels ride along the fence and require no other control. Feed narrow pieces with a push stick.

Long, wide panels require additional support (Illus. 696). The panel shown in Illus. 696 replaced a damaged panel at a local bank (Illus. 697). Because of its size, I chose to cut it with the planer head. If I had tried to cut it on a table saw, it would have hit the shop ceiling or lights. After the setup stock was planed (Illus. 698), I clamped a scrap in my bench vise and added a support (Illus. 699). This allowed the panel to be planed safely and without damage (Illus. 700).

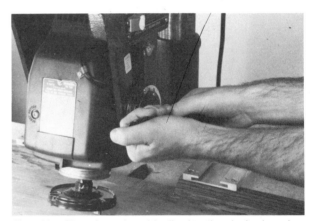

Illus. 691. The planer head is tilted to the desired angle. This is usually about 6°–10°.

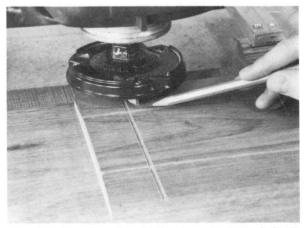

Illus. 692. The planer head is lined up with the kerf after it has been tilted to the correct angle.

Illus. 693. The end grain is cut first. Use a push block or mitre gauge to control the stock. Do not force the work.

Illus. 694. The second cut gives the panel edges an inclined edge. Push sticks sometimes work best when planing edge grain.

Illus. 695. Take light cuts when you approach the layout line. This will reduce the amount of sanding.

Illus. 696. A long, wide panel requires additional support. It would be difficult to turn this panel vertically on the radial arm saw. There would be little control when cutting the inclined edges.

Illus. 697. The panel in Illus. 696 was installed here on the front of a bank in my hometown.

Illus. 698. The large panel was planed after this piece was used as a setup.

Illus. 700. The support made the planing job safer and easier.

Coving Coves can be made using the planer head. The head is tilted in the direction of feed to make this cut. The table and fence are used to control the stock. Tilt the planer head 10 to 20°(Illus. 701) and make a test cut. Keep the width of the cove slightly less than one half the diameter of the planer head (Illus. 702). For a flatter look, use a tilt of 6 to 8°. Take light cuts (Illus. 703) and finish up with an extremely light cut (1/64"). Feed very slowly to make the surface as smooth as possible. This will reduce the amount of sanding. Always use a push stick to control stock. Hold-downs may also be helpful.

This procedure can also be used to make raised panels (Illus. 704). The planer head is moved closer to the fence. A half cove is now formed along all 4 edges of the work. These half coves produce a raised panel. Light cuts and a push stick are used when making these cuts (Illus. 705). The light cuts are extremely important here, since half of the planing is done on end grain (Illus. 706). Make a few test cuts before actually cutting your work. This will help

you to ensure that the cove or raised panel is actually what you desire.

Illus. 701. For coving with the planer head, the planer head is tilted 10°–20°.

227

Illus. 702. The planer head is lowered for a light cut and the guard is adjusted accordingly. A shallow cove is formed.

Illus. 703. As you go deeper, the cutting area gets wider. Cuts should be lighter when the planer head is lowered. Readjust the guard after each cut.

Illus. 704. The planer head can be adjusted to cut cove-shaped raised panels. Note that the fence always controls the work.

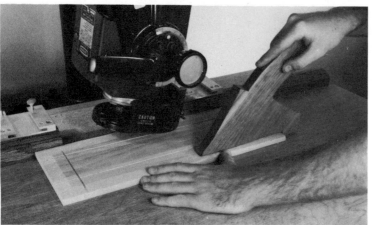

Illus. 705. As with other planing operations, light cuts produce the best results.

Illus. 706. One more light cut should finish this panel. Feed slowly for improved smoothness.

Drilling

The radial arm saw can be used for horizontal drilling. A chuck is mounted on the drill motor or on the auxiliary arbor. Usually the motor moves on the carriage to drill a hole, but the work can be pushed into a stationary bit. A special drill table is needed to elevate the work. This keeps the motor clear of the radial-arm-saw table.

Drill Setup Mount the chuck according to manufacturer's instructions. The saw blade, arbor washers, and nut must be removed. In most cases, the guard is also removed. Set up the drill table according to the type of drilling you plan to do. Install the desired bit in the chuck and turn it over by hand to be sure it is centered. Do all these things with the power disconnected.

End-Drilling End-drilling is usually done by moving the work into the bit (Illus. 707). Position the bit in

Illus. 707. End drilling is usually done by moving the work into the bit. Adjust the bit's position and secure all clamps before drilling.

relation to the work and lock the clamps that hold the bit in position. A fence can now be clamped to the auxiliary table to locate the bit horizontally. Turn on the motor with the bit clear of the work. Slowly push the work into the bit (Illus. 708). Retract the work occasionally to clear the chips. A collar can be attached to the bit to control the depth of cut (Illus. 709). Drill all holes at this setup before changing the setup.

Jigs and control devices can be built for radial arm saw drilling. These are designed to suit the job. In most cases, they will make the job more efficient and accurate. In some cases, they can make the job safer.

Illus. 708. The work is slowly pushed onto the bit. Retract the work occasionally to clear the chips.

Illus. 709. The carriage is moved when drilling in edges. A stop can be used to position the work.

Edge-Drilling Edge-drilling is done for many purposes. Two of the most common are dowelling and mortises. Dowel-joining of boards requires precision-drilling. The radial arm saw is well-suited to this job.

Layout all holes in mating parts. Position the bit and

clamp a stop to the auxiliary table. The stop will help position the stock.

Turn on the saw and push the carriage (and bit) towards the work. Allow the bit to cut its way into the work. Do not force the bit into the work (Illus. 710). Retract the bit occasionally to clear the chips. If the bit becomes packed with chips, it can push the bit off course. A depth stop can be located on the bit or an arm stop can be attached to the arm (Illus. 711). Either stop will control the depth of feed. Drill all holes at this setting prior to changing the setup.

Holes can be drilled at an angle when necessary (Illus. 712). The arm is turned and locked at the desired angle. Holes are drilled in the same way when the arm is turned. It may be necessary to clamp the work when drilling to keep it from creeping.

Mortises are made on the radial arm saw by drilling a series of holes. After the holes are drilled, the mortise must be cleaned out with a chisel. The work is positioned in the same way as it would be for edge-drilling. A mortising-type drill bit (Illus. 713), router bit (Illus. 714), or regular twist bit can be used for this operation.

When cleaning out a mortise, check it frequently with the mating part. Remove only enough stock to get a good fit (Illus. 715). It is good practice to custom-fit the joints and then mark the parts. When the work is glued up, mating parts will fit well and gluing will be easy.

Drilling Practices   There is one disadvantage to using the radial arm saw for drilling. The radial arm saw turns at 3,750 rpms. This speed is far higher than that of most portable drill motors. The larger the bit diameter, the *slower* it should turn.

When drilling with the radial arm saw, do not use bits larger than ½″ in diameter. Large spade bits, fly cutters, and hole saws should not be used. Their size and/or shank length can cause them to grab and throw the work. This could bend the bit's shank or damage the radial arm saw. A bent bit can be hazardous.

When drilling, use clamps to hold the work more securely. This minimizes the chance of the bit grabbing. The larger the bit, the greater the need for clamping. Keep loose sleeves away from the turning bit. The bit could grab your sleeve and cause injury.

Illus. 710. Do not force the bit. Allow the bit to clear the chips.

Illus. 711. A depth stop can be attached to the bit to control hole depth. An arm clamp or stop may also be used.

Illus. 713. This mortising bit is being used to cut edge mortises. Stops can be used to locate both ends of the mortise.

Illus. 712. Angular holes can be drilled by turning the arm. When large holes are drilled, stock should be clamped.

Illus. 714. A spiral router bit can also be used to cut edge mortises. The spiral bit clears chips in the same way as a twist drill.

Illus. 715. Remove only enough stock from the mortise to get a good fit. Mortise-and-tenon joints should be snug. Clamps can be used to hold the work securely while drilling. The larger the bit, the greater the need for clamping.

7

Useful Information About Radial Arm Saws

The more the radial arm saw is used, the greater your desire becomes to do a better, safer, more accurate job. This chapter is devoted to aspects of radial arm saw use that will help you improve the job you do.

General Maintenance

Maintenance of your radial arm saw is an important job. A saw that is out of adjustment makes the job more difficult and usually yields poor results. In addition, the job becomes more time-consuming and wasteful. The most common maintenance area on the radial arm saw is the blade (Illus. 716). Keep the blade clean (free of pitch) and sharp. Use the correct blade for the job. Review Chapter 3 for blade selection and maintenance procedures.

Keep the table and fence in good shape. When the fence has many cuts in it, replace it (Illus. 717). A true fence with a minimum of cuts will make all jobs easier, safer, and more accurate. When an auxiliary table is used, the radial-arm-saw table rarely needs to be replaced. In fact, it is good practice to have several auxiliary tables for any type of job at hand. The auxiliary table may be clamped, nailed, or screwed in place. Remember to keep metal fasteners out of the blade's path.

As the sheet stock gets old, the accumulated stresses cause the table to droop at the ends. Some woodworkers replace the table when the ends droop. This can affect the accuracy of the cut. Make sure the brackets that hold the table to the base of the saw are in the same plane before mounting the table. This will eliminate any irregularity in the cut.

A drooping table can be replaced with a reinforced table. This will control the drooping problem. Cut two pieces of ¾" veneer-core plywood to the size of the front table. Cut a ⅛" kerf 1" from all edges on the worst face of both pieces (Illus. 718). This kerf should be ⅜" deep. Now put a piece of ⅛ × ¾" steel bar into the 4 kerfs (Illus. 719). Line up the pieces and screw them together from the underside (Illus. 720). The steel will strengthen the table and control sagging. If you cut into this table, keep your cuts light; you do not want to hit the steel bar or fasteners. A thin auxiliary table will help protect any front table (Illus. 721).

Illus. 716. Change the blade whenever it is dull or incorrect for the job. The best and safest work is done on a well-maintained saw.

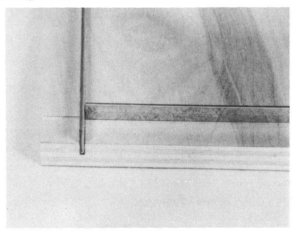

Illus. 717. Any fence with many cuts in it should be replaced with a new one. A smooth, true fence makes the job safer and more accurate.

Illus. 718. The reinforced table is grooved on all edges to accommodate a steel bar. Kerf depth should equal half the bar width.

Illus. 719. The steel bars are cut to length and inserted in the kerfs.

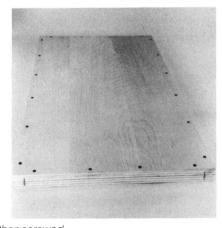

Illus. 720. The other sheet of plywood is located over the steel bars. The pieces are then screwed together. This makes a rigid front table.

Some front tables are simply replacements made from sheet stock. If you have a hand crank, you can rout away the area around the crank to provide some knuckle clearance (Illus. 722). Use the old table as a model for the new table (Illus. 723). This will help you drill the holes accurately.

If you wish to make a router or sabre saw base out of the front table, rout away an area to accommodate the tool (Illus. 724 and 725). Make sure their position does not interfere with the mounting brackets.

Illus. 722. If you make a front table, you may wish to rout away the area around the elevating crank. This will keep your knuckles from hitting the table.

Illus. 724. The front table has been routed away to accommodate a router base. This makes the radial arm saw more versatile.

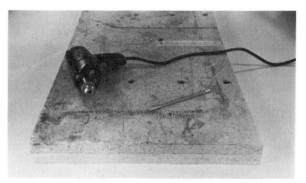

Illus. 723. The old table will help you locate the holes in the new table. Lay out the holes carefully for accurate placement of the new table.

Illus. 725. The front table has been routed away to accommodate a sabre saw. This allows the radial arm saw to make irregular cuts.

Save the old table. You can take a rip or two (Illus. 726) from the outer edge. These rips make good fences and back or spacer tables. Measure the old parts carefully, so that the rips are the correct width.

Illus. 726. Take a rip or two off the old front table. These can be used as rear tables, table spacers, or fences.

Clean the radial arm saw frequently. Keep sawdust from accumulating around the motor, elevating-and-tilting mechanisms, and tracks or carriage. When sawdust accumulates, problems can result. The motor may not get proper ventilation and could overheat. Sawdust packed around elevating-and-tilting mechanisms can make the saw difficult to operate. When sawdust accumulates on the tracks or carriage bearings, it can cause increased stress. This causes wear and could split the bearings on some machines.

Lubricate the saw according to the manufacturer's specifications. Generally, no lubrication is required on the tracks or carriage bearings. A drop of oil may be used to lubricate the yoke, column, and elevating mechanism, but use it sparingly. Overlubricating can cause chips to become impacted on contact surfaces. This could crack a gear or split a bearing. Some paste waxes and silicone spray lubricants will work as a substitute for oil. They do not attract sawdust the way oil does.

When lubricating the control mechanisms, inspect all contact areas (especially the tracks and carriage bearings) for sawdust accumulation. Use pitch remover and a brass bristle brush to remove any accumulated sawdust.

A visual inspection of the saw during lubrication can identify potential problems. Look at the cord, plug, and electrical supply lines. Make sure they are not cut, worn, or frayed. Check any castings and the stand for cracks or loose nuts and bolts. These are potential causes of failure, increased vibration, and wear.

Surface rust can be removed from the column or other surfaces with auto rubbing compound and a wool bonnet. Work slowly and carefully. Protect the wood surfaces with newspaper and masking tape. After the metal surfaces are clean, apply a coat of paste wax. If the saw is to be stored for any length of time, lightly oil any surface that may rust before storing. The oil can be removed later with mineral spirits or other solvents. The oil is much easier to remove than the rust.

Adjusting the Radial Arm Saw

Adjustment and maintenance of adjustment can be the most challenging and vexing part of radial-arm-saw maintenance. Adjustment problems can be minimized, however, if you use the saw correctly. However, many operators jerk the carriage through the work with no concern for the tool. The blade climbs the work and throws the saw out of adjustment. Also, some carpenters carry their saw from job to job; they pay no attention to how the saw is loaded or transported. These are a few examples of how mistreatment can throw the radial arm saw out of adjustment.

Blade selection can also affect the saw. A saw blade with a great deal of hook can cause climbing when crosscutting and kicking when ripping. The blade itself may cause adjustment problems. Sometimes the saw is adjusted properly, but a thin blade deflects during the cut. This may suggest an adjustment problem; but when a more massive blade or a saw collar is used, the problem goes away. It is good practice to think through your problem before undertaking major adjustment of your saw. Chapter 3 discusses blades and accessories in detail.

The following adjustment steps are generalizations for all radial arm saws. They will help you diagnose and make adjustments to your saw, but they are not a substitute for the manufacturer's specifications or owner's manual. Read all of the steps through before beginning. Work carefully, and with the power disconnected. Most tests are done with all stops and clamps engaged. When adjustments are made, however, the clamps must be released to allow movement or readjustment.

1. Table Should Be Parallel to the Arm. Begin by removing the blade and guards. Turn the arbor to the vertical position. Lower the arbor so that it is about 1/16" away from the table. Pull the carriage so that the arbor is over the front table. Look at the arbor and table; observe any deviation of space between the table and arbor. Now swing the arm to various positions while pulling the carriage through its stroke. Note any deviation of space between the table and arbor (Illus. 727–729). If there is deviation, the table is not parallel to the arbor. Check the table to see if it is true. Use a straightedge to check for warp (Illus. 730).

If the table is warped, most saws provide some mechanism for adjustment. Usually the table can be raised or lowered in the middle by tightening or loosening a threaded device (Illus. 731). Straighten the table and then check the table with the arbor again.

If deviation still exists, the table should be removed. The arbor can then be used to true-up the table brackets. A spacer may be used between the arbor and the brackets. This will allow movement without raising of the arbor. When the brackets are in the same plane, the table can be replaced.

2. Table Edge Should Be Perpendicular to Blade Travel. Turn the arbor to the horizontal position and mount a blade. Lock the column perpendicular to the table and move it over near the blade. Slowly pull the carriage through its stroke. Watch the blade and the square. The blade and the square should remain parallel throughout the saw's stroke (Illus. 732). If the two are not parallel, loosen the table and move it slightly. When the square and blade remain parallel through the stroke, the table should be tightened. Some machines also provide adjustment at the column. This method moves the arm instead of the table. In most cases, it is easiest to shift the table. Through practice, you will be able to determine which is best with your saw.

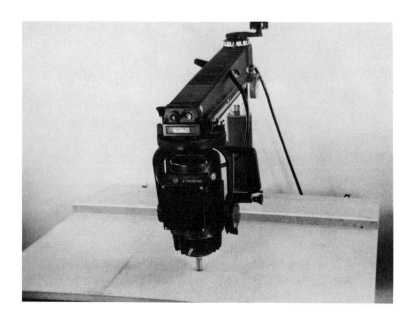

Illus. 727. Turn the arbor to the vertical position and lower it to the table.

Illus. 728. Move the arbor to another position to check the table for trueness.

Illus. 729. Continue moving the arbor to check for a true table. All clamps should be locked when checking for trueness.

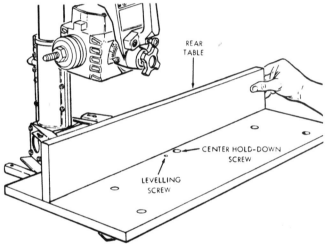

Illus. 730. Use a straightedge to check for table warp.

Illus. 731. The levelling screw can be raised or lowered to remove any table warp.

Illus. 732. Check the front table to see if the edge is perpendicular to the arm and the blade's path.

237

3. The Blade Should Be Perpendicular to the Table. Set a try square on the front table and move it up against the blade. Make sure the bevel pin or latch is engaged. The lock knob or clamp should also be secured. The blade of the square should be up against the body of the blade (Illus. 733). Do not let the tooth set affect your reading. If the blade is not perpendicular to the table, adjustment is necessary.

Most saws are adjusted adjacent to the bevel latch and lock knob. The adjusting screws are found within the bevel angle indicator. On some saws, the angle indicator plate must be removed for access to the adjusing screws.

The procedure requires that the bevel clamp or lock knob be loosened. The bevel pin or latch remains engaged. The set screws are loosened slightly. There may be 2, 3, or 4 set screws depending on the brand of machine. The motor is then turned so that the blade is perpendicular to the table. The set screws are now tightened. Check the square frequently while tightening the set screws. As the screws are tightened, the motor and blade may shift slightly. Tighten the screws uniformly. Do not tighten one screw completely. Tighten all screws gradually.

4. The Blade Should Not Heel. Heel is a condition where the rear of the blade does not follow the same path as the front of the blade (Illus. 734). Heeling can be observed when crosscutting. As the rear half of the blade enters the work, the kerf becomes wider. This can also cause tear-out. When ripping, heel can push the board towards or away from the fence. This can cause burning in the kerf or kickbacks. Check for heeling by placing a square against the fence and across the blade (Illus. 735). Any space between the square and the blade indicates a heeling condition.

Heeling is eliminated by adjusting the carriage on some machines. On other machines, the rear motor mount is moved in the yoke. When the square butts to the blade, heeling should be eliminated.

5. Align Splitter With Saw Kerf. For accurate and safe ripping, the splitter must be in the same plane as the blade. Most manuals recommend the "eyeball" approach for aligning the splitter with the blade. It can also be done with a piece of stock.

Clamp a scrap of plywood about 6 to 10″ wide to the table. Make a crosscut through about 8 inches (Illus. 736). Return the carriage to the column and shut off the saw. Disconnect the power and pull the carriage back until the blade is in the kerf. Now drop the splitter and adjust it so that it is centered in the kerf (Illus. 737).

Illus. 733. The blade should be perpendicular to the table. Any deviation must be corrected for accurate cutting.

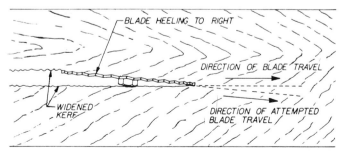

Illus. 734. Heeling occurs when the front and back of the blade are not in the same plane. This can cause tear-out when cutting.

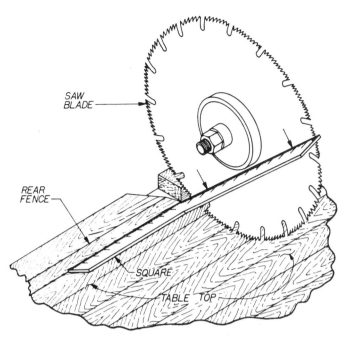

SAW BLADE

REAR FENCE

SQUARE

TABLE TOP

Illus. 735. A square is placed diagonally against the blade and fence. Any deviation indicates a heeling condition.

Illus. 736. Clamp a piece of plywood to the table and cut about half its length. Return the carriage to the column and shut off the saw.

Illus. 737. Move the blade back into the cut and adjust the splitter to the kerf. Do this with the power disconnected.

Compensating for Wear Most machines have adjustments that allow you to compensate for wear. The most common places wear is shown are: loose column, loose carriage, and yoke clamping. Most machines have provisions for tightening the column on the back side. It is possible to tighten these fasteners so tight that the column will not move. Exercise care when tightening the column clamps (Illus. 738).

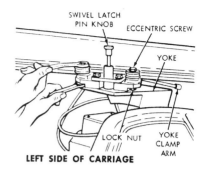

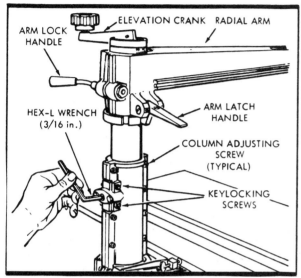

Illus. 738. When tightening the column, exercise caution. It is possible to overtighten the column. The column must be loose enough to move.

Illus. 740. Avoid overtightening the bearing. This could cause the bearing to split.

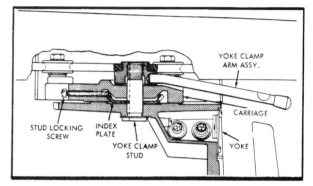

Illus. 741. The yoke clamp usually has a provision for tightening in the stud. This is under the yoke clamp.

A loose carriage can be tightened by adjusting the carriage roller bearings. Two of the bearings on the carriage have an eccentric center hole (Illus. 739). This allows them to be tightened against the arm (Illus. 740). This eliminates carriage slop.

A loose yoke will not pull up snugly against the carriage. After being cycled numerous times, the clamp mechanism begins to wear. Access for tightening is usually provided immediately under the yoke clamp (Illus. 741). Refer to the manufacturer's instructions for specifics.

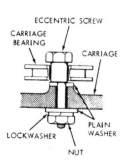

Illus. 739. The bearings on the carriage can be tightened to compensate for wear. These bearings are eccentric, so adjustment is easy.

Layout Techniques at the Saw

Many errors in measurement are caused by an incorrect layout or setup at the saw. For example, when a rabbet is cut, the distance between the fence and blade (rip position) or stop and blade (crosscut position) is set to the thickness of the piece that fits in the rabbet. First the thickness of the piece is measured, and then the fence is set to that measurement. A ruler is used twice. This means there are two opportunities to make a measurement error.

A better approach would be to set the distance using a piece of stock. This allows the setting to be made without the use of a ruler. Two chances of making an error have been eliminated.

Cutting lap joints or other joints where the blade must cut to the center of the piece provides several chances for measurement errors. Use 2 scraps of the correct thickness to set the blade height. No measurement is needed.

Set the blade slightly below the center of the pieces and make a cut on both pieces. Flip one piece over and push the cut ends together. The space between the 2 ends is exactly twice the distance that the blades must be elevated.

240

Raise the blade slightly and check the pieces. Continue the process until the blade is adjusted (Illus. 742–744). It is important that the final setting be made with the blade being elevated. Lowering the blade may cause creep. The slop or lash in the gears will allow the column to slowly drop from its adjusted height. As you practice this method of setting blade height, you'll find it easier and more accurate than any measuring method.

Illus. 742. The cut is past the halfway mark. Raise the dado head half the distance between the pieces.

Illus. 743. The cut has been adjusted correctly. Lap joints can now be cut correctly.

Illus. 744. The dado head is too high. When it is readjusted, make sure the last adjustment raises the dado head. This will take any lash out of the adjusting threads or gears.

Getting the Best Cut

In working with the radial arm saw, I have observed that the best cutting action for advanced cuts usually takes place when the blade remains stationary and the work is fed into the blade. Shaping, dadoing, and the like are cuts usually best made when the work is fed into the blade or cutter. Experience will suggest the best and safest cutting.

When working with the cutter in a stationary position, make sure that it remains stationary. Some clamps and locks cannot be tightened securely enough by hand. In some cases, the hand knob may be replaced with a hex head bolt (Illus. 745).

Illus. 745. When shaping or performing heavy cuts, I lock the carriage with a hex bolt. Some hand knobs cannot be locked securely enough.

Regardless of whether the cutter remains stationary or not, there are other problems that can affect the cut. They include:

1. *Workpiece Irregularities.* The edge of the work will not butt to the fence or rest on the table in a true plane.

2. *Chips or Sawdust.* Sawdust or chips of wood get between the work and fence or table. This can affect accuracy or the quality of the cut.

3. *Stock is Not Held Securely.* The workpiece moves during a crosscut angular cut. This affects the quality of the cut as well as the accuracy. When in- or out-ripping, the stock can flutter, causing accuracy and quality problems. Commercial hold-downs or featherboards can help eliminate the problem.

4. *Blade Problems.* A dull blade can usually affect quality and accuracy. A blade with too many teeth may cause burning in some rips and crosscuts, and a blade with too few teeth or too much hook can cause tear-out. A blade that flutters can make an uneven cut. Sometimes a saw collar cures this problem. A complete discussion of saw blades is presented in Chapter 3.

While working with the saw, you may discover other causes for a poor cut. The more you work with your saw, the more obvious any decrease or increase in quality will be. The ability to perceive these differences is almost as satisfying as a quality cut.

Minimizing Tear-Out Problems

Grain tear-out when sawing is an annoying problem. Tear-out may occur on the face or back of the work, or on the edge next to the fence. If the wrong blade or a dull blade is used, tear-out is sure to occur. Heeling will usually cause tear-out on the upper face of the work. There are other causes of tear-out: a rip blade or a blade with a great deal of hook; dull blades, which pound their way through the wood; and pulling the blade into the wood too fast. Moderate cutting speed will reduce tear-out.

One of the best ways of eliminating tear-out on the edge next to the fence is by installing an uncut fence or moving the present one over to an uncut area. The uncut fence supports the work everywhere except the kerf. This controls tear-out on the edge against the fence (Illus. 746).

Illus. 746. The fence and table have been moved. The blade now makes a fresh cut in the fence and table. This will control tear-out.

Tear-out through the top and bottom can be controlled by taping or scoring the stock. Generally, the cause of tear-out on the bottom face is a lack of support for the work; that is, the table has been cut away, and the wood fibres have no support. The lack of support makes it easy for the fibres to tear. Tape applied over the area to be cut holds the fibres in place. The blade cuts through the tape, and the tape holds the fibres down on both sides of the kerf.

Scoring the layout line with a utility knife will cause the wood fibres to break evenly at the line. A sharp utility knife must be used. The wood should be scored to a depth of $\frac{1}{16}''$ or greater. Scribe both faces and edges to completely control tear-out (Illus. 747).

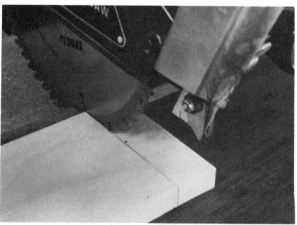

Illus. 747. Scribing or scoring the stock with a utility knife will control tear-out.

How Safe Is a Guard?

Unlike a table saw, one guard is always in place on the radial arm saw. The upper guard holds the splitter and is considered a necessary part of the saw for correct operation. The lower portion of the blade is exposed unless a lower guard is used. Anyone pushing work towards the blade could slip and come in contact with the side of the blade. It is very difficult to cut yourself when both the upper and lower guard are in position.

The guard is not perfect, however. Some operations cannot be done with the lower guard in place. Bevel crosscuts tend to catch the lower guard and make cutting difficult. During ripping, cutoffs can get caught between the blade and one side of the lower blade guard. This could cause a kickback. In many shops, the radial arm saw is not operated with the lower blade guard. Many operators feel that the lower guard is a hazard. Three common complaints about the lower guard are that they limit the operator's vision, are kickback hazards, and make it difficult to do accurate work. For extremely accurate work, the guard makes it difficult to trim a "hair" off the work.

When working with the arbor in the vertical position, use the shaper guard. The shaper guard limits contact with the shaper head or dado head. In fact, if you use an 8″ blade or smaller, use the shaper guard with a saw blade. This allows you to use it as a guard when performing grooving operations with a saw blade.

Use all guards whenever possible. When any of the guards cannot be used, ask yourself if there is another way to do the job. Review Chapter 4 periodically and make it part of your work philosophy. Approach every job cautiously and with the proper work philosophy. This will minimize your risk on the job.

Bringing the Saw to the Job The radial arm saw is usually the carpenter's saw of choice. For this reason, it must be portable. Rolling casters make the tool more portable (Illus. 748), but saws that have a removable stand are easier to maneuver on the job. The radial arm saw featured in Illus. 749 is clamped to the folding saw horses. When the clamps are removed, it is easily transported. The oak handles make it easy for 2 people to lift and carry it. Note: All locks and clamps should be secured before attempting to move any radial arm saw.

Larger radial arm saws are sometimes needed on the job. The 12″ saw shown in Illus. 750 was hauled into this savings and loan building. It was used to cut the oak beam above (Illus. 751). Unfortunately, one of the stops on the column was broken off during transport. This repair will put the saw out of commission for at least one day and require one day's labor for repair. A lesson to learn: Careful handling of the saw pays off.

When working on the job, be sure the electrical supply is compatible with your saw. If the motor does not have an overload protector (Illus. 752), extra amperage could burn out your motor. This is a very expensive mistake.

In the shop, portable stands make movement of the radial arm saw easier. Some of these stands have fold-out rollers on either end of the saw. Others use quick-disconnect or fold-up tables. All of these devices allow you to get closer to the job and make the radial arm saw more versatile.

Some people build their radial arm saw into a bench (Illus. 753 and 754). This makes an ideal table for long cutoffs and provides extra storage under the table. Some people add doors to keep out dust.

When a saw is built-in, it usually sits against the wall. This makes it difficult to get behind the saw for specialty setups. Stationary benches also make it difficult to get close to the saw when ripping. If you use your radial arm saw as a cutoff saw only, building-in the saw will not hamper use. Remember, though, you are using the saw for about 10% of its potential.

A saw that can be moved and has quick-disconnect tables for either end allows the greatest use. In most cases, it is best to keep the radial arm saw away from the wall. This allows you to work all the way around it. Making a work island with a radial arm saw on one side and a drill press, mortiser, or pedestal grinder on the opposite side makes better sense. Takeoff tables can be stored when not in use and the saw is available for all operations (Illus. 755–759).

Illus. 748. Rolling casters make the saw more portable. This allows you to move it easily from job to job.

Illus. 749. Note the oak handles attached to this saw. The saw can be carried easily to the next job. The oak handles are clamped to the sawhorses.

Illus. 750. This 12" radial arm saw was used on location in this savings and loan building. It was one of the last tools removed after the job was completed.

Illus. 751. This huge oak beam was cut with the radial arm saw in Illus. 750. Two cuts were required due to the thickness of the beam.

Illus. 752. An overload protector is important. It will protect the motor from burnout.

244

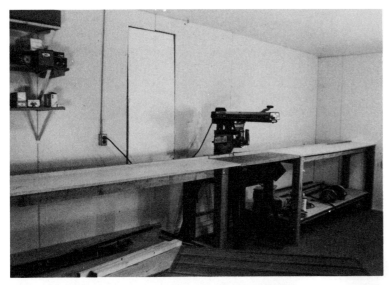

Illus. 753. These tables extend the radial arm saw and make crosscutting easier. Since the machine sits against the wall, the saw's capabilities are limited.

Illus. 754. The threaded rods pull the tables against the radial arm saw. This provides added rigidity.

Illus. 755. This radial arm saw is in a lumber supply shop (The Hardwood Connection). Note the built-ins for hardwood cutoffs and the shelves for "high and dry" veneer storage.

Illus. 756. This double-overarm saw can be moved anywhere in the shop. Note the small wheels for movement.

Illus. 757. This radial arm saw is in a school workshop. Note the curved plywood extension. This provides a table for the entire blade at the end of its stroke.

Illus. 758. Note how the softwood plywood splinters. It is a poor choice for a radial-arm-saw table. Hardwood plywood and particle board are much better.

Illus. 759. Note how the extension tables fold up when they are not needed. This provides easy access to the saw.

246

Dust Collection

Dust collection around your radial arm saw is very important. Sawdust is ejected out the side of the upper guard and in front of the blade. Unlike a table saw, there is no stand to trap sawdust. A blade that is smaller than standard on your saw also minimizes the effectiveness of the upper guard. This leaves more dust in the air and allows more chips to drop on your work.

A dusty shop is a hazard. It could have a very detrimental effect on your respiratory system. At the very least, protect your respiratory system with a dust mask or respirator (Illus. 760). It's a good idea to have a dust collection system.

Most radial-arm-saw manufacturers sell dust chutes that will collect the dust behind the blade and at the guard (Illus. 761, left). The connection at the guard is attached to a vacuum so that the chips clear correctly (Illus. 761, right). With this attachment, the operator can improvise some type of dust hood. Regardless of the design, it should contain the dust.

Illus. 760. At the very minimum, a dust mask should be used to protect you from wood dust.

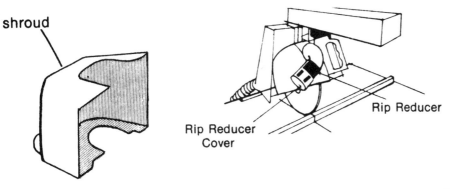

shroud

Rip Reducer Cover

Rip Reducer

Illus. 761. (left) A shroud can be located behind the radial-arm-saw column to collect dust. This controls dust and provides for vacuum collection. (right) When ripping, attach a connector to the upper guard to vacuum-collect the dust.

Buying a Radial Arm Saw

Buying a radial arm saw is similar to buying a car. When buying a new car, you know what options you want, and how much you are willing or able to pay. When buying a used car, your choice is limited to what is available. You may not get exactly what you want, but you save money.

The same is true of a radial arm saw. A new saw can be equipped to suit your needs. Everything is under warranty, and no one has abused the tool. A used radial arm saw, however, is like a used car. You must take the previous owner's word about the condition of the saw and how it was used. There is no warranty, and all repairs will be the responsibility of the owner.

A New Saw   When buying a new saw, remember that the saw should fit your needs. The following questions will help you determine the type of radial arm saw that's best for you.

1. What type of stock will I be cutting? What is the thickest, widest, and longest piece I will cut?

2. How large a table and blade will be needed to handle the stock I will be cutting?

3. Is the shop space large enough to accommodate the radial arm saw? A clear space 8 feet wide by 16 feet long is desirable. Smaller areas can be used, but stock size will be limited.

4. What type of electrical service is available? What voltage, amperage, and phase? For home use, a 110-volt circuit of 20 amps is needed. A 220-volt circuit of 10 amps will also work. A single-phase system is used exclusively in the home. A three-phase system is available for industrial use. It is used at voltages of 220 or higher.

5. Under what budget constraints am I working? What price range is desirable? Can I get a bank loan to buy a better quality saw? Could options be added later to keep the initial price lower?

6. Do I prefer a single-overarm (Illus. 762), double-overarm (Illus. 763), or sliding-overarm (Illus. 764) saw? Will it make any difference for the work I do? (See Chapter 1 for more details.)

7. Do I prefer an open or closed yoke (Illus. 765 and 766)? Will it make any difference for the work I do? (See Chapter 1 for more detail.)

8. What accessories are standard, and what other accessories will I need? Most radial arm saws come with an upper and lower guard. Accessories like a moulding head, dado head, shaper guard, router bracket, and commercial hold-downs will raise the initial cost of the saw.

9. What horsepower is needed to power the radial arm saw adequately? This will depend on the stock being cut and the blade diameter used on the saw. The discussion of horsepower in Chapter 1 will help you determine needed horsepower.

10. What type of elevating mechanism is used? Some elevating mechanisms are mounted on top of the column, while others are under the front table. Some people feel that the mechanism on the column is best, but it is more awkward to operate.

Illus. 762. This single-overarm-type saw may be your preference.

Illus. 763. A double-overarm-type radial arm saw may be your preference. Consult Chapter 1 for a discussion of its qualities.

Illus. 764. This sliding-overarm saw may best suit your needs. Consult Chapter 1 for a discussion of its qualities.

Illus. 765. An open-yoke radial arm saw has support at one end of the motor.

Illus. 766. A closed-yoke radial arm saw has support at both ends of the motor.

11. Where is the arm-turning clamp and stop located? Some are mounted on the column and others are mounted on the front of the arm. The ones on the column are more awkward, but some saw users feel the lock on the column is more positive. Others report no difference.

12. What materials were used to fabricate the column base and arm on the saw? How rigid are these materials? The column base should be cast. The more massive the casting (Illus. 767), the more rigid the machine. It should also be mounted securely to the base (Illus. 768). The arm itself should be rigid. Some are cast (Illus. 769), while others are made of rigid bar stock or assembled components (Illus. 770).

Illus. 767. This massive column casting makes the machine more rigid. The cast iron also dampens vibration.

Illus. 769. This rigid arm is made of cast iron. This arm will hold its tolerances and resist wear.

Illus. 770. This arm is made of bar stock and assembled components. The bar is usually hardened to resist wear.

Illus. 768. The column should be anchored securely to the base. This keeps the arm rigid when the carriage is completely extended.

13. What type of bearings are used between the column and carriage (Illus. 771)? They should be massive and ride in a machined track (Illus. 772) or on hardened rails.

14. Does the radial arm saw have provisions for wear? All contact points should be adjustable to maintain the saw's accuracy.

15. How do the fence, rear table, and table spacer clamp into position? Some clamping mechanisms work easier and are better.

The planning sheet (Fig. 5) will help you evaluate and compare various radial arm saws. Compare your needs to the features of the various radial arm saws. List price and cost of certain options may vary. Compare costs of various suppliers.

After determining which radial arm saw(s) will meet your needs, ask some experts for their opinion of the saw. People who use the saw will be candid with their remarks, and will be able to tell you about adjustment problems, ways to repair the saw, and general operating techniques. Cabinetmakers, carpenters, and woodworking teachers are usually willing to share their knowledge of woodworking equipment. This knowledge will help you make a wiser purchase.

The list price is a guideline of price. Not all sales agents hold that price, so it pays to shop. The last new radial arm saw I purchased was bought from a local agent. This agent was reputed to be a high bidder. He saved me about 10% off list and delivered the machine to my shop. This brings up shipping charges and sales tax. They can be hidden costs when comparing prices. Sales tax varies in cities and states. A 30-mile ride could mean 2% less sales tax. Picking up the radial arm saw at the factory or distribution center could also reduce the actual cost of the saw. Be ready to bargain; radial-arm-saw suppliers know an informed buyer. They may be willing to compromise to make the sale.

Illus. 771. These bearings ride in a machined cast-iron arm. This provides smooth carriage travel on the arm.

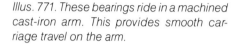

Illus. 772. These massive bearings ride on hardened rails. The rails can be replaced easily in the event of wear.

RADIAL ARM SAW

PLANNING SHEET

Desired saw
Brand _____ Model _____ Suggested list price _____
_____ Blade diameter   _____ Table size
_____ Widest crosscut   _____ Largest out-rip
_____ Weight   _____ Largest in-rip

Desired motor
_____ Volts   _____ Amps   _____ Phase   _____ Horsepower   _____ 24 V. switch

Design features
Arm type (check one)
_____ Single overarm   _____ Double overarm   _____ Sliding overarm

Yoke type (check one)
_____ Open yoke   _____ Closed yoke

Arm fabrication (check one)
_____ Cast   _____ Bar stock   _____ Assembled

Locks and clamps (rate saw + √ −)
_____ Positive   _____ Fast-acting   _____ Easily adjusted

Control location (check one)
_____ Mechanisms on front of saw   _____ Mechanisms on column

Fence and table board clamps (check one)
_____ Clamp at front of saw   _____ Clamp at back of saw

   Rate clamps (+ √ −)
   _____ Positive   _____ Fast-acting   _____ Easy to use

Options included or available (list)
                    Option   Cost
_____   _____
_____   _____
_____   _____
_____   _____

Parts availability
Distributor who can order parts
Name _____ Address _____ Phone _____
Regional manufacturer's warehouse where parts are available
Name _____ Address _____ Phone _____

List price _____ + Options _____
Other costs _____ + Sales tax _____ =

TOTAL COST _____

Fig. 5. This planning sheet will help you decide what type of radial arm saw you need for your work. Photocopy it and use it as a work sheet.

A Used Saw The cost of a new saw may be beyond your means. In this case, a used radial arm saw may be more appealing. Though the planning sheet will still help you focus in on your needs, the used radial-arm-saw evaluation sheet (Fig. 6) can help you determine the value of any radial arm saw you consider buying. It will help you compare 2 or more used radial arm saws when shopping.

The brand and age of the saw are important indicators of value. Some radial arm saws have higher resale value because of the manufacturer's reputation or the features of the saw. The fact that parts are still available for the radial arm saw is important too. It is very costly and sometimes impossible to have parts custom-made for a used radial arm saw. The part could cost more than the saw is worth.

Listing accessories helps determine value. A saw that has extra blades, a dado head, and a moulding head may be worth more than a basic table saw. The quality of the accessories must be medium to high, or they are nothing more than scrap metal. Be sure the accessories have value before you list them.

Electrical information is also important. Some 110-volt and 220-volt systems are interchangeable; that is, they may be used on either system by changing a couple of wires on the motor. A three-phase motor is not interchangeable. This means a three-phase motor cannot run on a one-phase current. Make sure you can use the saw before you buy it.

Features or options, such as a dust collector or extension tables, can also add to the value of the saw. Be sure to list all options, features, and accessories offered for sale with the radial arm saw. Remember, these things only have value if you can use them or resell them.

Comparing today's list price with the seller's asking price helps determine value. If the saw is 10 years old and the price difference is small, the value may be questionable. Consider this information carefully before you buy.

The general condition of the saw is obvious. Look over the table and check the column and other castings for cracks. See if there is any evidence of repair work on the saw. Parts of a different color or a part with no rust on a rusty saw suggests some repair work has been done. Check for slop in the carriage and column. Make sure there are provisions for adjustment. Look at the column to see if there are any saw kerfs in it. Sometimes the blade will contact the column when it is in the horizontal position.

If the saw is 5 to 10 years old and the owner still has the manual, the saw has probably been well-maintained. The manual should show some signs of wear. Pencil marks circling replacement parts or oily thumb prints indicate the manual was used on the job. If the radial arm saw needs repair, estimate the cost of the repair. Make sure the seller's price reflects the repair, and that replacement parts are available.

When buying a used table saw, decide on a fair price before making the seller an offer. Some woodworkers refuse to pay more than 60% of retail price for any used woodworking tools regardless of age or condition. Their rationale is that you can buy so much more with the extra 40% that the used tool is not worth the gamble. The 60% rule does not fit all sales, but it is another guideline. Others feel older radial arm saws are more valuable because they were built much better.

When shopping for a used radial arm saw, there are many places to look. Suppliers of new radial arm saws often take used saws as trade-ins. These saws are usually reconditioned and sold. Sometimes a warranty is included. Used saws from a supply house are usually more expensive and in better repair.

The auction advertisements often have radial arm saws. An estate auction or a woodworking shop auction might have a radial arm saw that fits your needs. Be careful when buying at an auction. Sometimes the excitement of the auction will cause the bidding to reach a price close to that of a new saw. Decide on your top bid before the auction begins and stick with it. Auction-bought tools are not always inspected carefully before purchase. The radial arm saw you thought was a bargain may turn out to be a poor investment.

The want ads in tabloids and newspapers often have radial arm saws for sale. Price and quality will vary with each ad. Inspect and compare the merchandise to determine value.

It is also possible to advertise for a radial arm saw in the "wanted to buy" section of the want ads. A person who wishes to sell a radial arm saw will find it easier to call you than place an ad. This gives you a better bargaining position because the seller does not have other buyers coming to inspect the saw. The seller has only one offer—yours.

When I wrote this book, I bought one new and three used radial arm saws. I used an ad for the used saws. This ad caused the phone to ring off the hook. There were 45 calls; my wife made me cancel the ad. I used my evaluation sheets to determine value, and bought what I thought were the best saws. They ranged from 15% to 40% of new list price. The one I purchased for 15% needed work (Illus. 773). I began by cleaning the saw. I got a manual and ordered parts. The saw had to be readjusted and tightened up (Illus. 774–783). This took approximately 16 hours. The saw works well now, and I've taken it to a few jobs.

Some of the things I learned about buying used radial arm saws are listed here.

USED RADIAL-ARM-SAW EVALUATION SHEET

Name of seller _____

Address _____

Phone number _____

GENERAL INFORMATION

Table saw brand _____

Model number _____   Year manufactured _____

Arm type _____

Company still makes saw: Yes _____   No _____

Repair parts available: Yes _____   No _____

Owner's manual included: Yes _____   No _____

Accepts standard-sized blades and accessories: Yes _____   No _____

Volts _____   Amps _____   Phase _____   Horsepower _____

Length of carriage stroke _____   Maximum blade diameter _____

GENERAL CONDITIONS CHECK-OFF

Tables	Poor __	Fair __	Good __
Clamping and locking mechanisms on column and carriage (work easily, lock positively)	Poor __	Fair __	Good __
Condition of carriage tracking mechanism and bearings (wear evident; slop or deflection)	Poor __	Fair __	Good __
Blade elevation and lowering mechanism (smooth and positive)	Poor __	Fair __	Good __
Clamping device for table boards (straight, undamaged, works smoothly)	Poor __	Fair __	Good __

Description of conditions and estimated cost of repairs: _____

_____

_____

_____

Options, features, accessories includes (list and estimate value): _____

_____

_____

_____

Price information

Cost of same radial arm saw, brand new _____ + sales tax _____ = _____

Asking price of seller _____ + cost of repair parts _____ = _____

Price difference = _____

Value rating (circle one)

Considering general saw condition, value of options, features, accessories, and machine qualities, I would rate the value of this saw:

10	9	8	7	6	5	4	3	2	1
high				moderate					low

Fig. 6. This used radial-arm-saw evaluation sheet will help you evaluate any used machine. Photocopy it several times and bring a copy with you every time you look at a used radial arm saw.

1. Used radial arm saws are always out of adjustment.

2. It will take a minimum of 8 hours to get the used (and maybe new) radial arm saw into good working order. Hurrying will only produce poor results.

3. Repair parts are expensive. A threaded carriage knob (Illus. 784) may cost $4. A stock hardware item will do the job and cost only 45¢. A particle board table, which is about ¼ of a sheet, will cost more than a full sheet of particle board. Make sure you know what repair parts cost before running up a large bill.

4. It is difficult to set up the radial arm saw correctly without an owner's manual. This is one item you cannot afford to be without.

5. It pays to double-check all adjustments before you begin using your saw. Many adjustments are dependent on other adjustments being made correctly.

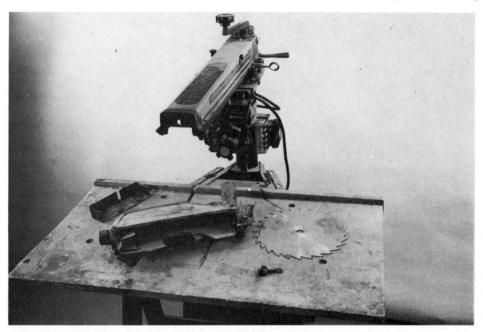

Illus. 773. (above) This saw was purchased for about 15 percent of list price. As you can see, it needed work. (below) Note that the fence had been nailed to the front table. There was no rear table or table spacer.

Illus. 775. The table brackets must be on the same plane. The saw arbor is used to check this.

256

Illus. 776. The bearings were cleaned and loosened with a commercial cleaner.

Illus. 777. After the table was installed, it was checked with a straightedge. The table should not droop or crown.

Illus. 778. The table was adjusted so that it was square with the carriage stroke. This is the easiest way to make this adjustment.

Illus. 779. The blade is not square with the new table, so adjustment is needed.

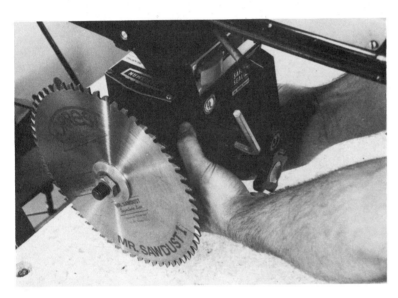

Illus. 780. The motor is turned and adjusted so that the blade is perpendicular to the table. Using a blade with very little hook will help keep the saw in adjustment.

Illus. 781. A check for heeling suggests that the blade is not travelling parallel to the carriage.

Illus. 782. The carriage is adjusted to eliminate the heeling condition.

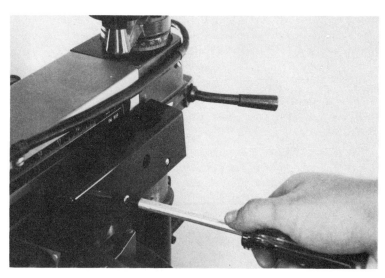

Illus. 783. The carriage covers are replaced, and the machine is ready to cut. Always check your adjustments a second time to be sure they are correct.

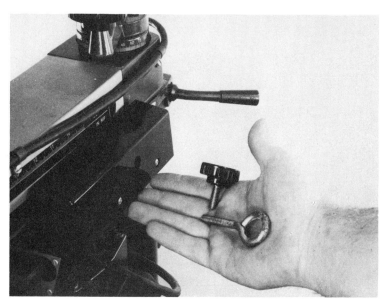

Illus. 784. This repair part cost roughly nine times as much as the standard hardware item. Sometimes it is best to gather parts for your saw in local shops.

Radial Arm Saws in the Future

With the development of various motorized mitre boxes and other crosscutting saws, it seems that today's radial-arm-saw buyer will want a very accurate machine. People who use the radial arm saw only for crosscutting will probably buy a different type of saw. The person who buys a radial arm saw will expect it to rip, mitre, shape, and crosscut. This requires a solid, well-maintained, accurate machine. Fortunately, some of these machines already exist.

Today, some saws have incorporated electronic controls (Illus. 785). These saws have electronic accuracy built-in, and can be programmed to a previous setup with little effort (Illus. 786). This should make duplicate parts easy to produce.

Many new fences, hold-downs (Illus. 787), guards (Illus. 788), and cutters (Illus. 789) have also been introduced into the market place. These devices make using the radial arm saw safer, and/or improve the quality of your work.

The newest saws on the market are both portable radial arm saws. The one manufactured by INCA has a steel bar as an overarm (Illus. 790–797). The table turns on this saw. The arm remains stationary. For bevel crosscuts, the bar is turned. The entire motor is turned 90° for in-ripping or out-ripping. This machine is capable of a 24″ crosscut with the longer overarm.

The Black and Decker machine has an arm that folds down for travel (Illus. 798). This makes the machine far easier to carry to the job (Illus. 799). Other features are essentially the same as the rest of the DeWalt line.

The guard shown in Illus. 788 is being produced in late 1985 by Mr. Sawdust™ Products. It is an all-metal guard designed for shaping, and dadoing or sawing with cutters 8″ in diameter or smaller. When used for any operation, the shoes on the guard act as hold-downs and keep the stock from lifting.

The twisted shaper cutters pictured in Illus. 802 are also being marketed by Mr. Sawdust™ Products. The twist in the 3/16″ steel gives it the rigidity needed for shaping. These cutters are made of tool steel, so they are only suited for use in solid stock. The tool steel may be honed on the flat side to resharpen them after use. The angular sides should not be honed. The cutters have been machined to plus or minus .005 inch for balanced cutting Any metal removal on the clearance edges could affect the balance.

Illus. 785. This radial arm saw has electronic controls. The blade height can be programmed. The height can be returned exactly to a previous setting.

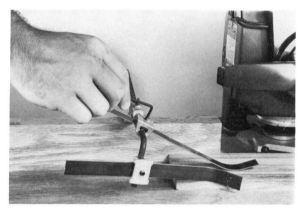

Illus. 786. The digital display shows blade elevation to .005″ and bevel and mitre angles to ½ degree.

Illus. 787. These commercial hold-downs are now available to all woodworkers. They make most jobs safer and more efficient.

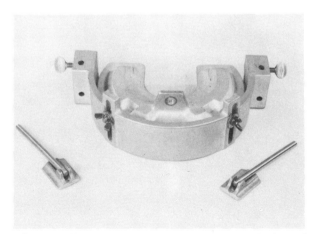

Illus. 788. This all-metal guard for shaping and horizontal blade work is now in production for most radial arm saws. This guard offers far more protection than a plastic guard.

Illus. 789. These cutters are being marketed for shaping on the table saw or radial arm saw. The cutters cannot be ejected since they are one solid piece.

Illus. 790. The INCA saw has a base and frame made of square tubing.

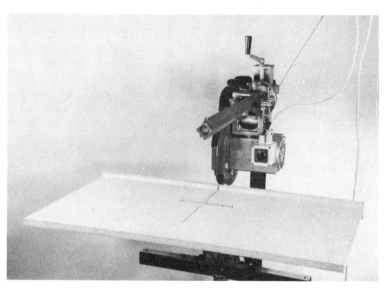

Illus. 791. The short overarm has been installed here. A wider crosscut can be made with the long overarm.

Illus. 792. The table is turned for angular cuts. The overarm remains stationary.

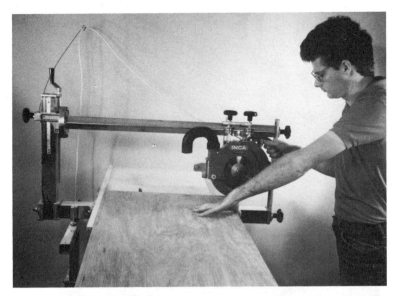

Illus. 793. The long overarm allows a cross-cut of over 24". Note that the front support bar is attached to the arm for rigidity.

Illus. 794. The lower guard release is depressed to allow the lower guard to lift over the fence and work.

Illus. 795. The motor unit is turned 90° on the overarm for ripping. When it is replaced, the lower guard release is depressed. This allows the work to be fed under the lower guard.

Illus. 796. The saw is ready for ripping. Note that the splitter has been positioned.

Illus. 797. A special router mount can also be used with the radial arm saw.

Illus. 798. The arm on this radial arm saw folds down for travel.

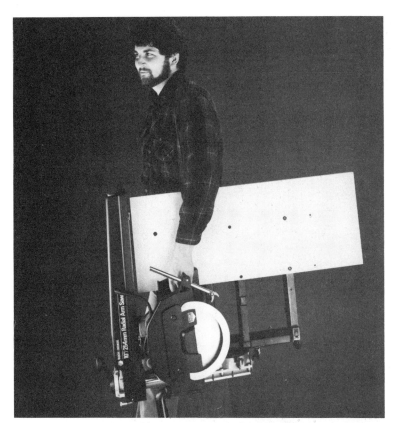

Illus. 799. The folding arm makes the radial arm easier to carry and transport.

Illus. 800. This guard is an effective aid while you shape on the radial arm saw.

Illus. 801. The shoes on this guard control and hold stock down on the table.

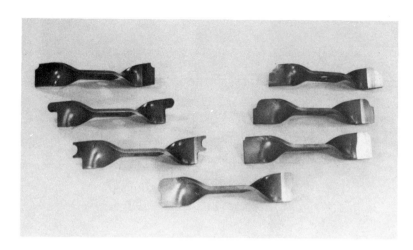

Illus. 802. These twisted shaper cutters are marketed by Mr. Sawdust products. They are machined carefully to hold their tolerances.

8

How to Build Radial-Arm-Saw Accessories and Items for Your Home

The projects in this chapter can be divided into 2 groups. The first group is jigs or accessories. These are devices you can make for your radial arm saw. The second group consists of projects for general use. These projects make nice gifts or accessories for your home or shop. They have been designed to help you practice the techniques presented in this book.

This project chapter is last for good reason. You must read, understand, and digest the material in the first 7 chapters before you begin building projects. If you begin a project without full understanding of radial-arm-saw operations, you could waste material or incur an injury. Plan projects carefully. Read the related sections in the book before beginning, and review the appropriate section before you begin any operation.

Tips for Building Projects

When building a project, consider the following tips. These tips will help you do a better job with fewer mistakes.

1. Study the plans carefully. Check the dimensions or scale on the plan to be sure all parts will be cut and machined correctly. Make allowances for joints or trimming on all parts. Remember, some jigs are dimensioned for a particular saw. These dimensions may have to be changed to fit your saw.

2. Develop auxiliary sketches when needed. When plans are modified or an assembly is complex, develop an auxiliary sketch. Take this sketch to the radial arm saw. It will help you determine how parts must be cut. Extra sketches will make radial-arm setups quicker and more accurate.

3. Develop a bill of materials. A bill of materials is a list of all parts needed to build the project. The list includes the part's dimensions (thickness, width, and length). The bill of materials makes stock selection easier. It also helps set stops on the radial-arm saw when cutting parts to length.

4. Write a plan of procedure. The plan of procedure is a list of steps one should follow to build the project. The plan is an orderly list or series of events. For example, the drawer opening would be made before the drawer front was cut to exact size. It is not considered good practice to make the drawer and then build the opening. It is also poor practice to cut drawer parts to exact size before the opening is made.

5. Think before making any cuts. Plan your cutting to reduce the chance of error. When cutting parts, cut the longest parts first. Any parts cut too short can then be used for shorter parts on the bill of materials.

Before making a cut in the work, test the setup in a scrap. Be sure it is correct before beginning. Mark complex cuts: Drawers and cabinets have a right- and left-hand side. The sides are not the same. They are mirror images of each other. Cut them carefully.

When several operations are being performed on a number of parts, mark the control edge. The control edge is the edge on the parts that always rides against (or away from) the fence. These marks will minimize the chance of reversing the parts after a few operations have been performed. The mark is important on parts such as moulding, picture frame parts, and cabinet sides.

6. Check the fit of all parts before assembly. Fit the parts together dry before gluing. Tight or loose fits can cause problems. A tight fit will be impossible to assemble when

267

glue is applied. Glue will cause both parts to swell and require that they be forced together. Sometimes the glue sets before the parts set. This stops the entire assembly.

A loose fit will mean a weak glue joint. It can also cause alignment problems since the mating parts can shift. Remember, it is easier to make minor adjustments and trim or shim when there is no glue on the parts.

7. *Plan ahead for finishing.* Sand all internal surfaces before assembling a box or cabinet. These surfaces may be difficult or impossible to sand after assembly. It may also be easier to stain and finish these surfaces before assembly.

Watch for glue smears on the wood. They can make your stain and finish appear blemished. Circle glue smears with chalk when you notice them. This will help you eliminate them during surface preparation. Scrape or sand away these smears before applying stain or finish.

8. *Keep your radial arm saw well-maintained.* A poorly maintained radial arm saw seldom cuts accurately. It is difficult to get good cuts from a saw that is not maintained correctly. It is well worth the extra time involved to readjust a radial arm saw. Using a saw that is out of alignment can damage the blade and will yield poor work.

Radial-Arm-Saw Devices

Most jigs designed to be used on a radial arm saw are controlled by the table (Illus. 803) or the fence (Illus. 804–806) by moving the position of the arm, carriage, or jig. When making a jig for your radial-arm saw, select stock carefully. Most sheet stock resists warping, swelling, and wear. Sheet stock is a good material for jig construction. Make the cleats on your radial arm saw jigs out of a dense hardwood. This will keep the control surfaces from wearing and will prevent crushing of the cleat when clamped between the table boards.

Always consider safety when designing a jig for the radial-arm saw. Many times the saw owner builds the jig carelessly because it is regarded as a means to an end rather than an end itself. A well-made jig will be an accurate device that can be used for many different operations. A poorly made jig may be dangerous, yield poor results, and be used only once.

A safe jig is planned carefully. It is built as an accessory to the radial-arm saw. It fits correctly and can be mounted or installed easily. When building jigs for your radial arm saw, ask yourself, "What if?" Be sure you know the blade's path and how you can keep clear of the path. Vision is also important. You have to be able to see the work and the blade. Clear plastic can be used as a barrier between you and the work or blade. Clear plastic limits personal contact but does not limit vision.

Any jig you build can probably be made safer, but careful planning will help you begin with a safe, accurate jig. Follow the basic safety rules in Chapter 4 when operating any jig on the radial-arm saw.

Illus. 803. The spindle-sanding jig is controlled by the table. Clamps hold it securely in position. Movement of the arm or carriage locates the spindle.

Illus. 804. This compound mitre jig is clamped between the table boards in place of the fence. A cleat extends down off the end of the jig. It fits in the opening made when the fence is removed.

Illus. 805. Note the cleat on this commercial mitre jig. It also clamps in the opening made when the fence is removed. This jig must be aligned carefully with the blade. Contact between the blade and jig could cause damage.

Illus. 806. This tapering jig is controlled by both the fence and table. It rides on the table and against the fence.

Building Basic Jigs and Accessories

Many jigs and fixtures were presented in the first 7 chapters. You may wish to make some of them for your radial arm saw. Some of the first items you should make for your radial arm saw include push sticks, push blocks, featherboards, auxiliary front tables, and extra fences.

Push sticks and push blocks are presented in Chapter 2. This is because they should be made as soon as you begin working with your saw. Use a scrolling attachment to cut out some of the push sticks. Then use the spindle-sanding attachment to smooth the edges (Illus. 807). Rout the edges to round them over (Illus. 808). A round edge is not as likely to cut you in the event of a kickback. Drill a hole in them so that they can be hung near the saw. Make some hooks that can be mounted on the radial arm saw (Illus. 809). These hooks assure that a push stick will be where it is needed at all times.

Study the procedure to make a featherboard (Illus. 810) in Chapter 2. A featherboard helps control stock when

Illus. 807. Use the spindle-sanding attachment to smooth the edges of a push stick. Take light cuts and keep the work moving. This will make the abrasives last longer.

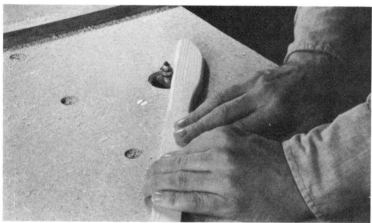

Illus. 808. Rout a radius on your push-stick handles. This makes them safer and more comfortable. A round edge is not as likely to cut you in the event of a kickback.

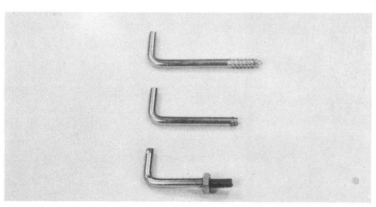

Illus. 809. Hooks like these can be used to hang push sticks on the radial arm saw. Wood screw threads can be used in a wooden base. For a metal base, cut the wood screw threads off and replace them with machine screw threads. Anchor them to the saw with two nuts, or thread the base and use one nut.

Illus. 810. The featherboards are being used to help control stock. They keep the stock positioned correctly. Make several of these and keep them ready for special setups.

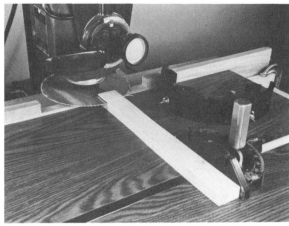

Illus. 812. This laminated auxiliary table is quite thick. It has been dadoed to accommodate a mitre gauge. This allows greater control of the work in some operations.

Illus. 813. Laminated surfaces are best cut with the laminated face closest to the table. Refer to Chapter 6 for more information on cutting laminates.

ripping or shaping on the radial arm saw. Make several while the saw is set up. Keep them handy for future use.

Auxiliary front tables are also an important accessory. Extra front tables can be made of sheet stock. They will protect the actual radial-arm-saw table from deterioration. In addition to sheet stock tables, you may wish to have a couple of laminated tables (Illus. 811 and 812). Laminated tables are usually special-purpose types. They can be used for ripping or shaping or other specialty operations. The laminated surfaces resist wear and provide a very smooth work surface. Review the section on cutting plastic laminates (page 175) before you make a laminated auxiliary table (Illus. 813).

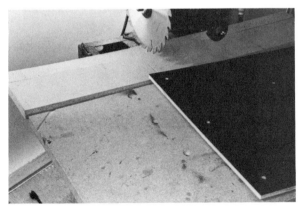

Illus. 811. This laminated auxiliary table can be used for ripping operations. The laminated surface allows the work to glide over it.

A typical laminated auxiliary table is presented in Illus. 814. Use the scale to determine working dimensions. The table is usually laminated first, then machined. Carbide saw blades, router bits, and dado heads must be used when working with laminated surfaces. Cut the mitre slot to accommodate the mitre gauge from your table saw, shaper, or other machine. The fences on this table were used with a planing head. It was designed for cutting raised panels. (See Illus. 696–700.)

You can modify this laminated auxiliary table to suit any specific purpose. Make a few sketches before you begin. Work carefully and accurately. Avoid stock that is warped. If you begin with a poor piece of stock, the jig cannot be any better. Be sure to test-cut the dado on scrap before making the mitre slot dado (Illus. 815).

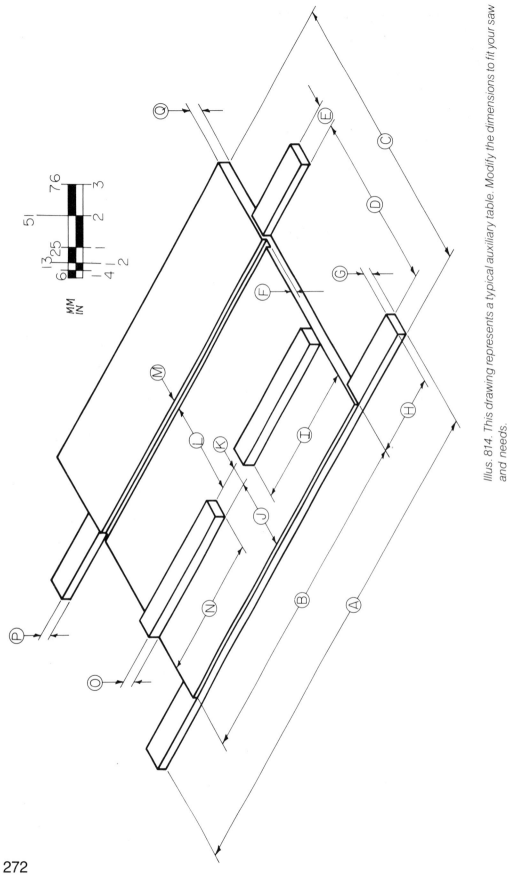

272

Illus. 814. This drawing represents a typical auxiliary table. Modify the dimensions to fit your saw and needs.

Illus. 815. Make a test dado in scrap before cutting the mitre-slot dado. This dado should be snug. A loose-fitting mitre dado reduces the jig's accuracy.

Extra fences are also an important thing to have on hand. Some fences are just a simple piece of wood that clamps between the table boards (Illus. 816), while others serve a special function. The fence in Illus. 817 is used for shaping or dadoing when the arbor is in the vertical position. Note that a small amount of fence is above the table in the cutout area. This allows control of the work along the entire length of the fence. Note also the metal tracks. These provide for the use of commercial hold-downs when needed.

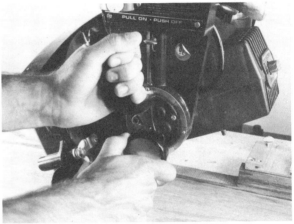

Illus. 817. This fence is used for shaping and dadoing operations. A small amount of fence is above the table in the cutout area. This allows control of the work along the entire length of the fence.

The fence may also be used to hold small pieces when crosscutting (Illus. 818). This fence and handle combination allow you to keep your hand clear of the blade yet maintain control of the workpiece. This makes crosscutting of small parts much safer.

The most common fence used on the radial arm saw is ¾" thick and wide enough to be about ¾ to 1" above the front table. Most new radial arm saws come equipped with a particle board fence. Some woodworkers prefer a fence of solid stock, while others have no preference. After the saw has been used for a while, either fence will be in a deteriorated state.

Rip several extra fences so that they will be available when they are needed. The shaping fence is somewhat thicker than the regular fence. This allows the top edge to be bevelled for the commercial hold-down tracks. The shaper fence must be dadoed away to accommodate the shaper or dado head and guard. If a thicker fence cannot

Illus. 816. The typical fence is made of particle board or solid stock. It clamps between the table boards.

be clamped between the table boards, the bottom edge of the fence may be rabbeted to the thickness of a normal fence.

If you plan to make a hold-down type of fence (Illus. 819), study the drawing carefully (Illus. 820). Modify the dimensions (if necessary) to fit your saw. Plan your operations in sequence so that the fence can be made safely and easily. Begin by cutting the fence to its rectangular shape. Lay out the arc, but do not cut it yet. Now cut the handle to its rectangular shape and lay out the curves. Do not cut these curves either.

Set up the dado head to cut the grooves in the fence. Mark the position of the grooves on the end of the fence (Illus. 821). This will make setup much easier and faster. After all the grooves are cut (Illus. 822), the piece can be set aside for later scroll work. While the dado head is set up, cut the protrusion on the handle. This is done in the crosscut mode. Note that this protrusion is not centered. This means that 2 separate height adjustments must be made when dadoing. The offset protrusion makes the hold-down device more versatile. By using different grooves in the fence and by turning the handle over, just about any stock thickness can be accommodated. If the

protrusion were in the middle of the handle, the jig would not be as versatile.

Set up the scrolling attachment or use a sabre saw to cut the irregular shapes on the fence and handle. Leave the layout line so that it can be sanded away using the disc- or spindle-sanding attachment (Illus. 823). After the fence and handle are smooth, you may wish to rout the handle with a roundover bit (Illus. 824). This will make it more comfortable to use.

Clamp the fence between the table boards, being careful to line it up in relation to the blade and motor. The high side of the fence will not allow the motor to clear. Clamp the fence securely. This will prevent the fence from lifting as you exert force on the hold-down handle.

An industrial clamp may be affixed to a lower fence to achieve the same holding action (Illus. 825). This device is simply attached to the fence with hexhead sheet-metal screws (Illus. 826). The drawback to this type of holding fence is that it must be adjusted for stock thickness (Illus. 827). If all stock is the same thickness (as in production work), this is not a problem. The fence-and-handle approach might be better in a nonproduction or job shop.

Illus. 818. This fence-and-handle combination make crosscutting safer because your hand is clear of the blade when cutting smaller pieces.

Illus. 819. This hold-down-type fence uses a handle that engages with the grooves in the fence to hold work securely while crosscutting. It also allows your hands to remain clear of the blade.

274

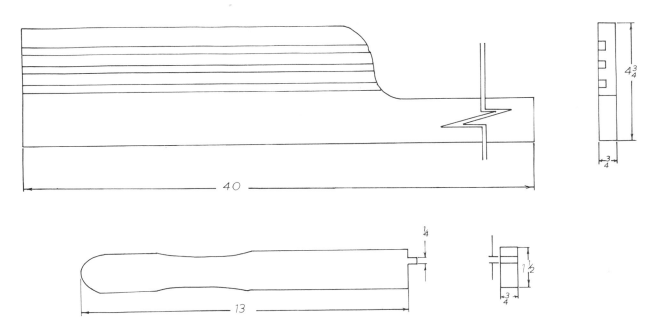

Illus. 820. Study the drawing carefully before making the fence and handle. Note that the protrusion on the handle is not centered.

Illus. 821. Mark the grooves on the end of the fence before you begin. This will make setup much easier.

Illus. 822. After cutting the grooves, set the piece aside for scrolling. Note the layout line pencilled on the work.

Illus. 823. Sand the handle using the spindle- or disc-sanding attachment as needed. Sand until the layout line is removed.

Illus. 824. Use a roundover bit to rout the handle. The handle will feel more comfortable in your hand.

Illus. 825. This industrial snap clamp holds stock securely while crosscutting. Your hand does not need to be near the blade.

Illus. 826. The snap clamp is affixed to the fence with hex sheet-metal screws. Use an awl and a push drill to make pilot holes for the screws.

Illus. 827. The snap clamp must be adjusted for every change in stock thickness. This may be considered a drawback in the job shop.

When doing production crosscutting, remember to allow for sawdust accumulation. A groove cut in the fence (Illus. 828) at the table level will keep the sawdust from affecting accuracy. The groove will have to be cleaned periodically, but not as frequently as a saw with a solid fence.

An arm stop or clamp is another useful accessory for your radial arm saw. The stop bolts to the arm to control the travel of the carriage (Illus. 829). This allows you to cut blind dadoes accurately. It also controls the stroke on repetitive cuts. By limiting the stroke, you always know where the blade will be. This can minimize the chance of error or accident.

Select 2 pieces of hardwood about 1½″ thick and about 4″ wider than the arm at its widest point. Clamp the 2 pieces together and drill 2 holes to accommodate the hex-head clamping bolts. Drive T-type nuts through the holes on one of the pieces with a hammer. Select bolts of the appropriate length and mount the stop or clamp on the arm. Tighten it securely at the desired setting.

When crosscutting, a length gauge or stop can frequently be useful (Illus. 830). Fine adjustments can be made by turning the flathead machine screw in or out. Tightening the hex nut against the T-shaped nut locks the adjustment (Illus. 831). Select a piece of stock about 1″ square and 10″ long.

Set up the radial arm saw for drilling, and drill a hole in the middle of one end (Illus. 831). The hole should be about 1½″ deep and large enough to accommodate the T-shaped nut (Illus. 832). Drive the T-shaped nut into the wood with a hammer. Thread the machine screw through the hex nut and into the T-shaped nut (Illus. 833). The length gauge is ready to use.

If you've ever been annoyed by the small chuck keys furnished with an electric drill, you may want to leave the radial arm saw set up for drilling. Bore a hole in a piece similar to the one you used for the length gauge (Illus. 834). The bit should be the same diameter as the shaft on the chuck key. Drill the hole as deep as the shaft is long (Illus. 835). Now epoxy the chuck key into the piece of wood and allow it to cure well.

The wooden handle may then be sanded or carved to a shape that is comfortable in your hand (Illus. 836). Use the disc- or spindle-sanding attachments on your saw to help shape the handle. You may even wish to carve your initials in the handle. This tool is quite useful. Much more torque can be gained with the handle, and the key is not as easy to lose.

If your radial arm saw is moved frequently, you may wish to make a set of handles similar to the ones on the saw in Illus. 837. Select a species of wood that is stiff so that it will hold the weight. Quarter-sawn stock would be the best for this handle. Use the drawing (Illus. 838) to help you make a pattern for the handles. Cut and shape the handles. Use a roundover bit in a router to break all sharp corners. Be sure the overall length of the pieces is long enough to clear the table on both ends. This makes the handles less cumbersome to use. I have found that clamping the handles to a pair of sawhorses gives the saw excellent support.

Illus. 828. The groove cut in this fence along the table will keep sawdust from interfering with the accuracy of your crosscuts.

Illus. 829. This arm stop bolts to the arm to control the stroke of the carriage. It is useful for blind dadoes and repetitive cuts.

Illus. 830. A length gauge like this one can be useful for crosscutting. The screw can be moved in and out for fine adjustment.

Illus. 831. Use the drilling attachment to drill a hole in the end of the length gauge. The hole should be large enough to accommodate the T-shaped nut.

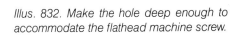
Illus. 832. Make the hole deep enough to accommodate the flathead machine screw.

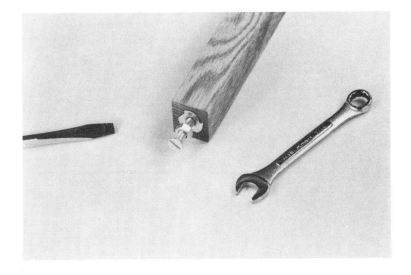

Illus. 833. Drive the T-shaped nut into the block of wood with a hammer. The screw is threaded through the hex nut and into the T-shaped nut.

Illus. 834. The same drilling attachment can be used for making a handle for your chuck key.

Illus. 835. Drill the hole the same diameter as the shank on the chuck key and as deep as the shank is long.

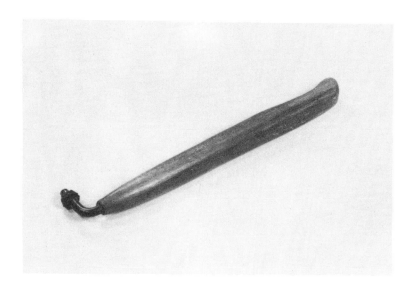

Illus. 836. Shape the handle so that it is comfortable in your hand. You can carve your initials in the handle.

Illus. 837. The handles attached to this saw make it easier to transport and allow it to be clamped to a pair of sawhorses.

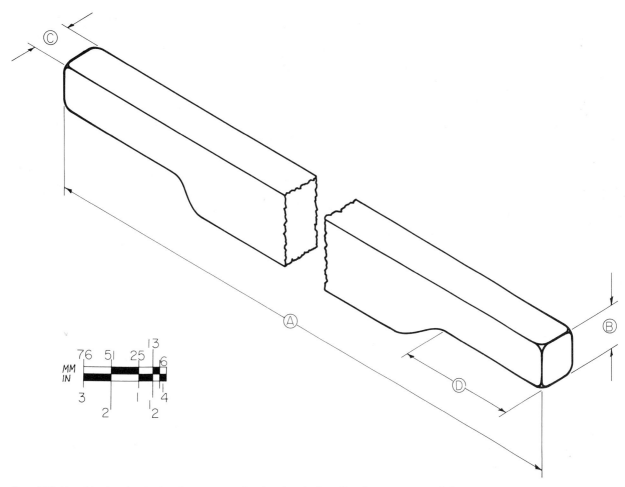

Illus. 838. Use this drawing to develop a pattern for shaping the handles. Be sure to rout all sharp corners.

Sanding Jigs

The radial arm saw lends itself to the use of several sanding jigs. In this section, plans for a disc, spindle- and circle-sanding jig will be presented. Constructing these jigs will increase the versatility of your radial-arm saw.

Disc-Sanding Jig Two different sanding jigs were presented in this book. One has a particle board top (Illus. 839), while the other has a laminated top (Illus. 840). The chief difference is that the laminated table houses the arbor and arbor nut, and it also has a larger table. The housed nut enables you to use the entire sanding disc. This can be helpful when sanding larger parts. The base on each jig is essentially the same. Study the drawing (Illus. 841) to see how the parts fit together. Adjust dimensions to suit your top and saw.

Cut the top to size and then notch it for the disc and arbor nut. Use a sabre saw (Illus. 842) or other device to notch the top. After the top is notched, adjust its fit relative to the base. Mark it, but do not attach it (Illus. 843). It must be dadoed to accommodate the mitre gauge (Illus. 844). If you plan on doing any pattern-sanding, install a T-shaped nut in the underside of the top. This will accommodate the pin for pattern-sanding (Illus. 845). The top may now be attached to the base. Use wood screws for this purpose (Illus. 846). Watch the screw placement. Make sure that the screws do not come up into the mitre slot.

281

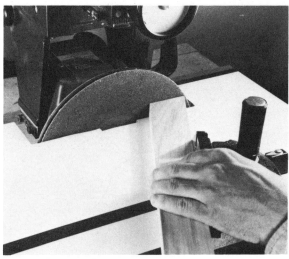

Illus. 839. The top on this disc-sanding jig is made of particle board. Note that the arbor nut and arbor are exposed.

Illus. 840. The laminated top on this sanding jig is larger, and it houses the arbor and arbor nut. This allows better use of the sanding disc.

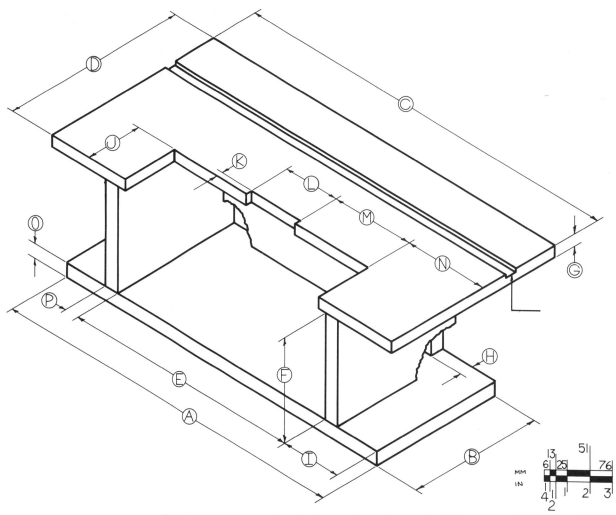

Illus. 841. Use this drawing to help you plan a disc-sanding jig for your radial arm saw. Adjust the dimensions as needed.

282

Illus. 842. The sabre saw under the front table was used to cut the notch in the top.

Illus. 843. Adjust the position of the top in relation to the base. Mark it, but do not attach it.

Illus. 844. Dado the top to accommodate a mitre gauge. Use a scrap to test the fit before cutting the top.

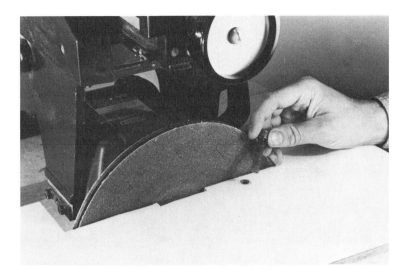

Illus. 845. If you plan to use a pin for pattern sanding, put a T-shaped nut in the underside of the top.

Illus. 846. Attach the top to the base with wood screws. Do not drive the wood screws up into the mitre slot.

Spindle-Sanding Jig A spindle-sanding jig has no mitre slot. This is because it is used to sand inside curves and other irregular shapes. Some spindle-sanding jigs have laminated tops (Illus. 847), while others have a sheet-stock top (Illus. 848). Study the drawing (Illus. 849) and modify the dimensions if desired. The spindle hole in the center of the jig should be large enough to accommodate the largest spindle. When smaller spindles are used, the jig can be moved close to the spindle. If you have a variety of spindle diameters, you may wish to make two jigs: one with a medium-sized hole and one with a larger hole. The two jigs would accommodate all spindles with a better fit. If you plan to spindle-sand with the spindle tilted, you will have to make an elliptical hole in the jig (Illus. 850).

After the hole has been cut in the top, the jig may be assembled with glue and screws. The jig is now ready to clamp to the front table of your saw for sanding.

Circle-Sanding Jig The circle-sanding jig is a specialty jig (Illus. 851). This jig can be used on a radial arm saw, band saw, or table saw. It is designed for sanding stock to a perfect circle. Study the drawing carefully (Illus. 852) before you begin to make the jig. The tongue is the most difficult part to make. Rout the groove down the center of the tongue first. Reduce its thickness with a series of dado cuts across the work. It is a good idea to tape a scrap in the routed groove while the dado is being cut. This will minimize the chance of breakage.

The base may now be constructed. Any sheet stock can be used for the base. It should be about ¾" thick. Cut the dado to accommodate the tongue, then attach the cleat. Fit the hardware to the tongue and base. Wax the moving parts for smooth operation. Drill a hole on the end of the tongue for a pivot pin. Use a dowel of a workable diameter.

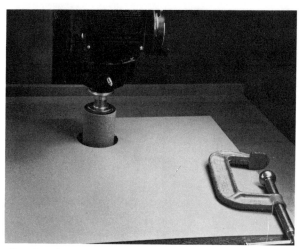

Illus. 847. Some spindle-sanding jigs have a laminated top. This increases wear resistance and reduces friction between the work and the jig.

Illus. 848. Sheet stock such as particle board may also be used for spindle-sanding jigs.

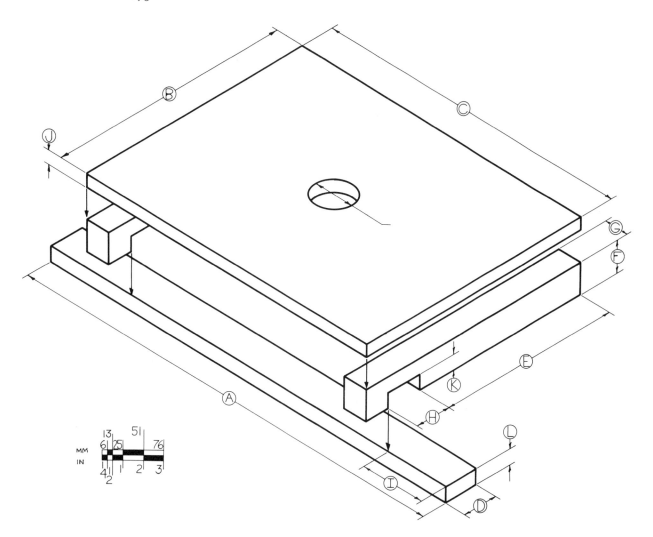

Illus. 849. Study this drawing carefully before making a spindle-sanding jig. Modify the dimensions to suit your saw and the spindle diameter.

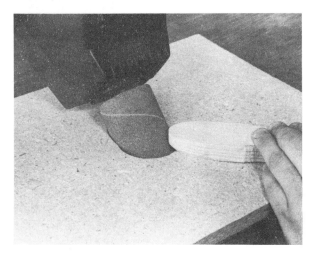

Illus. 850. If the spindle is to be tilted, the spindle hole will have to be elliptical.

Illus. 851. This circle-sanding jig can be used on the radial arm saw, band saw, or table saw.

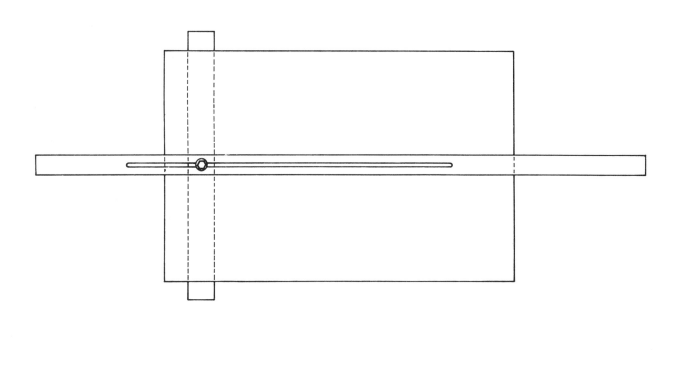

0 1 2 3   6
INCHES

I 10 30
02 20 40   80   150
MILLIMETRES

Illus. 852. Study the drawing before beginning. You may wish to modify the dimensions depending on the diameter of pieces you plan to sand.

Mitring Jigs

Mitring jigs are useful for frame work. The advantage of a mitre jig is that it has a 90° included angle. This means that all corners will form a right angle. It also means that the arm does not have to be turned. This eliminates any adjustment error.

Two jigs are presented here. One has low fences (Illus. 853). The other has high fences (Illus. 854). The high fences are used when doing compound mitres. Avoid making the fences too high, or they can hit the motor and interfere with the cut.

Flat Mitre Jig   The flat mitre jig is easy to build. Study the drawing (Illus. 855) first. Modify the dimensions as needed. Begin with a true piece of sheet stock ½" thick or greater. Cut it to the dimensions of the front table on your saw. A cleat is attached to the underside of the sheet on a long edge (Illus. 856). This cleat allows the jig to be clamped between the table boards.

Determine the blade's path on the sheet stock. This will dictate the placement of the fences. Note how the fences are staggered (Illus. 857). This keeps the fences from interfering with a mitre on a long piece.

Lay out the position of the fence nearest to the edge of the jig. It should be 45° off the long edge. Cut the end of the fence as specified and attach it to the sheet stock on the layout line. The other fence is cut as specified and attached to the sheet stock. It is offset from the first fence. It is important that the second fence be set perpendicular to the first fence (Illus. 858).

Compound Mitre Jig   The compound mitre jig is made the same way as the flat mitre jig except the fences are higher and on edge. This means that there must be a 90° angle between the edges and faces of the fence. Determine maximum fence height before cutting any stock. If the fence is too high, it will contact the motor. Locate the fences as you would for the flat mitre jig. Be sure the fences are perpendicular to each other (Illus. 859). In addition, they must be perpendicular to the sheet-stock base (Illus. 860).

The jig may now be clamped between the table boards ready for use. Be sure the jig is lined up with the blade. This will keep the jig from being damaged by the blade.

Illus. 853. The flat mitre jig has low fences for cutting simple mitres. The jig clamps between the table boards and replaces the fence.

Illus. 854. The fences on the compound mitre jig are much higher. This allows stock to be tilted during the mitre cut.

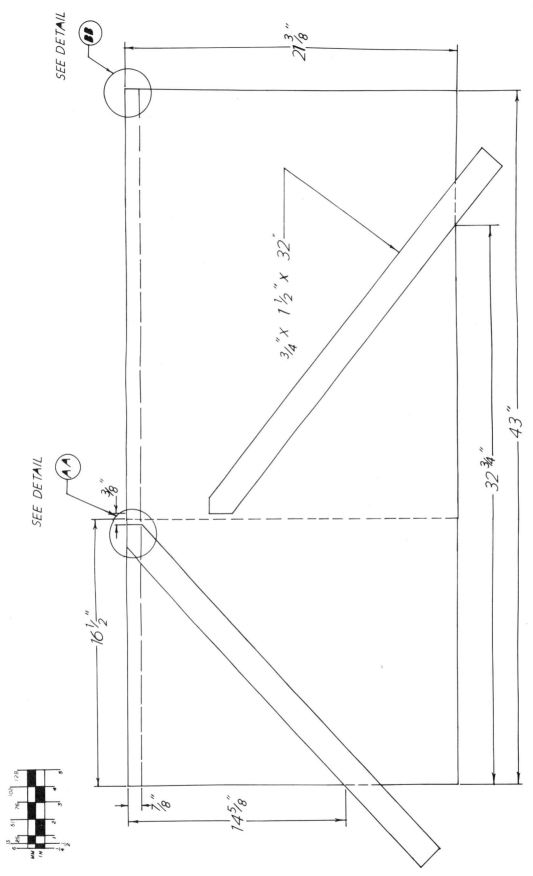

SEE DETAIL

SEE DETAIL

21 3/8"

3/4" X 1 1/2" X 32"

43"

32 3/4"

16 1/2"

3/8"

7/8"

14 5/8"

Illus. 855. Study the drawing before making a mitring jig. Modify the dimensions to suit your radial arm saw.

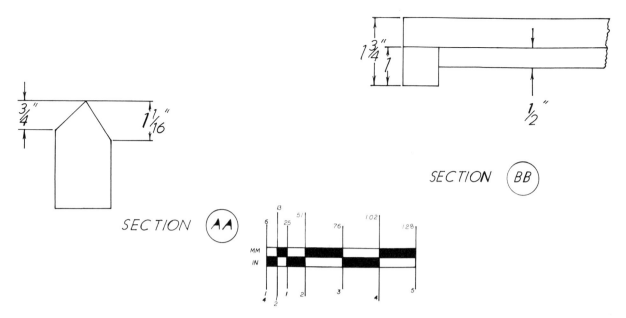

SECTION (AA)

SECTION (BB)

Illus. 856. These details show the cleat placement and the cutting detail for the end of the flat fences.

Illus. 857. The fences on the mitre jig are staggered. This keeps the fence from interfering with the work.

Illus. 858. Be sure the fences have true faces and edges. The fences must also be perpendicular to each other.

289

Illus. 859. Adjust the wide fences the same way as the flat ones. Note that the ends of the wide fences remain square.

Illus. 860. Be sure the wide fences are perpendicular to the sheet stock. The fences should be square and true.

Spline and Feather Jigs

The spline jig (Illus. 861) and the feather jig (Illus. 862) are very similar in design. In fact, if you study the 2 prints (Illus. 865 and 866), there are 2 differences. One is the opening between the triangular blocks attached to the top of the jig. The other is the method of holding the work to the jig.

The longer opening between the triangular blocks allows the splining jig to handle mitred ends (Illus. 863). Industrial clamps hold the stock while the splining operation is performed.

The smaller opening between the triangular blocks on the feather jigs positions a mitred corner correctly for the operation. A T-shaped nut and a hexhead bolt provide the clamping pressure (Illus. 864).

It is a good idea to build both of these jigs at the same time. The construction procedure and the dimensions are similar. Mark your parts to avoid confusion. Study the plans and develop a bill of materials. Select sheet stock that is true and free of voids. Cut the triangular blocks and locate them. Mark the position of the T-shaped nuts on the feather jig and drill the holes. Position the T-shaped nuts and then fasten the triangular blocks. Drill the holes for the handles and cut dowels to the appropriate length. Round one end of the dowels and glue them in position.

Attach the industrial clamps to the splining jig. Sheet metal screws work well for this job. The industrial clamps will have to be adjusted to the height of your work before the jig is used. A piece of hardwood must be cut for the feathering jig. It acts as a hold-down when the frame is positioned.

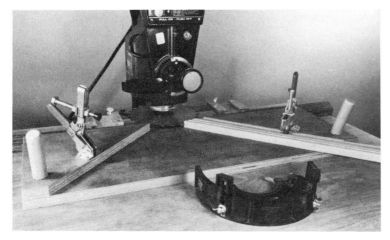

Illus. 861. The spline jig holds mitred parts for the splining operation. Industrial clamps secure the work to the jig.

Illus. 862. The feather jig uses a hex bolt and a T-shaped nut to hold frames securely while the kerf is cut.

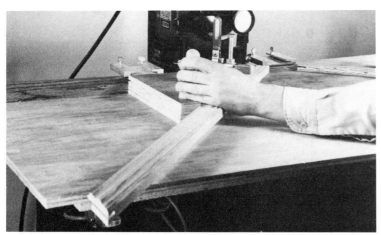

Illus. 863. The large opening between the triangular blocks allows the mitred ends to align with the edge of the jig.

Illus. 864. The hex bolt provides clamping pressure to the piece of hardwood. A T-shaped nut is pressed into the base of the jig. There are 2 positions for the bolt. This allows the jig to accommodate frame stock of various widths.

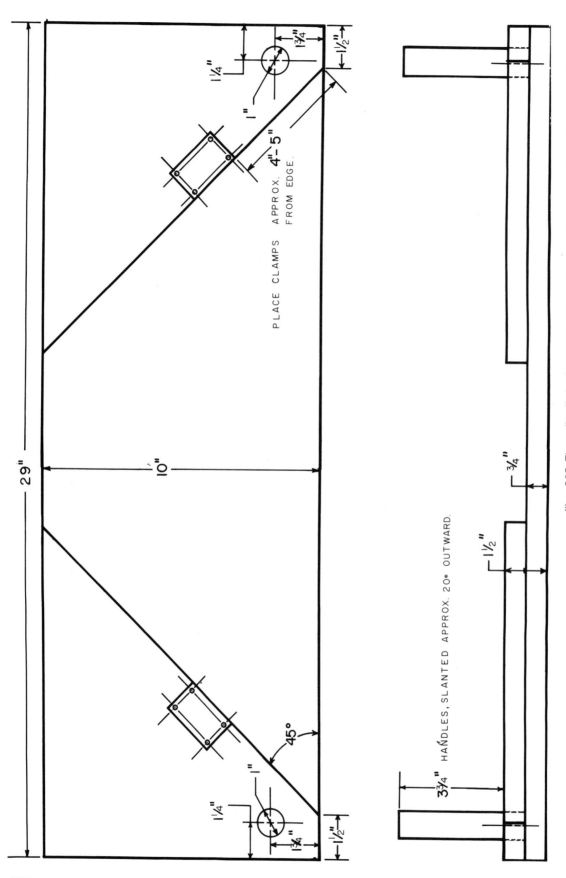

29"

1¼"

1¾"

1½"

1"

4"–5"

PLACE CLAMPS APPROX. FROM EDGE.

10"

45°

1"

1¼"

1¾"

1½"

3¾" HANDLES, SLANTED APPROX. 20° OUTWARD.

3¾"

1½"

¾"

Illus. 865. The spline jig is dimensioned here. Note the differences between it and the feather jig before you begin construction.

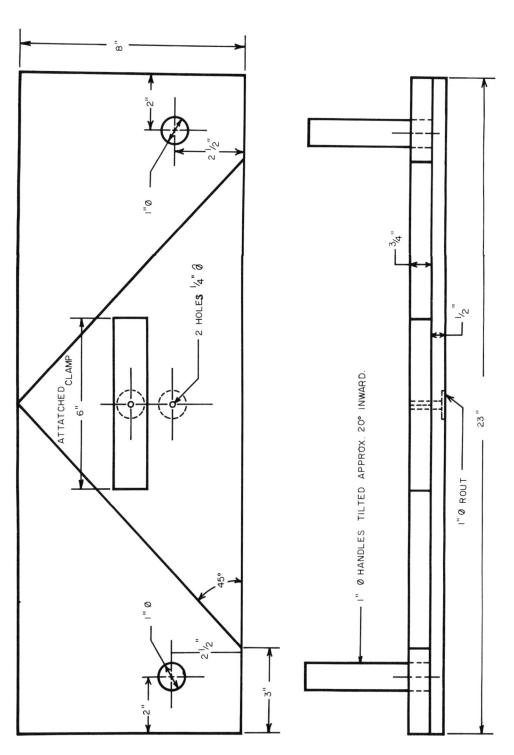

8"

2"

2 1/2"

1" Ø

ATTATCHED CLAMP

6"

2 HOLES 1/4" Ø

45°

1" Ø

2 1/2"

2"

3"

3/4"

1/2"

23"

1" Ø ROUT

1" Ø HANDLES TILTED APPROX. 20° INWARD.

Illus. 866. This drawing details the feather jig. Note the differences between it and the spline jig before you begin construction.

Tapering Jigs

Tapering jigs are useful for many projects you build with your radial-arm saw. Because of the possibility of stock lifting, I feel that the safest rip tapering jig should have a base (Illus. 867). The base allows the stock to be held securely while the cut is made. Industrial clamps are used with the jigs in Illus. 868, but many other types of hold-down devices may be used.

The notch or step cut in the jig determines the taper of the work. Lay out the notch or steps carefully. The notched board is then secured to a second board, which becomes the base. These pieces are usually made of sheet stock.

The handle is the same as the one shown on the push block on page 35 (Illus. 91 F). Cut it out and smooth the edges (Illus. 869). Radius all corners with a roundover router bit. This will make the handle more comfortable. Screw the handle to the jig. Placement should make the jig convenient to use and allow clearance past the motor or fence.

Some tapering jigs are used in the crosscut instead of rip mode (Illus. 870). These jigs are usually clamped between the table boards in place of the fence. The opposite end can be secured with a clamp.

These jigs do not require a base. The table acts as a base. Industrial clamps are used to secure the stock, but they also allow you to keep your hands well away from the blade. Note that the wide end of the taper is closest to the fence. This gives the work a wider base for control when the cut is made. Plan your crosscut tapering jigs with this in mind.

Illus. 867. Rip taper jigs are safest when they have a base. The base allows the work to be clamped securely while the cut is made.

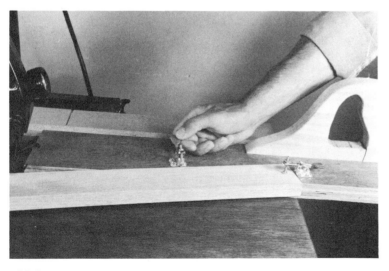

Illus. 868. Industrial clamps can be adjusted for maximum clamping pressure. They work well on radial-arm-saw jigs.

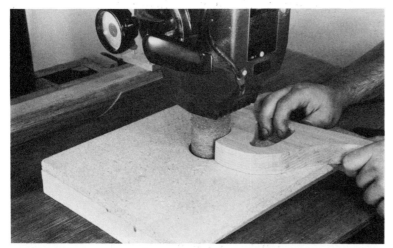

Illus. 869. Smooth the edges and rout the corners of the handles you put on any tapering jig.

Illus. 870. This taper jig is used in the cross-cut mode. It is held in place by the table boards and a clamp. Note that the wide end of the taper is closest to the column. This gives better control over the work.

Parallel Cove Layout Guide

The parallel guide is used for cove layout (Illus. 871). This is a simple project to build. Study Illus. 873 to see how the parts fit together. Stock is ripped to 1¼", and then cut to length. The corners are drilled through to accommodate the bolts and then the bottom of the hole is counterbored to hold the T-shaped nut (Illus. 872).

Position the parts and drive the bolts through the parts into the T-shaped nuts. Tighten the bolts until movement is stiff. This will allow the guide to hold its setting.

Illus. 871. This parallel guide will make cove layout easier and more accurate.

Illus. 872. The bottom of the holes is counterbored to accommodate the T-shaped nuts. These nuts must be driven in with a hammer.

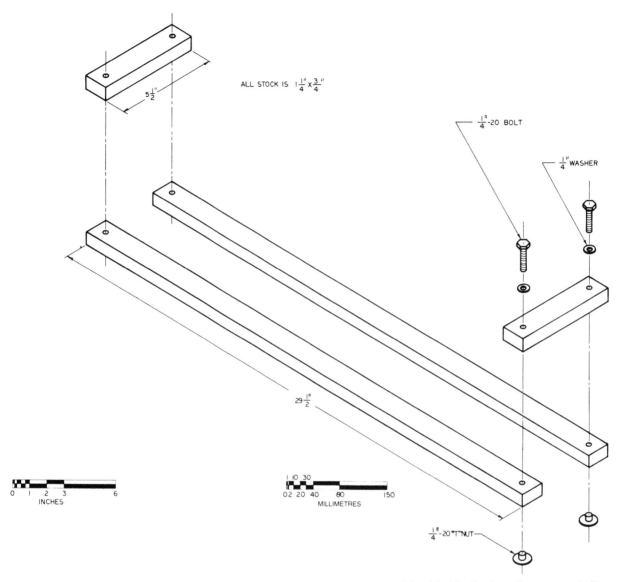

ALL STOCK IS $1\frac{1}{4}$" $\times \frac{3}{4}$"

$5\frac{1}{2}$"

$\frac{1}{4}$"-20 BOLT

$\frac{1}{4}$" WASHER

$29\frac{1}{2}$"

INCHES
0 1 2 3 6

MILLIMETRES
1 10 30
02 20 40 80 150

$\frac{1}{4}$"-20 "T"NUT

Illus. 873. Study the drawing before making a parallel guide. Modify sizes, if necessary, to fit your needs.

Building Projects

Clocks In most books, I include a clock project. This is because the design potential is limitless. Clocks are displayed with pride, and most homes need more than one clock. They also make nice gifts for most occasions.

Heptagon Clock. Who says a clock must have an even number of sides? This heptagon clock (Illus. 874) is a 7-sided challenge. The clock provides a chance to do the following operations: edge-shaping, dadoing, end-mitring, and pattern-sawing.

Begin this project by studying Illus. 876 on page 298.

Make any modifications you wish. Typical modifications include the length of the mitred parts and the position of the clock face. Changing the length of the mitred parts affects the clock size. Changing the position of the clock face is dependent on the size of the clock motor. The motor should be completely housed inside the frame.

Begin by selecting true, straight-grained stock. Rip the mitred parts to width and crosscut them to rough lengths. It is best to keep the rough lengths 24″ long or longer. This makes them easier to handle when routing or shaping them.

Set up the radial arm saw for dadoing, and dado the inside face of the mitred parts. Be sure the dado is wide enough to hold the clock face. The mitred parts are now ready for shaping or routing.

Set up the radial arm saw for routing or shaping and rout or shape the front edge of the mitred parts. After they are shaped, the end mitres may be cut. Adjust the saw carefully. Control part length so that the mitres will fit snugly. If there are problems with the fit, recut the mitres after adjusting the angle.

Use a band clamp to hold the mitred parts together. While they are clamped, develop a pattern and take measurements for the clock face.

You may wish to pattern-saw the clock faces (Illus. 875). This requires that you make an auxiliary fence (Illus. 877) and a pattern (Illus. 878). The pattern will be smaller than the clock face to allow for the auxiliary fence. Be sure to drive some sharp points through the pattern (Illus. 879). These points will hold the clock face firmly to the pattern while it is cut.

Fit the face to the frame. If the fit is correct, glue the frame together with the face in place. Band clamps work best for this job (Illus. 880). After the glue cures, locate the center and bore a hole for the clock motor (Illus. 881). Locate and glue the numerals in position. The 12 should be at the junction of a mitre. This allows the clock to hang correctly.

Illus. 874. This clock has an uneven number of sides (seven). Note how the 12 is located at the junction of a mitre. This allows it to be hung correctly.

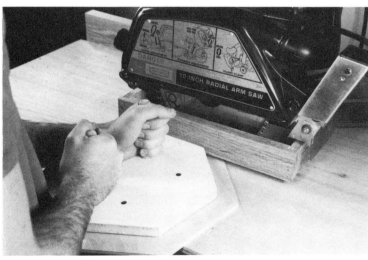

Illus. 875. The clockfaces may be pattern-sawn if you plan to make a large quantity of them. A sabre saw can also be used for limited production.

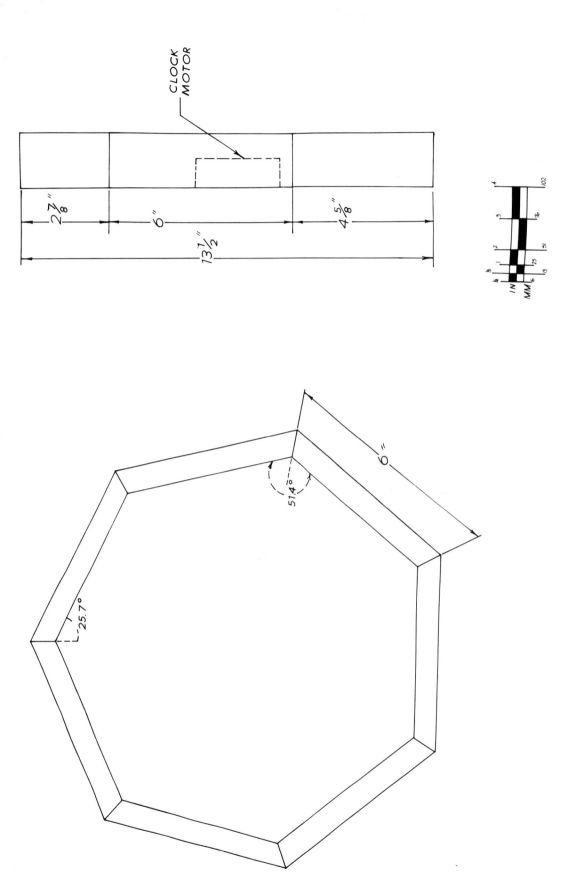

CLOCK
MOTOR

2 7/8"

6"

13 1/2"

4 5/8"

51.4°

25.7°

6"

Illus. 876. Study this plan before building the clock. Make any needed modifications in the dimensions.

Illus. 877. For pattern sawing, you must make an auxiliary fence like the one shown here.

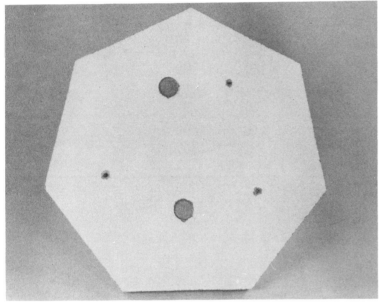

Illus. 878. The pattern for the clockface will be smaller than the actual clock face. This allows for the thickness of the auxiliary fence.

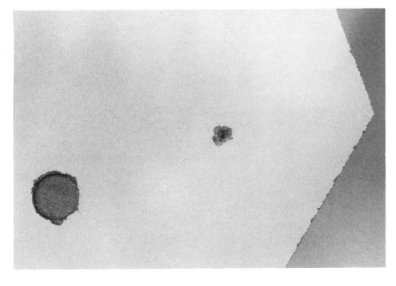

Illus. 879. The pattern should have sharp points protruding through the bottom. They allow the pattern to hold the work securely while the cuts are made.

Illus. 880. Use band clamps to hold the parts together while the glue cures.

Illus. 881. Locate and glue the numerals in position. Be sure the 12 is at the junction of a mitre. This allows the clock to hang correctly. Install the motor and fit the hands.

24-Hour Clock. The 24-hour clock (Illus. 882) uses the nautical or military approach to telling time. It requires a special motor and clock face. After the clock face is purchased, clock diameter can be determined. Draw up the appropriate templates, and then glue parts together (Illus. 883). Mitres are cut on the ends of the frame parts using the radial-arm saw. A template is used to lay out the outer circle and inner circle (Illus. 884). The outer circle is cut first (Illus. 885). Then the inner is cut. You may be able to see the layout line in Illus. 886. Use the sabre-sawing attachment to cut out the circles, or work on the band or jig saw.

After the pieces have been cut out, spindle-sand the inner circle and disc-sand (Illus. 886) the outer circle. The frame is now ready for decorative router cuts. A portable router can be used (Illus. 887), or the router bracket can be mounted on the radial arm saw. A curved fence, such as the one on the router, must be used with the router bracket.

To rout the rabbet for the clock face, a special guide must be used with the router (Illus. 888). This guide controls the depth of cut. The guide rides along the inner edge of the circle (Illus. 889). The bit then cuts the rabbet. The rabbet locates and holds the clock face in position. It is best to finish the clock before securing the clock face. This keeps stain and finish from damaging the clock face.

Illus. 882. This 24-hour clock uses the military approach to telling time. A special motor and clockface are needed for this clock.

Illus. 883. The frame is mitred and glued together. A band clamp holds the parts in position until the glue cures.

Illus. 884. Templates are used to lay out the inside and outside circles.

Illus. 885. Cut out the clock with a sabre saw, scrolling attachment, band saw, or jigsaw. Leave the layout line so that the parts can be sanded.

Illus. 886. The disc-sanding attachment is used to transform the clocks into a perfect circle. Keep the work moving so that it does not burn and damage the abrasives.

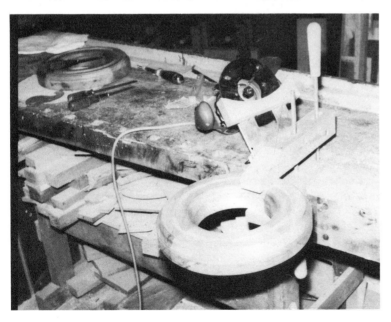

Illus. 887. The clock is routed to give it a decorative look. A special edge guide is attached to the router for this purpose.

Illus. 888. A special guide is used to cut the rabbet on the inner edge of the clock.

Illus. 889. The inner edge rides on the special guide while the rabbet is cut. Take light cuts for best results.

Frame Clocks. Frame clocks are similar to picture frames. Instead of having an odd number of sides, these frames have 4 sides (Illus. 890). These clocks can be made a number of different ways depending on which motor, face, and hands you decide to use. Study Illus. 891 to see the most common methods of holding the clock face in position. Use these drawings to decide what type of clock you wish to make. Adjust the dimensions to suit your hands, face, and motor.

Use any of the mitre-cutting methods presented in Chapter 5 to cut the end mitres on your frame members. Cut the parts accurately so that they will fit together well. Sand and finish the inside of the frame members before assembly. This will keep finishing materials off the clock face. Additional frame clocks can be found in *Table Saw Techniques* and *Woodworking Principles and Practices*, both by this author.

303

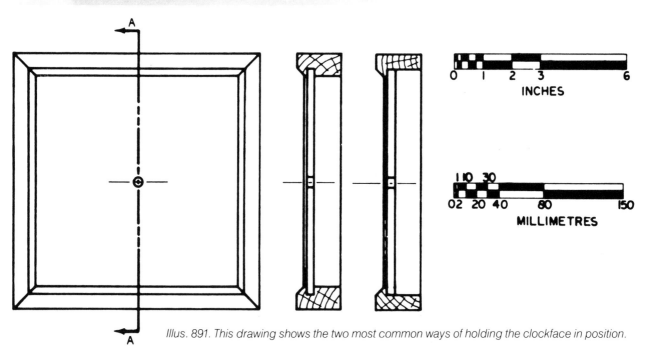

Illus. 891. This drawing shows the two most common ways of holding the clockface in position.

Picture Frames Picture frames provide many challenges on the radial arm saw. They provide opportunities to cut coves, dadoes, and rabbets. They allow practice with flat and compound mitres, and also allow you to use the shaper head to form fancy frame moulding. Begin with simple frames that require flat mitres (Illus. 892). Be sure you allow enough space in the rabbet for the glass. Make the rabbets as deep as possible. Shallow rabbets may not allow enough room for the photo, glass, and backing. Allow for the total thickness of these materials.

Jigs may be used to help you cut simple (Illus. 893 and 894) and compound (Illus. 895) mitres. Review the section on mitre-cutting before beginning. Select a technique that will work with your saw and available equipment. You may even wish to make the mitre-cutting jigs presented earlier in this chapter. The frames should have tight mitres (Illus. 896) when assembled. Accurate layout is very important.

When you decide on a particular moulding shape, this shape can be attached to your work (Illus. 897). Use the drawing to help you set the saw up correctly. For an added decorative effect, you may wish to put a key in the corners of the frame (Illus. 898). This will require construction of the feather-cutting jig described earlier in this chapter. Trim the feathers off even after the glue cures. They look decorative and also reinforce the joint.

Illus. 892. Flat mitres are easiest; begin making frames with these. Be sure to allow room in the rabbet for the glass.

Illus. 893. This jig makes it easier to cut mitres. Chapter 5 discusses how this jig works.

Illus. 894. This commercial jig makes mitre cutting very accurate. Make sure the saw blade does not contact the metal parts of the jig.

Illus. 895. This commercial jig may also be used for compound mitres. There is also a shop-made jig earlier in this chapter. It is designed for compound mitres.

Illus. 896. Picture frames will have tight mitres if they are laid out correctly.

Illus. 897. A pattern can be glued to your work to make saw layout easier.

Bath Accessories Bath accessories are popular wood-working projects. The towel bar and robe hooks (Illus. 901 on page 309) look lovely in any bathroom. The mirror shelf (Illus. 902) makes a nice accent in the bathroom. If you look in the mirror, you may notice another cabinet. This cabinet is detailed in *Table Saw Techniques*. The trim around the small window you see in the mirror was made on the radial arm saw. It matches the rest of the trim in the house.

Towel Bar. The towel bar is an easy project to make because there are only 4 parts. Study the drawings (Illus. 899 and 900) to see how the parts fit together. The backing board is the easiest part to make. Most woodworkers begin by ripping and crosscutting it to size.

Make a template for the backing board (Illus. 903) and lay out all parts. Make the line heavy enough to see. It will be a guide line when sanding.

Use the scrolling attachment (Illus. 904), a scroll saw, or band saw to cut the arc on both ends of the backing board. If you plan to make several towel bars, you could pattern-sand the ends using a jig (Illus. 905 and 906). If you are only making a few, freehand-sand the ends using a disc-sanding attachment.

The backing board can now be routed along its outer edge. Work carefully (Illus. 907), especially on end grain. Remember, it is better to take 2 light cuts than one heavy cut. After the edge is routed (Illus. 908), the piece is ready for final sanding.

The dowel fits into 2 sockets (Illus. 900). These sockets are blind holes that are drilled into the 2 ends (Illus. 909).

It is best to make these ends out of a longer piece, and then crosscut them to length. The radius on the ends is scrolled, then disc-sanded in the same way as the backing board. Use a spade bit or Foerstner bit to drill the blind holes.

The bar or dowel can be purchased, or it can be made out of a piece of 1"-square stock. Chamfer the edges with a router bit until the square piece becomes an octagon. Now shape the octagon into a dowel with a block plane. Sand the dowel and fit it to the blind holes.

Attach the ends to the backing board with wood screws. Remove the ends from the board and finish-sand all the parts. The towel bar can be reassembled and then stained and finished.

Robe Hooks. The hooks are attached to a simple backing board. This board is 6½" wide and 15" long. Lay out any decorative cuts on the backing board first. Use a scrolling attachment or scroll saw (Illus. 910) to make the cuts. Spindle-sand (Illus. 911) or disc-sand the decorative cuts. After the cuts have been smoothed, the work may be routed. Use a routing attachment or router table (Illus. 912) to rout the edges.

Locate the metal (Illus. 913) or wooden hooks (Illus. 914) and attach them carefully. Brass screws are soft and they break easily. Be certain the pilot hole is big enough. If you wish to make the wooden hooks, complete plans are found in *Woodworking Principles and Practices*.

Remove the hooks and finish-sand the board and other wood parts. Stain and finish to match the towel bar.

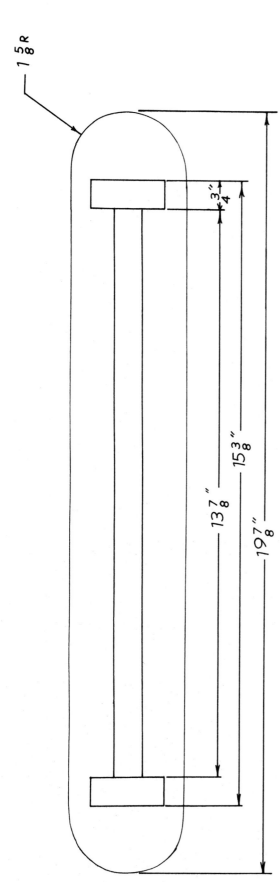

$1\frac{5}{8}R$

$\frac{3}{4}''$

$13\frac{7}{8}''$

$15\frac{3}{8}''$

$19\frac{7}{8}''$

Illus. 899. The front view of the towel bar shows all four parts: the backing board, the ends, and the bar or dowel. Modify the dimensions to suit your needs.

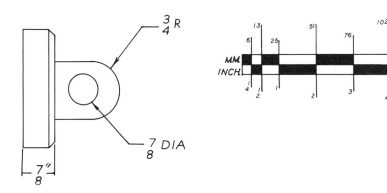

Illus. 901. The towel bars and robe hooks make a lovely accent in any bathroom.

Illus. 902. The mirror shelf is a custom product you can make for your bath or dressing area. It has a cove shelf to hold brushes and combs.

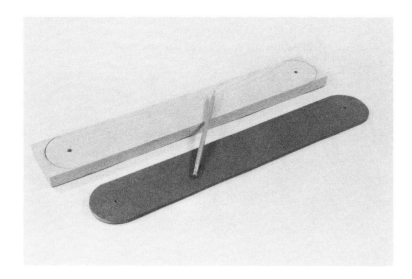

Illus. 903. A template may be used to lay out the backing board. This will ensure that all parts are uniform.

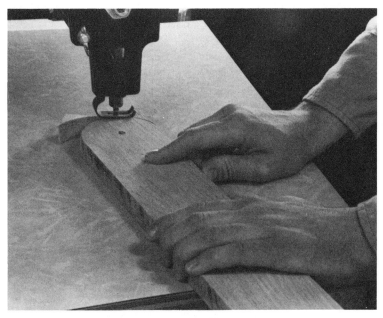

Illus. 904. The scrolling attachment can be used to cut ends on the backing board.

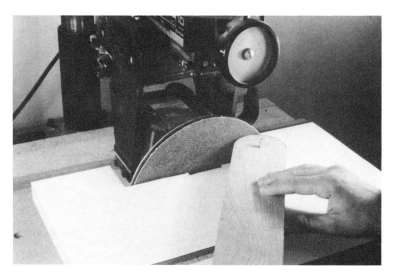

Illus. 905. A pattern or jig can be made for pattern-sanding the backing boards. This will ensure that all backing boards will be the same.

Illus. 906. The pin controls the sanding depth by rubbing against the pattern. The two holes in the backing board locate it on the pattern.

Illus. 907. A router is mounted under the front table for routing the backing board. Remember to take light cuts.

Illus. 908. After the piece has been routed, it is ready for final sanding.

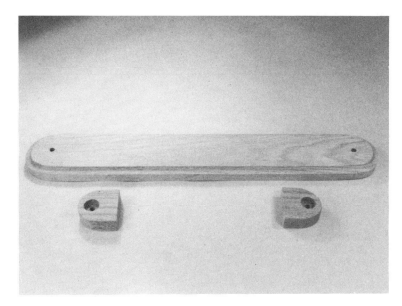

Illus. 909. The holes in the ends are blind. They hold the bar in position.

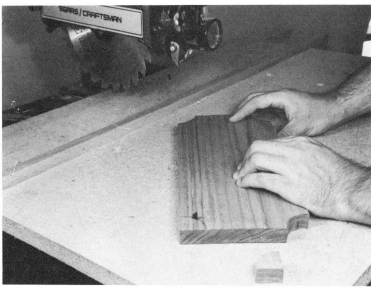

Illus. 910. A scroll saw has been mounted under the front table. It is used to cut the backing board to shape.

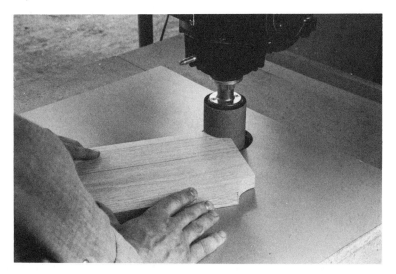

Illus. 911. Spindle-sand the saw marks away. Work slowly and keep the work moving. This will prevent burning.

Illus. 912. The routed edge is made with a portable router that is mounted under the front table.

Illus. 913. The metal hooks are positioned and marked with an awl.

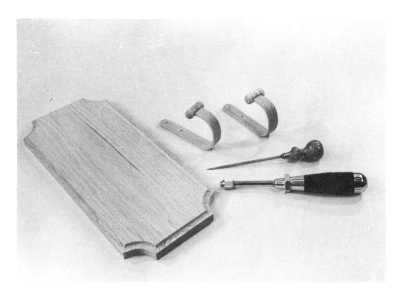

Illus. 914. If you make wooden hooks, the marking procedure is the same. Drill a large pilot hole. Brass screws break easily.

Mirror Shelf.　The mirror shelf must be designed according to your needs. The top and bottom are rabbeted to hold the mirror. The valance is located far enough away from the top to accommodate a fluorescent bulb. The tray on the bottom has been coved out to hold brushes and combs. Making this shelf will give you a chance to work with coves. Read the section on cutting coves (page 190) before starting. The brush shelf in Illus. 578 also allows cove practice. Plans for this project can be found in *Table Saw Techniques.*

After cutting the cove, sand it carefully so that there are no saw marks visible when you stain and finish. The cove shelf is attached to the mirror bottom with wood screws. All parts are then stained and finished to match the towel bars.

Blox Box　This set of toy blocks (Illus. 915) was made as a gift for my nephew. Can you guess his name? This project is relatively simple, but there are grooving and dadoing operations, as well as scrolling and sanding. Begin by studying the plan (Illus. 917) and the detail (Illus. 916).

Rip the parts for the box and cut them to length. Cut the grooves on the ends and center handle. Cut the arcs and opening in the center handle. Sand and rout the center handle with the desired bit.

Cut the bottom pieces to size and drill holes in each. The position is located on the plan. These holes allow easy removal of the blocks. They can be pushed out from the bottom.

Assemble the box after the dadoes are cut. The ends are screwed in position. Be sure to drill pilot holes of adequate size. You may wish to disassemble it for final sanding and finishing.

Make the blocks fit the box. The size is specified on the print. If you have thick stock available, these blocks may be solid. If not, stock will have to be glued up. Smooth the pieces and crosscut them to length. Disc-sand the ends if needed and round all sharp corners or edges. Test the fit of the blocks in the box.

For an added touch, you can burn letters, numbers, or designs into the blocks (Illus. 918). Remember, this is a child's toy. If you apply a finish, be certain that it is nontoxic. If in doubt, use no finish at all.

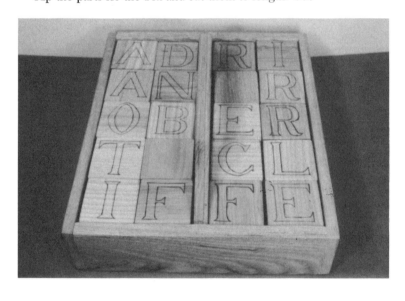

Illus. 915. The Blox Box makes an excellent gift and it needs no batteries.

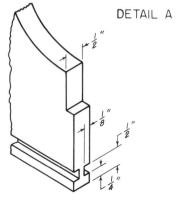

DETAIL A

Illus. 916. This detail shows you how the ends of the center handle are cut. See Illus. 917 on the following page.

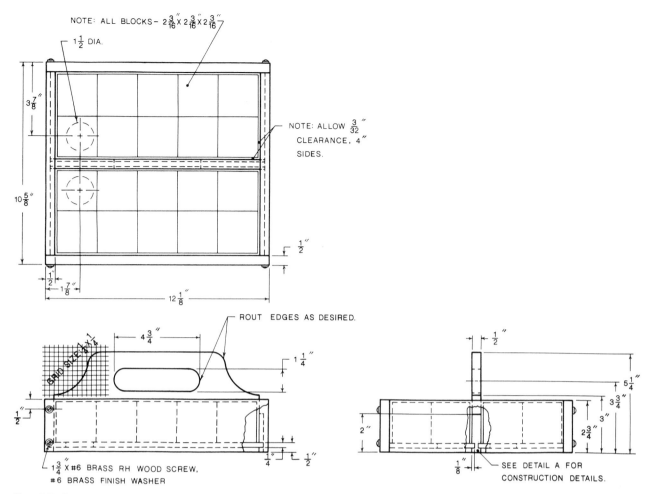

NOTE: ALL BLOCKS – 2 3/16" X 2 3/16" X 2 3/16"

1 1/2 DIA.

3 7/8"

NOTE: ALLOW 3/32" CLEARANCE, 4" SIDES.

10 5/8"

1/2"

1/2"

1 7/8"

12 1/8"

ROUT EDGES AS DESIRED.

4 3/4"

GRID SIZE: 1/4" X 1/4"

1 1/4"

1/2"

1/4"

1/2"

1 3/4" X #6 BRASS RH WOOD SCREW,
#6 BRASS FINISH WASHER

1/2"

5 1/4"

3 3/4"

3"

2 3/4"

2"

1/8"

SEE DETAIL A FOR CONSTRUCTION DETAILS.

Illus. 917. Study these three views of the Blox Box to see how the parts are oriented.

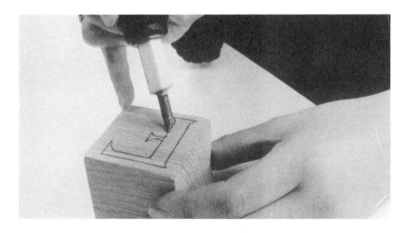

Illus. 918. The blocks can be lettered, numbered or designed using a woodburning tool. This adds a personal touch to the set.

Plant Stand The plant stand (Illus. 921 on page 318) is a nice table for the hallway or other living area. The table is semicircular, so it sits against the wall. There is no apron on this table, but one could be bent around the edge using the kerf-bending technique in Chapter 6.

Study the plans (Illus. 919 and 920) before you begin. Develop a bill of materials. The table height is 30", so the legs are 29¼" long. The method of joining the legs to the "T" support is your decision. One side (Illus. 920) is shown with a mortise-and-tenon joint; the other side is shown with a dowel joint. The mortise-and-tenon joint is the strongest, but the joint you use will be determined by what tools you have. This decision will affect your bill of materials.

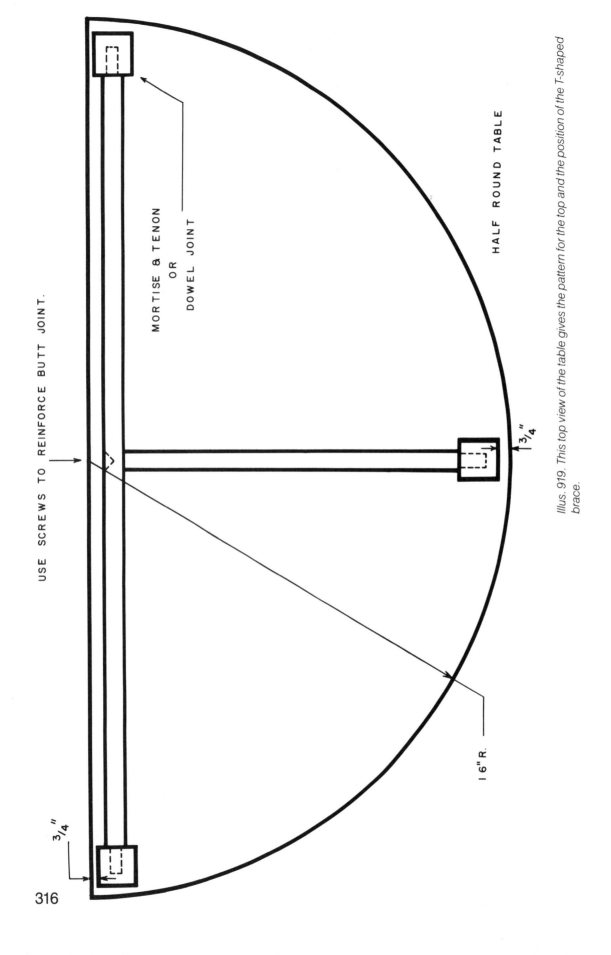

USE SCREWS TO REINFORCE BUTT JOINT.

MORTISE & TENON
OR
DOWEL JOINT

HALF ROUND TABLE

3/4"

3/4"

16" R.

316

Illus. 919. This top view of the table gives the pattern for the top and the position of the T-shaped brace.

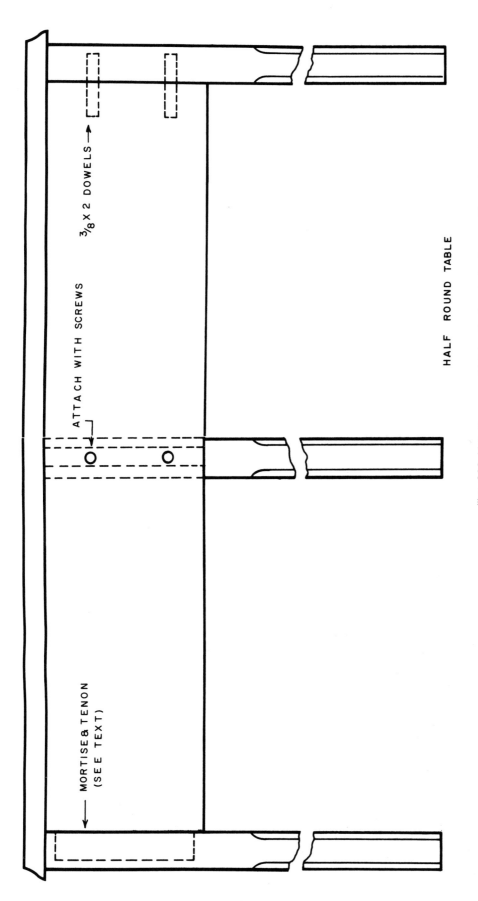

3/8 X 2 DOWELS →

ATTACH WITH SCREWS

MORTISE & TENON
(SEE TEXT)

HALF ROUND TABLE

Illus. 920. Note the ways of joining the legs to the braces. The tools you have are a determining factor for the best approach to take.

Illus. 921. The plant stand is a semicircular table that looks good in the hall or other area.

Begin by gluing up stock for the top (Illus. 922) and the legs. Rip the parts for the "T" brace and cut them to length. Cut the legs to length and rout the lower portion of them (about 18-20″). This gives the legs a tapered look. Join the legs to the "T" brace and set aside for final sanding.

Make a template for the top, and lay it out (Illus. 923). Make the line broad enough so that it can be used as a sanding guide. Use a scrolling attachment (Illus. 924) or other device to cut the top to rough size. Use a disc-sanding attachment (Illus. 925) to bring the top to exact size. Use the pencil line as a guide.

Rout a decorative edge on the curved side of the top, but leave the flat side square. Fit the top to the leg assembly with square cleats and wood screws. Make the screw holes in the cleats large enough to allow for expansion and contraction of the top.

Remove the top and finish-sand all parts. Stain and finish your plant stand with the finish of your choice.

Illus. 922. Glue up stock for the top carefully. Remove glue and sand the top smooth.

318

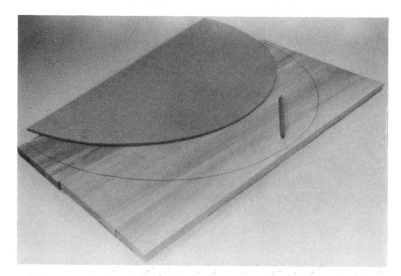

Illus. 923. A template has been used to lay out the top. Use a heavy pencil line.

Illus. 924. The top is being cut out using the scrolling attachment. Be sure to leave the pencil line.

Illus. 925. Disc-sand the pencil line away. The top will form a true arc. It is now ready to be routed.

Portable Workbench The portable workbench (Illus. 926) was designed to fold up for compact storage and easy transportation to the job. The clamping device holds stock securely for sanding or other operations. When it is not in use, it can be stored in the tool trough (Illus. 927).

Study the cutaway drawing (Illus. 930 on page 322). This will help you see how the parts fit together. Decide how large you wish to make the table and develop a bill of materials. The top is made of sheet stock, the borders are made of hardwood, and the cleats that stiffen the table and anchor the brackets are made from framing material.

It is best to buy all the hardware before you begin. This way, you can make allowances for the position of the folding legs, the vise, and the hold-down clamp.

Begin by cutting the top to size. Build up one edge and screw the bottom of the tool trough to the spacers (Illus. 928). The ends can then be glued and nailed in position. Position the stiffeners and glue them in position. Nails or screws can be used for reinforcement. Locate the legs on

the stiffeners and screw them in position (Illus. 929). Round-head wood screws work best for this task (Illus. 931).

Decide on the position of the hold-down bolts, and drill the appropriate holes. First counterbore a hole for the head of the bolt, then drill a pilot hole for the bolt (Illus. 932). Counterbore the stiffener to accommodate the nuts and washer (Illus. 933), and adjust the bolt correctly (Illus. 934).

Chisel away the stock (if necessary) for correct fit of the vise (Illus. 935). Attach the vise with wood screws (Illus. 936) and line the jaws with a hardwood such as birch or maple (Illus. 937). This protects the work when it is secured in the vise (Illus. 938).

Sand the bench as needed. Radius the sharp corners and apply a finish. I selected an oil finish (Illus. 939) because it does not chip off or discolor the work. The oil also resists the adhesion of any glue that may be spilled.

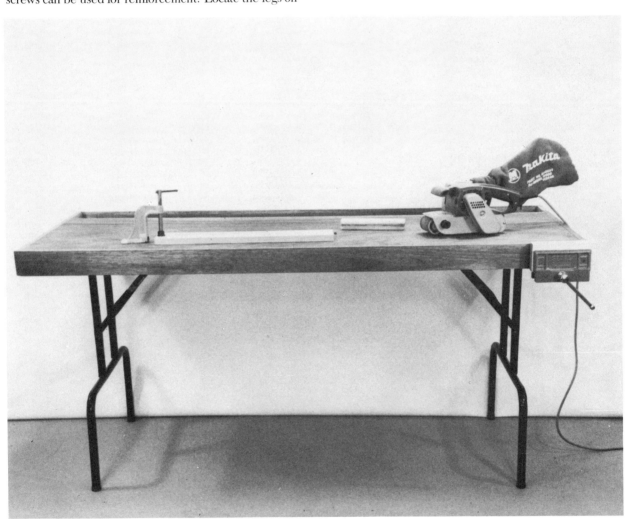

Illus. 926. This workbench folds up for easy storage and transportation. It also has a hold-down clamp and vise for holding stock.

Illus. 927. The tool trough allows tools to be stored and keeps the work surface clear.

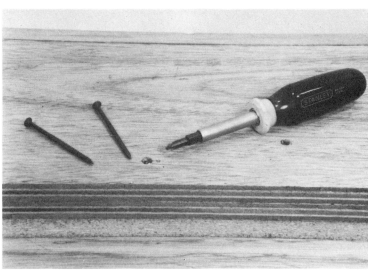

Illus. 928. The bottom of the tool trough is screwed to the spacers. The tool trough is about 2¼" deep.

Illus. 929. The legs are located on the stiffeners and pilot holes are drilled.

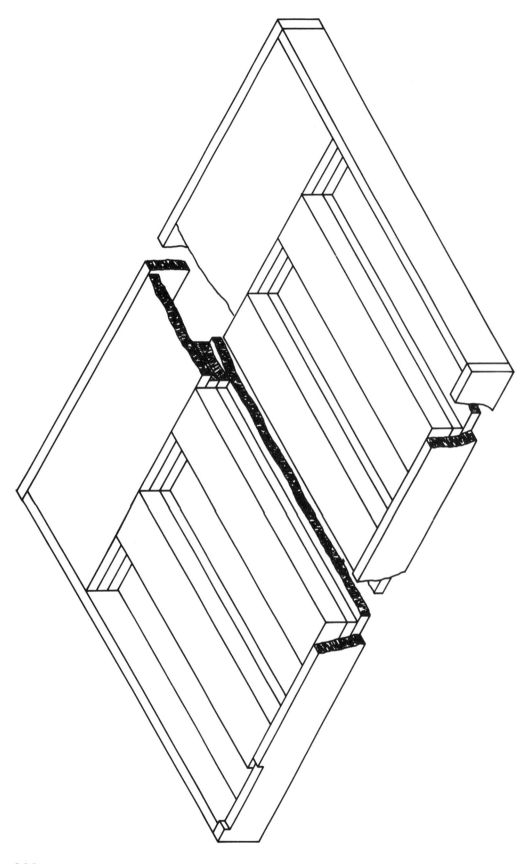

Illus. 930. This cutaway drawing will help you visualize how the parts fit together. The hardware purchased and the desired bench size will determine your bill of materials.

Illus. 931. Round-head wood screws work well for securing the legs to the stiffeners. Sheet-metal screws may also be used.

Illus. 932. A pilot hole is drilled in the middle of the counterbored hole. The counterbored hole holds the bolt head when the clamp is not in use.

Illus. 933. The stiffener is counterbored to accommodate the washer. The pilot hole drilled from above keeps all holes aligned.

Illus. 934. The bolts are adjusted so that the bolt head rises the correct distance above the workbench.

Illus. 935. Stock is chiselled away for the correct fit of the vise. Additional blocking may be required to reinforce the vise.

Illus. 936. Lag bolts hold the bottom of the vise in position, and wood screws hold the front of it in position.

Illus. 937. The vise jaws are lined with hardwood to protect the work.

Illus. 938. Make sure the hardwood liners line up. Also, be sure the jaws extend beyond the end of the bench. This allows clearance for sawing.

Illus. 939. An oil finish works well on a workbench. It is easy to repair, it does not chip, and glue does not stick to it.

Stereo Cabinet The stereo cabinet (Illus. 940) is a product that can be tailored to your stereo equipment. The doors have a rabbet on 3 sides (Illus. 941). The doors keep dust off the albums and stereo components. Notice that this cabinet does not have a back. This allows heat from the components to escape. A back with some holes in it would be an alternative to this design. The shelves are adjustable on 2″ centers, but this could be modified to suit your equipment.

You may wish to add drawers for cassette tape storage or disc storage. Measure your equipment and list your storage needs. Study Illus. 942 and 943. Modify the dimensions or design to fit your components and storage needs.

Cut the plywood for the sides and shelves first. Drill the holes for the adjustable shelves in both sides. Make the top and assemble the carcass. Do all internal sanding before assembly. Edge-band the carcass and attach the shelf nosing.

Measure the opening and determine the size of the doors. Study the details and begin to make them. These doors were made using lap joints. The inner and outer edges were then routed to make the lip and glass rabbet.

Make some moulding to hold the glass in position. Stain and finish the moulding and doors before installing the glass. Be sure to stain the rabbet well. It will be visible through the glass.

Illus. 940. This stereo cabinet has adjustable shelves. It can be tailored to your stereo equipment.

Illus. 941. The doors have a rabbet on three sides. They keep dust off your albums and components.

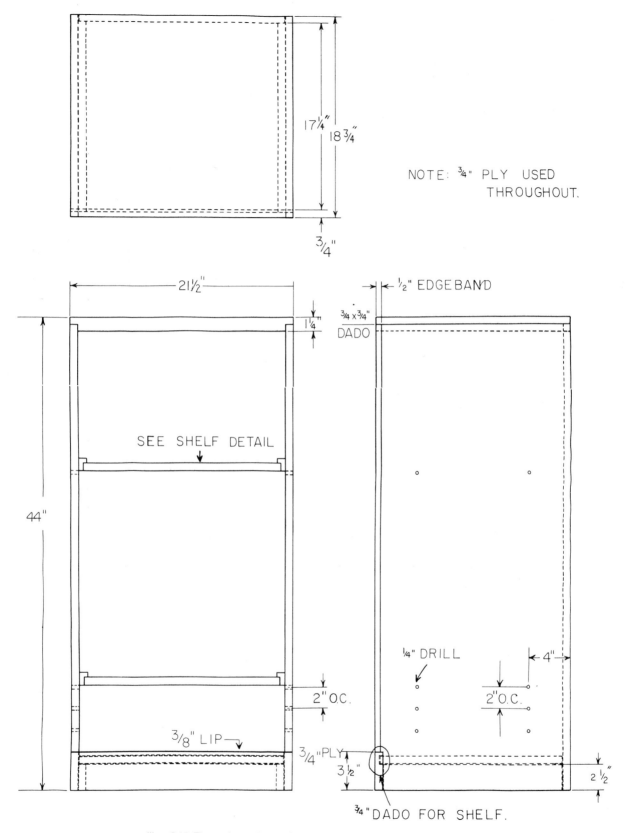

17¼"
18¾"

¾"

NOTE: ¾" PLY USED
       THROUGHOUT.

21½"

½" EDGEBAND

1¼"

¾" x ¾"
DADO

SEE SHELF DETAIL

44"

¼" DRILL

4"

2" O.C.

2" O.C.

3/8" LIP

¾" PLY

3½"

¾" DADO FOR SHELF.

2½"

Illus. 942. These three views of the stereo cabinet will help you visualize how the parts fit together.

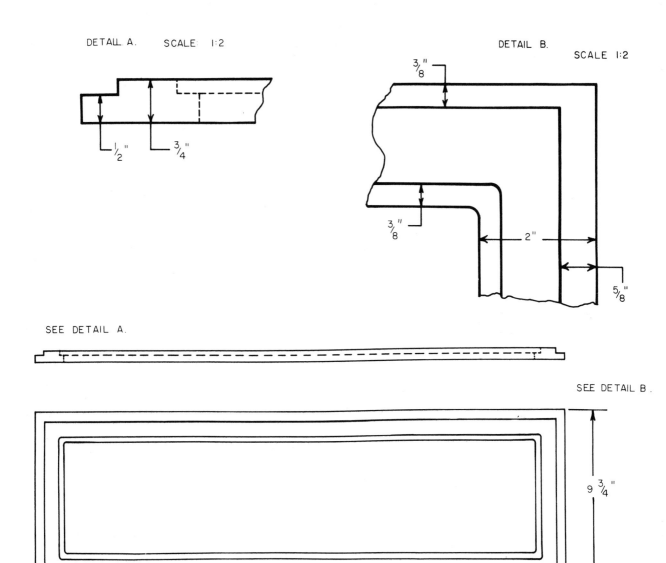

DETAIL A.   SCALE 1:2

½″

¾″

DETAIL B.   SCALE 1:2

⅜″

⅜″

2″

⅝″

SEE DETAIL A.

SEE DETAIL B.

9 ¾″

40 ½″

HALF SCALE

Illus. 943. These details will help you see how the doors were constructed.

329

Hope Chest The hope chest (Illus. 944 and 945) is my favorite radial-arm-saw project. It is easy to build, and it provides many opportunities for you to use the techniques in this book.

The plans (Illus. 946–948) provide the necessary details for you to develop a bill of materials and plan of procedure. Study the plans to be sure you know how the parts fit together. Begin by cutting the plywood to size and ripping the solid stock parts. Crosscut the solid stock leg parts to length.

Set up the radial arm saw for rabbeting in the rip position. Use a dado head to cut away part of the fence. Rabbet the bottom edge of the ends and sides (Illus. 949). The sides must also be rabbeted on both ends (Illus. 948 and 950).

One side of the legs must also be rabbeted (Illus. 951). When I made the hope chest, I made the rabbet a little deeper than stock thickness. This allowed it to be trimmed to exact size later.

Start assembly by clamping up the box (Illus. 952). You can also nail the box together since the legs will hide the joint. While the glue cures, select the appropriate clamps and clamp pads for gluing the legs together (Illus. 953). Do not use nails on the legs since they will be routed.

After the box cures, the bottom can be fitted to the rabbet (Illus. 954). When the fit is correct, glue it in position (Illus. 955). Use the glue sparingly so that it doesn't drip inside the box. Use nails to secure it in position (Illus. 956). After the glue cures, turn the box over and edge-band the exposed plywood edges. Use mitre joints at the corners of the edge band. This will give the box a more professional look.

Trim the overlap from the rabbet on the legs (Illus.

957). Use a laminate-trimming bit for this job. Next, radius the corners with a roundover bit. This will ease the corners and make the hope chest appear more professional.

The scallops should now be cut on the decorative moulding (Illus. 958). This goes at the top of the front. Follow the procedures outlined in Chapter 6 for this job. Careful layout is essential to this job. Attach the legs and other mouldings to the box. These may be glued, or they may be reinforced with nails and screws from the back side.

Determine the size of the lid and cut it to size. Make up the edge-banding material and rout as desired. A straight edge band is used on the back. This allows it to accommodate the hinge. The sides are decorative edge bands that are mitred to the front. Before attaching the front edge band, rout it on the underside (Illus. 959). This provides a finger pull for lifting the lid.

Rout the rear edge band to accommodate the piano hinge (Illus. 960). Square-out the corners with a sharp chisel (Illus. 961). Note: If you nailed the edge bands in position, drive the nails below the routing depth with a nail set.

Attach the hinge to the box and mark its position on the lid. Screw the hinge in position on the lid and box (Illus. 962). Use a clamp to hold the lid open while the lid support is attached (Illus. 963). Adjust the tension on the lid support. This will ensure that the lid does not slam shut.

For a final touch, cedar may be added to the inside of the box (Illus. 964). It is best to do this after the box has been stained and finished. That way no stain or finish can be spilled on the cedar.

Illus. 944. The hope chest is my favorite radial-arm-saw project. It is easy to build, yet it offers many challenges.

Illus. 945. This project offers challenges such as scalloping, mitring, and routing.

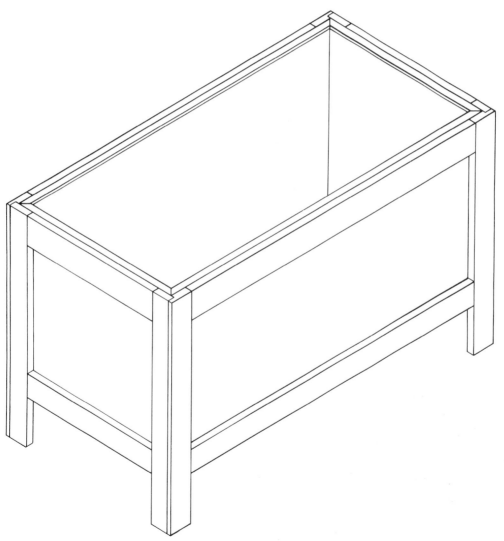

Illus. 946. This isometric view gives you an idea of how the parts fit together.

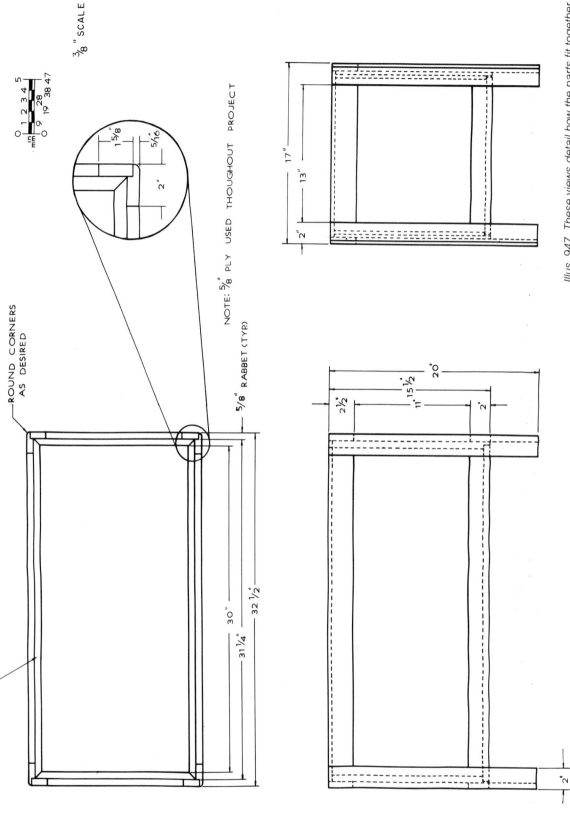

ROUND CORNERS
AS DESIRED

⅝" × ¼" EDGEBAND

31¼"
30"
32½"

5/8" RABBET (TYP.)

NOTE: ⅝" PLY USED THOUGHOUT PROJECT

1⅝"
5/16"
2"

⅜" SCALE

0 1 2 3 4 5
9   19 28 38 47
mm

17"
13"
2"

20"
2½"
11"
15½"
2"
2"

Illus. 947. These views detail how the parts fit together.

332

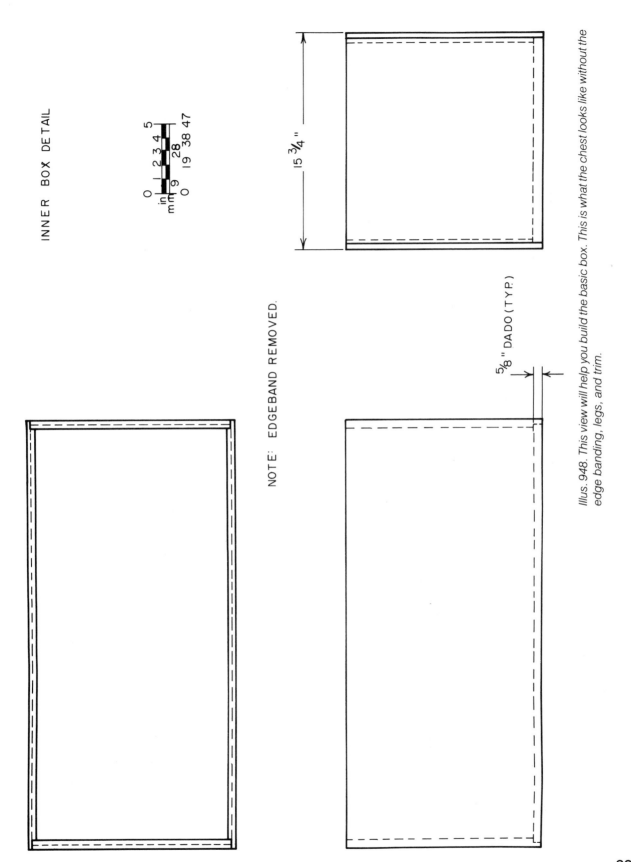

INNER BOX DETAIL

NOTE: EDGE BAND REMOVED.

15 3/4"

5/8" DADO (TYP.)

Illus. 948. This view will help you build the basic box. This is what the chest looks like without the edge banding, legs, and trim.

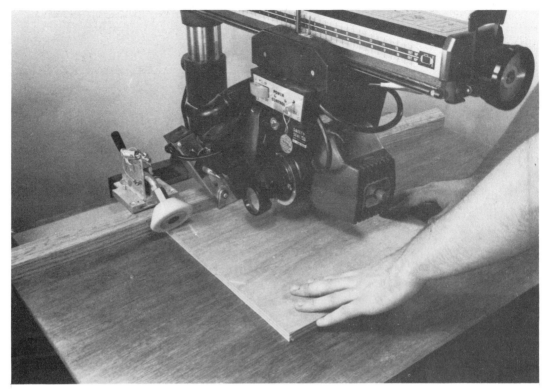

Illus. 949. The ends are rabbeted only on the bottom.

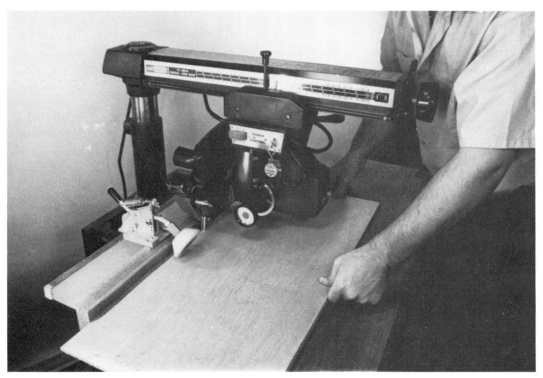

Illus. 950. The sides are rabbeted on the bottom and both ends. The same setup is used for both rabbets.

Illus. 951. Rabbet the legs while the saw is set up for rabetting. The rabbet dimensions will change slightly. Replace the guard after you make the setup.

Illus. 952. Clamp the box together after gluing. Nails may also be used since they will be hidden by the legs.

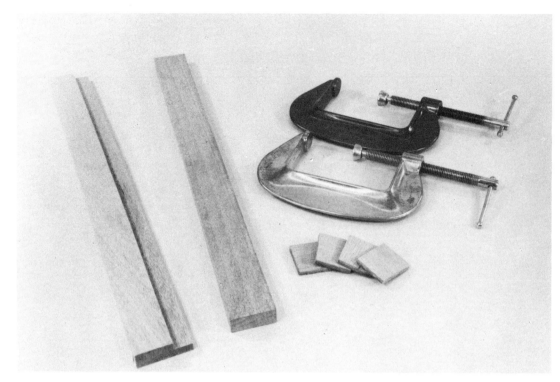

Illus. 953. Clamps and clamp pads are used to hold the legs after gluing. The pads protect the surface.

Illus. 954. Fit the bottom carefully to the box. Make sure the box is square when the bottom is dropped in position.

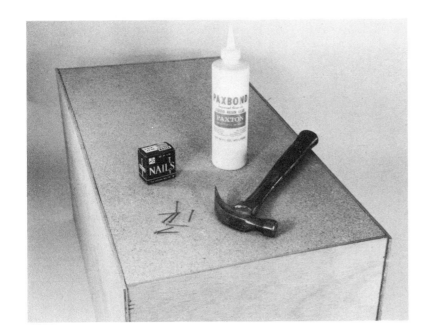

Illus. 956. Nail the bottom into the rabbet. Keep nails centered in the plywood so that they do not come through the inside or outside of the box.

Illus. 957. Remove any overlap with a laminate trimming bit. The corners are then routed with a roundover bit.

Illus. 958. The scallops can now be cut on the decorative moulding. Follow the procedure outlined in Chapter 6.

Illus. 959. Rout the edge band that goes on the front of the lid before installation. This provides a finger pull for lifting.

Illus. 960. The rear edge band is routed to accommodate the piano hinge.

Illus. 961. A sharp chisel is used to square up the gain cut for the piano hinge.

Illus. 962. The hinge is joined to the lid and box. Use pilot holes to keep the screws from breaking.

Illus. 963. A clamp is used to hold the box open while the lid support is positioned and attached. Be sure to adjust the support tension. This will keep the lid from slamming.

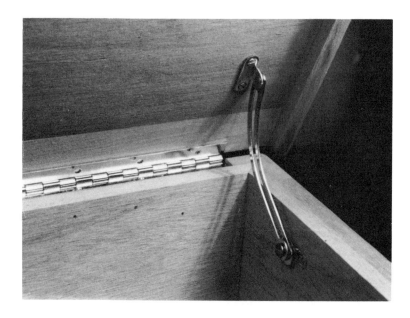

Illus. 964. Cedar has been added to the bottom of this hope chest. The cedar was added after the finish was applied. This keeps stain and finish from damaging the cedar.

METRIC EQUIVALENCY CHART

MM—MILLIMETRES   CM—CENTIMETRES

INCHES TO MILLIMETRES AND CENTIMETRES

INCHES	MM	CM	INCHES	CM	INCHES	CM
⅛	3	0.3	9	22.9	30	76.2
¼	6	0.6	10	25.4	31	78.7
⅜	10	1.0	11	27.9	32	81.3
½	13	1.3	12	30.5	33	83.8
⅝	16	1.6	13	33.0	34	86.4
¾	19	1.9	14	35.6	35	88.9
⅞	22	2.2	15	38.1	36	91.4
1	25	2.5	16	40.6	37	94.0
1¼	32	3.2	17	43.2	38	96.5
1½	38	3.8	18	45.7	39	99.1
1¾	44	4.4	19	48.3	40	101.6
2	51	5.1	20	50.8	41	104.1
2½	64	6.4	21	53.3	42	106.7
3	76	7.6	22	55.9	43	109.2
3½	89	8.9	23	58.4	44	111.8
4	102	10.2	24	61.0	45	114.3
4½	114	11.4	25	63.5	46	116.8
5	127	12.7	26	66.0	47	119.4
6	152	15.2	27	68.6	48	121.9
7	178	17.8	28	71.1	49	124.5
8	203	20.3	29	73.7	50	127.0

YARDS TO METRES

YARDS	METRES	YARDS	METRES	YARDS	METRES	YARDS	METRES	YARDS	METRES
⅛	0.11	2⅛	1.94	4⅛	3.77	6⅛	5.60	8⅛	7.43
¼	0.23	2¼	2.06	4¼	3.89	6¼	5.72	8¼	7.54
⅜	0.34	2⅜	2.17	4⅜	4.00	6⅜	5.83	8⅜	7.66
½	0.46	2½	2.29	4½	4.11	6½	5.94	8½	7.77
⅝	0.57	2⅝	2.40	4⅝	4.23	6⅝	6.06	8⅝	7.89
¾	0.69	2¾	2.51	4¾	4.34	6¾	6.17	8¾	8.00
⅞	0.80	2⅞	2.63	4⅞	4.46	6⅞	6.29	8⅞	8.12
1	0.91	3	2.74	5	4.57	7	6.40	9	8.23
1⅛	1.03	3⅛	2.86	5⅛	4.69	7⅛	6.52	9⅛	8.34
1¼	1.14	3¼	2.97	5¼	4.80	7¼	6.63	9¼	8.46
1⅜	1.26	3⅜	3.09	5⅜	4.91	7⅜	6.74	9⅜	8.57
1½	1.37	3½	3.20	5½	5.03	7½	6.86	9½	8.69
1⅝	1.49	3⅝	3.31	5⅝	5.14	7⅝	6.97	9⅝	8.80
1¾	1.60	3¾	3.43	5¾	5.26	7¾	7.09	9¾	8.92
1⅞	1.71	3⅞	3.54	5⅞	5.37	7⅞	7.20	9⅞	9.03
2	1.83	4	3.66	6	5.49	8	7.32	10	9.14

INDEX

Photo Credits

The illustrations in this book display the products, creations and photography of many people and business organizations. Represented among them are: *American Design and Engineering*, Illus. 271–273, 274–276; *Black & Decker*, Illus. 2, 6–8, 16, 25, 29, 43, 48, 64, 65, 68, 72, 100, 141, 175, 187, 192, 233, 279, 343, 708, 762, 768, 769, 771, 798, 799, 816; *Boice-Crane Industries, Inc.*, Illus. 74; *Clemson Group (Sanblade™)*, Illus. 118; *CRC Concepts*, Illus. 17, 292, 293, 296, 297, 335–339, 382, 383; *Delta International Machinery Corporation* (formerly Rockwell), Illus. 3, 10, 11, 14, 42, 45, 51 right, 59, 61, 66, 69, 73, 153, 155, 227, 234, 278, 717, 763, 766, 767, 772 and Fig. 1; *DML, Inc.*, Illus. 120, 193; *Fisher Hill Products*, Illus. 87; *Foley-Belsaw Company*, Illus. 104–109, 111, 112, 114, 115, 125, 133, 134; *Forrest Manufacturing*, Illus. 128, 136, 137; *HTC Products*, Illus. 97, 756, 759; *Mertes Manufacturing*, Illus. 267–270; *Northfield Foundry and Machine Co.*, Illus. 19–21, 30, 47, 734, 735 and Fig. 3; *Sears, Roebuck and Company*, Illus. 4, 5, 18, 22, 23, 24, 26, 27, 31–33, 36–39, 50, 67, 70, 71, 85, 86, 89, 90, 91A and B, 98, 99, 101, 102, 124, 152, 162, 163, 169, 170–173, 189, 348, 349, 565, 653, 672–674, 682, 707, 712, 730, 731, 738–741, 748, 761, 785, 786; **Sharon Baazard**, Illus. 271–273, 276; *Wallace Kunkel*, Illus. 1; *Western Commercial Products*, Illus. 88.